JEWISH
Women
FICTION WRITERS

JEWISH Women FICTION WRITERS

Edited and with an Introduction by

Harold Bloom

CHELSEA HOUSE PUBLISHERS

Philadelphia

ON THE COVER: Edna Hibel, *Ruth*, 1978. 45" x 27", oil, gesso, and gold leaf on silk. Courtesy Hibel Museum of Art, Palm Beach, Florida.

CHELSEA HOUSE PUBLISHERS

EDITOR-IN-CHIEF   Stephen Reginald
MANAGING EDITOR   James D. Gallagher
PRODUCTION MANAGER   Pamela Loos
PICTURE EDITOR   Judy Hasday
ART DIRECTOR   Sara Davis
SENIOR PRODUCTION EDITOR   Lisa Chippendale

WOMEN WRITERS OF ENGLISH AND THEIR WORKS:
   Jewish Women Fiction Writers

PROJECT EDITOR   Robert Green
CONTRIBUTING EDITOR   Therese De Angelis
COVER DESIGNER   Alison Burnside
EDITORIAL ASSISTANT   Anne Hill
INTERIOR DESIGNER   Alison Burnside

Introduction © 1998 by Harold Bloom

First Printing
1 3 5 7 9 8 6 4 2

Library of Congress Cataloging-in-Publication Data

Jewish women fiction writers / edited and with an introduction by
   Harold Bloom.
      p.   cm. — (Women writers of English and their works)
   Includes bibliographical references.
   ISBN 0-7910-4477-7 (hc.). — ISBN 0-7910-4493-9 (pbk.)
   1. American fiction—Jewish authors—History and criticism.
2. Women and literature—United States—History—20th century.
3. American fiction—Women authors—History and criticism.
4. American fiction—Jewish authors—Bio-bibliography. 5. American
fiction—Women authors—Bio-bibliography. 6. Women authors,
American—20th century—Biography. 7. Jewish women—United States—
Intellectual life. 8. Jewish authors—United States—Biography.
9. Jews in literature. I. Bloom, Harold. II. Series.
PS374.J48J48 1998
813'.5099287'089924—dc21
                                                                                    97-32468
                                                                                    CIP

CONTENTS

JEWISH
Women
FICTION WRITERS

THE ANALYSIS OF WOMEN WRITERS

HAROLD BLOOM

I APPROACH THIS SERIES with a certain wariness, since so much of classical feminist literary criticism has founded itself upon arguments with that phase of my own work that began with *The Anxiety of Influence* (first published in January 1973). Someone who has been raised to that bad eminence—*The Patriarchal Critic*—is well advised that he trespasses upon sacred ground when he ventures to inquire whether indeed there are indisputable differences, imaginative and cognitive, between the literary works of women and those of men. If these differences are so substantial as pragmatically to make an authentic difference, does that in turn make necessary different aesthetic standards for judging the achievements of men and of women writers? Is Emily Dickinson to be read as though she has more in common with Elizabeth Barrett Browning than with Ralph Waldo Emerson?

Is Elizabeth Bishop a great poet because she triumphantly meets the same aesthetic criteria satisfied by Wallace Stevens, or should we evaluate her by criteria she shares with Marianne Moore, but not with Stevens? Are there crucial gender-based differences in the representations of Esther Summerson by Charles Dickens in *Bleak House*, and of Dorothea Brooke by George Eliot in *Middlemarch*? Does Samuel Richardson's Clarissa Harlowe convince us that her author was a male when we contrast her with Jane Austen's Elizabeth Bennet? Do women poets have a less agonistic relationship to female precursors than male poets have to their forerunners? Two eminent pioneers of feminist criticism, Sandra Gilbert and Susan Gubar, have suggested that women writers suffer more from an anxiety of authorship than they do from influence anxieties, while another important feminist critic, Elaine Showalter, has suggested that women writers, early and late, work together in a kind of quiltmaking, each doing her share while avoiding any contamination of creative envy in regard to other writers, provided that they be women. Can it be true that, in the aesthetic sphere, women do not beware women and do not suffer from the competitiveness and jealousy that alas do exist in the professional and sexual domains? Is there something in the area of literature, when practiced by women, that changes and purifies mere human nature?

I cannot answer any of these questions, yet I do think it is vital and clarifying to raise them. There is a current fashion, in many of our institutions of higher education, to insist that English Romantic poetry cannot be studied in the old way, with an exclusive emphasis upon the works of William Blake, William Wordsworth, Samuel Taylor Coleridge, Lord Byron, Percy Bysshe Shelley, John Keats, and John Clare. Instead, the Romantic poets are taken to

XIII

include Felicia Hemans, Laetitia Landon, Charlotte Smith, and Mary Tighe, among others. It would be heartening if we could believe that these are unjustly neglected poets, but their current revival will be brief. Similarly, anthologies of 17th-century English literature now tend to include the Duchess of Newcastle as well as Aphra Behn, Lady Mary Chudleigh, Anne Killigrew, Anne Finch, Countess of Winchilsea, and others. Some of these—Anne Finch in particular—wrote well, but a situation in which they are more read and studied than John Milton is not one that is likely to endure forever. The consequences of making gender a criterion for aesthetic choice must finally destroy all serious study of imaginative literature as such.

In their *Norton Anthology of Literature by Women*, Sandra Gilbert and Susan Gubar conclude their introduction to Elizabeth Barrett Browning by saying that "she constantly tested herself against the highest standards of male-defined poetic genres," a true if ambiguous observation. They then print her famous "The Cry of the Children," an admirably passionate ode that protests the cruel employment of little children in British Victorian mines and factories. Unfortunately, this well-meant prophetic affirmation ends with this, doubtless its finest stanza:

XIII
They look up with their pale and sunken faces,
    And their look is dread to see,
For they mind you of their angels in high places,
    With eyes turned on Deity.
"How long," they say, "how long, O cruel nation,
    Will you stand, to move the world, on a child's heart,—
Stifle down with a mailèd heel its palpitation,
    And tread onward to your throne amid the mart?
Our blood splashes upward, O goldheaper,
    And your purple shows your path!
But the child's sob in the silence curses deeper
    Than the strong man in his wrath."

If you read this aloud, then you may find yourself uncomfortable, on a strictly aesthetic basis, which would not vary if you were told that this had been composed by a male Victorian poet. In their selections from Elizabeth Bishop, Gilbert and Gubar courageously reprint Bishop's superb statement explaining her refusal to permit her poems to be included in anthologies of women's writing:

Undoubtedly gender does play an important part in the making of any art, but art is art and to separate writings, paintings, musical compositions, etc., into sexes is to emphasize values in them that are *not* art.

XIV

That credo of Elizabeth Bishop's is to me the Alpha and Omega of critical wisdom in regard to all feminist literary criticism. Gender studies are precisely that: they study gender, and not aesthetic value. If your priorities are historical, social, political, and ideological, then gender studies clearly are more than justified. Perhaps they are a way to justice, or at least to more justice than women have received throughout thousands of years of male domination and aggression. Yet that is a very different matter from the now vexed issue of aesthetic value. Biographical criticism, like the different modes of historicist and psychological criticism, always has relied upon a kind of implicit gender studies and doubtless will benefit, as other modes will, by a making explicit of such considerations, particularly in regard to women writers.

Each volume in this series contains copious refutations of, and replies to, the traditionally aesthetic stance that I have advocated here. These introductory remarks aspire only to a questioning, and not a challenging, of feminist literary criticism. There are no longer any Patriarchal Critics; they are all dinosaurs, fabulous beasts fit for revival only in horror films. Sometimes I sadly think of myself as Bloom Brontosaurus, amiably left behind by the fire and the flood. But more often I go on reading the great women writers, searching for the aesthetic difference that yet may prove to be there, but which has not yet been found.

INTRODUCTION

THE AUTHORS IN THIS VOLUME are very diverse, particularly in regard to the enigma as to whether some of them can usefully be considered as "Jewish writers." Certainly Gertrude Stein manifests nothing like an Hebraic ethos in her work, while Dorothy Parker owed far more to Hemingway's stories than to the Bible. Cynthia Ozick, with enormous deliberation, set out to be a Jewish storyteller, in a mode having affinities with the work of Bernard Malamud and Isaac Bashevis Singer. The dedication she has manifested in this difficult quest is evident in the thirty-year sequence that goes from her early novel, the rather Jamesian *Trust* (1966) through *The Puttermesser Papers* (1997), sub-titled a novel though actually a suite of tales. Ozick's masterwork, in my judgment, is *The Messiah of Stockholm* (1987), a wry novel that reads even better now than it did a decade ago. I return here though to her early novella, "Envy; or, Yiddish in America" (1969), which I have previously discussed in another context. "Envy" is very nearly of the aesthetic eminence of *The Messiah of Stockholm*; its style may not be as fully modulated as that of the later novel, but the novella seems as fresh and sharp to me today as thirty years ago. "Envy; or, Yiddish in America" is shockingly funny, with that painful kind of Jewish humor of which Philip Roth is the acknowledged master.

Hershel Edelshtein, the protagonist of "Envy," is a Yiddish poet who may be based upon Jacob Glatshtein, a major figure in the pantheon of American Yiddish poets that also included Moshe Leib Halpern and Mani Leib. Untranslated into English, Edelshtein particularly resents the novelist Yankel Ostrover (certainly based on Bashevis Singer), who is fully translated and has a large American following. Attending a public reading by Ostrover, Edelshtein meets a young woman, Hannah, who is one of Ostrover's translators from the Yiddish, but who declines to perform that office for him. Their mutual contempt explodes in a great passage that remains the essence of Ozick's art as a Jewish writer:

> Edelshtein's hand, the cushiony underside of it, blazed from giving the blow. "You," he said, "you have no ideas, what are you?" A shred of learning flaked from him, what the sages said of Job ripped from his tongue like a peeling of the tongue itself, *he never was, he never existed.* "You were never born, you were never created!" he yelled. "Let me tell you, a dead man tells you this, at least I had a life, at least I understood something!"
> "Die," she told him. "Die now, all you old men, what are you waiting for? Hanging on my neck, him and now you, the whole bunch of you, parasites, hurry up and die."

His palm burned, it was the first time he had ever slapped a child. He felt like a father. Her mouth lay back naked on her face. Out of spite, against instinct, she kept her hands from the bruise—he could see the shape of her teeth, turned a little one on the other, imperfect, again vulnerable. From fury her nose streamed. He had put a bulge in her lip.

"Forget Yiddish!" he screamed at her. "Wipe it out of your brain! Extirpate it! Go get a memory operation! You have no right to it, you have no right to an uncle, a grandfather! No one ever came before you, you were never born! A vacuum!"

"You old atheists," she called after him. "You dead old socialists. Boring! You bore me to death. You hate magic, you hate imagination, you talk God and you hate God, you despise, you bore, you envy, you eat people up with your disgusting old age—cannibals, all you care about is your own youth, you're finished, give somebody else a turn!"

The wonder of this is that Ozick is on both sides and on neither; the anguish is also her own, and she makes it ours. For this *is* storytelling, hilariously poignant and yet also very dreadful in its effect, since Edelshtein's hysteria transcends his own absurdist dilemma, that of a poet who writes, not in a dead language, but rather in a mother tongue almost all of whose children were murdered by Germans and their Ukrainian, Polish, Rumanian, and Croat assistants in slaughter. The terrible fury of Edelshtein and of Hannah is by no means fully provoked by one another. The enormity of the Holocaust's extermination of a people and its language is conveyed in the hyperbolic rage that old poet and young translator hurl at one another. Had Ozick written nothing more than "Envy; or, Yiddish in America," she still would have earned survival as a canonical author.

HORTENSE CALISHER

1911–

HORTENSE CALISHER was born in New York City in 1911 to a German-Jewish mother and a southern father of English descent. She attended Hunter College High School and Barnard College, then took a job counseling poor families after receiving her degree. In 1932 she married Heaton B. Heffelfinger, an engineer whom she had met in college; they had two children. During this period, she described herself as a "secret artist (for I continue writing poems in between the housework)," and composed her first published story in 1947 while walking one of her two children to school. Her first collection of short stories, *In the Absence of Angels* (1951), launched her into the forefront of American short fiction. She won Guggenheim fellowships in 1951 and 1953 and a State Department grant to tour Southeast Asia in 1958. Since 1957 she has taught at Stanford, Barnard, Brandeis, Columbia, Bennington, Sarah Lawrence, the University of Iowa, the University of Pennsylvania, and other institutions.

Calisher's short stories have been highly acclaimed and have won four O. Henry prizes. Her autobiographical stories feature Hester Elkin, a portrayal of the artist as a young girl. The merits of Calisher's novels, however, have been subject to debate. Calisher has created a unique world, which has both enthralled and puzzled readers and critics. Her works include *False Entry* (1962), *On Keeping Women* (1977), the science fiction works *Journal from Ellipsia* (1965) and *Mysteries of Motion* (1983), as well as *Textures of Life* (1963) and *The New Yorkers* (1969) and a sexual farce, *Queenie* (1971). There is more agreement on the high quality of her novellas, such as *The Railway Police* (1966) and *Standard Dreaming* (1972).

"I was never to be a conventional feminist; conventional thought is not for writers," Calisher once stated. "But I had always wanted to do a novel from within the female feelings I did have from youth, through motherhood and the wish for other creation." Critics have compared some of Calisher's short stories to brief life histories, for example, that of the successful Jewish lawyer, David Spanner in "One of the Chosen." In these fictional biographies, the reader observes the protagonist during a time of crisis and witnesses his or her transformations of character.

Calisher lives in New York with her second husband, the novelist Curtis A. Harnack. Calisher's nonfiction autobiography, *Herself*, was published in 1972.

1

CRITICAL   EXTRACTS

BRIGID BROPHY

Hortense Calisher is an American of European sympathies, taut artistry and stupendous talent. European culture in the very act of being déraciné—and letting out a mandrake shriek—is the motif Miss Calisher builds into a grand fugue in *False Entry*, published here last year, a huge novel you can nibble round for twenty or thirty pages before you are suddenly in, hurtling through its exciting plot, dazzled by its delicacy and stunned by its sheer Dickensian creativeness. Her effects are necessarily smaller but at their best just as cogent in *Tale for the Mirror*, which consists of thirteen stories, all bearing the marks of having had to earn their living. Literally, they are magazine stories: it is sad that the only one which could be called so derogatorily is the one from *The New Yorker*. The atmospheres range from suburban to Southern to Yiddish; there is even a superb period piece set at a 1918 victory parade, as condensed in its evocations as a bit of dusty bunting. The themes are mostly metaphors of loneliness. In the title story—the longest—the hero is led, through a Jamesian series of social scenes, to recognise that he himself is no less isolated in American society than his Indian and possibly charlatan neighbour. Loneliness is tied into a neat, rather Dorothy Parker parcel in a story about two solitary American women in Rome, and carried to a chill intensity in 'The Scream on 57th Street', a story about—or, I rather think, a story which achieves the classic expression of—widowhood.

Occasionally Miss Calisher's intricate prose flattens into doodling, her narrative swoops towards sentimentality or melodrama and she herself seems engulfed in a second's loneliness, where she cannot believe her own imagination. But she is only plummeting in an air pocket. One even comes to accept her scoopings, like those of a supreme soprano. Most of the time her decorative manner is as firm and economic as rococo wrought iron. Her talent is a naturally brilliant exotic, cutting a figure of stylish idiosyncrasy. Muscular and slender, it picks its fastidious way over the mudflats, leaving a print beautiful, elaborate and rare.

—Brigid Brophy, "Solitaries," *New Statesman* (21 June 1963), in *The Chelsea House Library of Literary Criticism: Twentieth-Century American Literature*, Vol. 2, Harold Bloom, ed. (New York: Chelsea House Publishers, 1986), 648

EMILY HAHN

Hortense Calisher has sometimes been called a writer's writer, an appellation that does not please her because it seems somehow limited, and that adjective certainly cannot be applied to her. It was her scope I noticed when I read her first published story, "The Box of Ginger" in *The New Yorker* in 1948. The style was unabashedly individual, the vocabulary was full; these were refreshing qualities at a time when most young writers, still in Hemingway's thrall, were reining themselves in and holding themselves down, deliberately employing the most poverty-stricken language possible. Miss Calisher knew where she was going, but would not be hurried. To make her point she took the way that seemed best to her, no matter if it wasn't a short cut. ⟨. . .⟩

⟨. . .⟩ *False Entry* is packed, and moves along so subtly that unless you pay close attention you lose the thread. It's not the usual easy reading: and some people were puzzled by it. Others, however, were enthusiastically in favor. ⟨. . .⟩

J. N. Hartt in the *Yale Review* called *False Entry* a beautifully written novel. "Both in style and disclosure it is vivid and luminous, and its powerful moral argument is given an expression as dramatic as it is poetic." The brilliant Brigid Brophy said, in London, "Hortense Calisher is an American of European sympathies, taut artistry and stupendous talent." As for *False Entry*, "You can nibble round for twenty or thirty pages before you are suddenly in, hurtling through its exciting plot, dazzled by its delicacy and stunned by its sheer Dickensian creativeness."

—Emily Hahn, "In Appreciation of Hortense Calisher," *Wisconsin Studies in Contemporary Literature* (Summer 1965), in *The Chelsea House Library of Literary Criticism: Twentieth-Century American Literature*, Vol. 2, Harold Bloom, ed. (New York: Chelsea House Publishers, 1986), 654–55

CHARLES THOMAS SAMUELS

Christina Stead and Jane Bowles are genuinely quirky writers. Hortense Calisher cultivated her oddness, but she is much too earnest to be more than a soggy sport. Confronted with her banal themes, reviewers customarily praise her style. But why? Her prose is witless, awkwardly shifting in tone, self-congratulatory. One scene in *Textures of Life*, in which the heroine, searching for a loft apartment, suffers traumas of class guilt when she must dispossess some starving beatniks, should make anyone immune to Miss Calisher's inflations.

In her most recent novel, *Journal from Ellipsia*, she envisages another planet whose inhabitants are so self-sufficient that they lack sex, yet so free from the interesting stresses of earthly life that at least one of them yearns to become earthbound. This is accomplished when a lady anthropologist working at a "think tank" in the Ramapo Hills decides to exchange places. Most of the novel consists of a journal recording the elliptoid's education in the ways of humanity. But Miss Calisher is less interested in the methods of interstellar turncoating than in making murky observations about love and woman's role. In place of plot, we get portentous earth-bound generalities and intergalactic patois.

Neither species speaks very clearly. Miss Calisher is devoted to the unfinished sentence, the cryptic utterance (the book, alas, is elliptical); when illumination threatens, she merely confuses her pronouns. Which is perhaps unavoidable; it's not only the elliptoids who lacks clear sexual differentiation. One of the human males thinks of his mistress as "a jampot for boys," and in a moment of passion, she expresses herself like this:

> . . . I've been thinking . . . I-me imperturbable in the world, the
> universe. But how could he, anybody be, as long as he still admits
> the I-me part?

Whereupon her lover, understandably wishing to shut her up, "plant[s] a kiss on the mouth and [seeks] its arch."

Breaking in on these bizarre erotic rites, Miss Calisher displays and displays her wisdom. A few examples:

> A philosopher can know better than to hunt the philosopher's stone,
> and yet suspect that the very act of knowing is as sad as it is wise.
> Nor is there anybody more humbly expectant of change than a
> man who despairs of the absolute.

From the elliptoid's ultimate discovery:

> And I said to myself the old message for messiahs that I now say to
> you. What is humane? The small distance. What is wild? The mortal
> weight. Wherever there is difference, there—is morality. Where there
> is brute death, there love flits, the shy observer. I had my feelings
> now, those mysterious pains which held them to living. And I said a
> blessing for all those who live in mystery. The wilderness was all
> before me—and I was glad that I had come.

Compared to such complacency, Nellie's raving ⟨in Stead's *Dark Places of the Heart*⟩ and Mrs. Bowles's moral lemmings ⟨in *The Collected Works of Jane Bowles*⟩ have a certain bright appeal.

—Charles Thomas Samuels, "Serious Ladies," *New York Review of Books* (15 December 1966), in *The Chelsea House Library of Literary Criticism: Twentieth-Century American Literature*, Vol. 2, Harold Bloom, ed. (New York: Chelsea House Publishers, 1986), 650

NORA L. MAGID

The New Yorkers and *False Entry* (1961) comprise a unit, or possibly two parts of what may become a still larger epic. In the earlier volume, an enigmatic character whose assumed name is Pierre Goodman (his mother's name—shades of *Everyman*—is Dora Cross), with a "strange history of third-hand listening and remembering," gains access to the lives of others by knowledge of their pasts. Himself he deems a blackmailer, "paid off in the currency of his need," but the implication is that truth has various faces and that false entry may be a form of truth. (In *The New Yorkers*, on the other hand, the woman who speaks only truth is possessed of a kind of vice; she cannot lie, therefore to her truth there is not beauty, no value.) Drawn by places, Goodman finds the Mannix home to be "one of those nucleal households that attract by virtue of their own warm enclosures." Reference is made to the secret of the Mannix daughter, Ruth. Eventually, to Goodman, but not yet to the reader, she unloads her peculiar burden, and is free of the house.

What she was, what her mystery is, is revealed in *The New Yorkers*, which is set further back in time. In other words, the author, having put cart before horse, focuses here on the Mannixes, and Goodman, the narrator of the other volume, is peripheral. Miss Calisher has always had a tendency to mark her characters with a flaw, and the defects are many and singular. Judge Mannix, the father, is unusually small. His son, David, is deaf. His daughter, Ruth, is symbolically dumb. David's closest friend, Walter Stern, is a hunchback who loses his luck when his hump is cut out. Edwin Halecsy, the stranger whom Ruth introduces because he was born of violence—"He's like me. . . . Everything's already happened to him"—has in turn to commit violence. Ruth as his savior and his victim lives out an idea that has obsessed her father: "Every martyr's always half self-made. . . . We all half choose to be victim—to be the chosen." ⟨. . .⟩

Everyone senses that in this close and loving house—much is made of the house physically and of the fact that it is a Jewish home—something is wrong. The judge has given up judging, the daughter has substituted movement for speech (she is a dancer), the dead mother speaks still. There are moments of power, of poetry, and of nervous, ornate elegance, but the secret the house must ingest is indigestible, and the characters are so entangled in the web of abstraction that they are impaired beyond the blows already dealt them by Miss Calisher. They lose another dimension, and the reader, sinking under the weight of bizarre mechanism and cumulative paradox, is in danger of succumbing to a peculiarly narcotic confusion. Miss Calisher seems to have experienced this, too. In the earlier book, Edwin was called Edgar.

—Nora L. Magid, *Kenyon Review* (1969), in *The Chelsea House Library of Literary Criticism: Twentieth-Century American Literature*, Vol. 2, Harold Bloom, ed. (New York: Chelsea House Publishers, 1986), 651

JOYCE CAROL OATES

Hortense Calisher's new novel, *The New Yorkers*, tells a very long, technically complex, claustrophobic story which is precipitated by an act of violence—the killing of a woman by her daughter, in the presence of her lover. To the genteel imagination, violence justifies itself because it is a rejection of the genteel; a murderer is always interesting. Those of us who are not genteel are more cynical, knowing that murderers are no more interesting than anyone else, and in literature they are no more interesting than their creators are able to make them. In fact, the danger with a murderer is that he never accomplishes anything else—one act, one crime, one glorious killing, and after that all he can do is think. . . .

The novel concerns itself not with facts but with the play of consciousness over facts. Nothing is real; everything is relative. Like the Judge, we become obsessed with the subtleties of guilt, responsibility, the "inter-penetrations of things." Therefore, chronological time is insignificant; we move freely back and forth from the novel's present (1955) to its important pasts (1943 and 1951), so that threads may be taken up, partly explained, different points of view may illuminate ambiguous events, or further darken them. The novel's structure is dictated by Miss Calisher's commitment to what seems to me an old-fashioned, but occasionally effective, means of keeping in the foreground an act that is not only historical, but confused as history; this "act," with its mythical aspirations, must dominate nearly every page of a novel of 559 pages. Who would want to take on such a burden as a writer? In order to keep prominent the theme of violence other violent acts are introduced, rather arbitrarily—a weird episode in which a meek, drunken assistant professor of English slashes his wrists on Ruth; an equally weird episode in which Judge Mannix's brilliant secretary-protégé beats and apparently rapes Ruth in her own father's house, with her father upstairs. Thus Ruth is associated with blood, violence, passivity, the fate of an eternal victim who can be depended upon to remain silent, daughterly, etc.

Miss Calisher has not a logical or intellectual imagination at all, as many critics believe. She is a primitive, a believer in magical powers, fantastic feats of consciousness, the uncanny confusion between inner will and outer history. There is nothing realistic in this novel apart from its concern with the law and its setting, which is done with care (New York City—the upper middle-class—cultured Jews—excellent furniture and antiques); everything is exaggerated, drawn out, worried over, teased, twisted, left dangling. Less direct than either Henry James or Djuna Barnes (an unlikely combination, but strangely suggested by this novel), Miss Calisher is concerned with presenting a kind of ballet which ties together the various characters of the novel into what the Judge calls the "inertia of family life . . . an underground spring neither diseased nor healthy. . . ." How to break free of this inertia? ". . . any man at a window now and then shivered at its argument, assassin deep in the breast. I must move. I must murder. Where is Joy?"

But the will to move, let alone murder, is not strong enough. Everything is dense, weighed down, opaque, slightly insane. *The New Yorkers* is not only a primitive novel, it is something of an insane novel, unfortunately weakened by its moments of sanity and the author's tendency to simulate realism through meandering conversations. There are too many words, too many subtle thoughts. Says the Harvard protégé, Edwin, who takes his place in the ballet as a rapist some years later:

> It wasn't only your possessions that I didn't know the names or uses
> of, that confused me. . . . It was you yourselves, sir, in your heads and
> souls. It was like I couldn't even tell secondary sex characteristics at
> first, or what was the age of who. . . . For a while, until I saw the
> sequence, you all scarcely *had* any actions. Just talk. Like magic
> powder—that explodes.

—Joyce Carol Oates, "Fiction Chronicle," *Hudson Review* (Autumn 1969), in *The Chelsea House Library of Literary Criticism: Twentieth-Century American Literature*, Vol. 2, Harold Bloom, ed. (New York: Chelsea House Publishers, 1986), 651

IRVING MALIN

Hortense Calisher is a shrewd observer of our social ills—displacements of youth, futilities of the rich—but she is more than a naturalist noting easy details, cataloguing crimes or sins. She is a maker of fictions; she insists upon private consciousness—even when this consciousness is extreme, obsessive and "poetic." Her new novel ⟨*Eagle Eye*⟩ is a powerful indictment of social wrongs by an odd hero who may see less (or more) than he believes.

The plot of *Eagle Eye* is superficially thin. The hero is a young man who discovers that his parents—the mother is Catholic, the father Jewish—have never been happy with each other. Their family life has been a series of deceptions and thefts. Bunty—his given name is Quentin Bronstein—confronts the loss of once-durable truths and "recovers" gradually from this shock of recognition.

Calisher begins with a convenient plot, but she refuses to structure her fiction in a straightforward manner. She knows that linear plots are lies that rarely get at the heart of perception. Thus there is for her no one Vietnam, no single youth cult, no simple family. Social "realities" are as "real" as *one mind perceiving them*. Radical truth is inevitably more alarming and convincing than editorial prescriptions.

The first paragraph alerts us to the structure and theme (and, yes, "plot") of the novel: "Did weather exist when nobody looked at it? Did it know? At dawn, say, on a summer Sunday in the financial district, in a suite on the forty-first floor? Whose only occupants were the owner minimally sleeping in his windowless private eyrie at the center of it, and his son here in the outer office lying naked and face down on a rug in front of a computer panel, not yet cracking an eye." These details are carefully chosen to suggest a dreamlike setting in which things are out of focus (or dazzlingly clear?). There is strangeness. When we read that "weather" may not exist unless someone looks at it, we recognize the urgency of private eyes, of inner perceptions and weathers. And the entire novel deals with this "given"—can Bunty ever marry his vision and routine details? Can he *conform*?

Look more closely at the quoted sentences. The setting is the financial district (of New York), but the district is viewed as unusual—the time is Sunday; the office is empty except for two sleepers. (We think of Melville's Bartleby.) There are references to eyes, visions, "windows." These references, along with the title of the novel, assert the supremacy of consciousness.

But the consciousness here seems "free-floating." Who is thinking? Who is shrewdly noting (and shaping) details? We don't know. Later we read about Bunty in the third person: "his own eyes saw so much of late there must be something wrong with them." He is the center of consciousness, but he sees so clearly that he is *blinded*.

As the novel "progresses"—the progress is spirit-bound, not time-bound—Bunty refers to himself in the first person. Third and first persons increasingly symbolize his divisions, his conflicts between family (super-ego?) and self. He finds it more and more difficult to reconcile the two, although he is on the surface as "hip" as his contemporaries. (Indeed his hipness hides a powerful, tic-ridden awareness.)

Bunty is drawn to heights. He would like to be above his parents' strife-filled world. He hopes for a kind of magic divinity. He longs to soar like an eagle, scrutinizing the patterns below him. He is an Icarus—the mythic element is continually suggested—and the higher he tries to go, the more removed he is from economic and social designs.

But, like the coins mentioned throughout the novel, Bunty is two-sided. He secretly wants to *fall away* from his family ties, his startling perceptions and his humanity. He, like many of his contemporaries, yearns to drop out—to die. At one point he informs us: "I think the flesh of apartment dwellers never really forgets at what height it lives. Or not the child who is bred to it, warned when near windows, or grabbed away from them before language, his sight grilled with curliced iron, or soft stone balustrade or glass, or nothing but nothing—between him and the people moving urgently down below. Down there is the empire. The eye is always making the magic, forbidden leap."

Calisher stuns us with the "magic, forbidden leaps" of her imagination. She forces us to enter—and withdraw from—her narrator's mind; she offers few clues to his ultimate condition. But by testing us with her sharp vision she emerges here as a true creator—an eagle of fiction-makers.
    —Irving Malin, "Supremacy of Consciousness," *New Republic* (3 November 1973): 652–53

ELLEN CRONAN ROSE

An *oeuvre*, as every critic knows, is the body of an author's work and in the autobiographical *Herself*, Hortense Calisher says that "if a writer's work has a shape to it—and most have a repetition like a heartbeat—the *oeuvre* will begin to construct him." The 36 short stories of Hortense Calisher ⟨in *The Collected Stories of Hortense Calisher*⟩ constitute an *oeuvre* and construct a portrait of the artist that her seven novels and four novellas neither modify nor significantly augment. . . .

It appears, in cameo form, in the most engaging of the stories, "Mrs. Fay Dines on Zebra," originally published in *Ladies Home Journal* and first collected in *Tale for the Mirror* (1962). Ostensibly a fantasy, the story is a revealing self-portrait of the storyteller Hortense Calisher, here disguised as the *diseuse* Arietta Minot Fay. Mrs. Fay is the last of the Hudson River Minots, a family distinguished by its unique and now outmoded talent for entertaining. "No Minot had ever had a salary." Instead they had attached themselves to various wealthy patrons as "jesters, *fonctionnaires* attending the private person only," prized for their wit, intelligence, charm, that *je ne sais quoi* called style. The widowed Mrs. Fay, her bank account standing at a somber $126.35, needs to find a rich husband; the Minot in her requires him to be a patron as well, who will appreciate her talents.

Watching Arietta Fay identify and capture her patrons, we are watching Hortense Calisher at work. Like the Minots, Calisher is "not a knave, beyond a certain French clarity as to the main chance." She has entertained her patrons superbly for 25 years, perhaps because—like the Minots—she has "attached herself to honorable patrons" who read *The New Yorker* and *Harper's Bazaar* and the best of the women's magazines. Arietta Fay procures a patron and a subsistence by her uncanny tact as a story-teller. Calisher's *Collected Stories* are a dazzling display of that tact at work.

The successful jester knows his patron, supplies his demand even before it is articulated. As Calisher says in *Herself*, "when you write under the likelihood that a magazine will take your work, you will not be able to prevent taking your tone from it." Reading the *Collected Stories*, you can identify the wry sophistication and sardonic detachment of the *New Yorker* stories, the well-bred and tasteful sentimentality of those that flattered the readers of *Mademoiselle* and *Charm*. Always you are conscious of the general public, represented for me by the anonymous librarian who pasted on the flyleaf of *Queenie* her handwritten judgment that "Hortense Calisher always *writes* well."

If Hortense-Arietta has an Achilles heel, it is just that. "Words!" she exclaims in "Little Did I Know," another story with a *diseuse* heroine. "I was drunk on language. I collected words in all shapes and sizes, and hung them like bangles in my mind." In *Herself* she admits that this may lead "to a rhetoric which, loving its own rhythms, may stray too far from sense," as it does when, in "The Rabbi's Daughter," a baby gazes at us, "with the intent, agate eyes of satisfaction." What is agate about satisfaction? What is satisfying about agate?

This rhetoric endangers the bulk of Calisher's fiction, the stories and novels representing "those flights from the subscribed-to-ordinary" that Calisher says are for her "the heights of literature." There remains a small and precious residue. Even Arietta Fay must have had some private moments, when she wasn't spinning tales for her patron.

"Imagination, which speaks in dithyramb, can never equal the rough, fell syllable of memory," says the narrator of *False Entry*. Calisher's tongue is restrained by the stringencies of memory in her autobiographical fictions, the Hester-Kinny Elkin stories that replicate her family, and the two novels, *False Entry* and *The New Yorkers*, that imaginatively build on that foundation. In the Elkin stories, that Calisher wisely put at the center of this collection "where they may radiate" (and do), verbal felicities are at the service of memory. Adjectives do not pirouette, but evoke the smells and tastes and atmospheres of childhood. In the best of these stories—"The Gulf Between," "The Sound of Waiting," "The Middle Drawer"—personal memory is transformed into universal truth as the child becomes "us" and the parents "them" in an eternal drama of growth and mutability.

Comparing the Elkin stories to the tales told by Arietta, one wonders why Calisher deserted the syllables of memory for the dithyrambs of the entertainer. Like Mrs. Fay, she performs superbly, knowing "every periphrasis" of her stories, "every calculated inflection and aside," every knack of pleasing. But even Arietta Fay knows that "in this taxable world," patrons are hard to come by and that the decline of the private patron signals the decline of "his factotum." Can a world which rations its fuel and chastens its cuisine afford a retainer who dines on her charm? Calisher's *oeuvre*, represented by the *Collected Stories*, constructs a portrait as exquisite as the full-length portrait in ivory of Arietta's forebear, Yves Minot—and just as out of date.

—Ellen Cronan Rose, *New Republic* (25 October 1975), in *The Chelsea House Library of Literary Criticism: Twentieth-Century American Literature*, Vol. 2, Harold Bloom, ed. (New York: Chelsea House Publishers, 1986), 648–49

DORIS GRUMBACH

Hortense Calisher has her own way with the story form. Her stories make a somewhat slow, decorous and stately progress, in the direction she destines for them, stopped only to be enriched in texture by complex, decorative words and phrases. They move on, ending so that we are struck each time by the inevitableness of her steps, by the exact rightness of her coda.

Curiously enough, it is from our realization of their difference from "real life" that we derive our satisfaction. In life, we are told the history of a man or a place to whose conclusion the teller has only rarely been a witness. We receive the story along the implacable, flat and incomplete lines of chronology—this happens and then that. Calisher's accomplishment is that she lifts the tale out of the commonplace, carrying it away from the harness of hard fact by her fine verbal textures. Seen through her eyes the real world is not prosaic. Placed in lyrical, poetic spaces, it is thick and rich with implication.

She has never been much for plot. What happens in her stories is what she defined as "an apocalypse, served in a very small cup." Sudden ⟨. . .⟩ epiphanies of character are her métier, which perhaps explains why, to my mind, her stories seem more impressive than her novels. Prophetic revelation does not extend well: the tea cup is the proper vessel for sudden, small visions into the spirit. In a blaze of light, as startling as Paul's Damascan vision, we see, not a string of events, but a tableau, frozen, static, inevitable—and instructive.

But if nothing happens in the traditional sense, there is another more solid kind of knowledge we acquire of the life and nature of her characters. She catches likeness with eerie accuracy ("calls up" might be more accurate: I have the image of a fakir, cross-legged, drawing upon his pipe, as characters slowly materialize out of smoke) and this may be the result of her choices. Almost a third of these stories are about her family—her father, mother, aunts, family hangers-on, servants, her brother. She is best, I think, with them because she allows herself to wander among them, an awkward, under-valued, sensitive child among proud, attractive, transplanted, late Victorian Southerners, living out their well-to-do "comfortable" lives in New York. No resentment ever clouds these firm portraits of her eccentric, charming father and her more critical, "grenadier" mother. She remembers their oddities and their essential differences with accepting love. These stories are literally the core of the book, having been moved here from other locations and order in other books. Now they form a chronological hub from which her perceptions on other subjects radiate so that, with very little further imaginative stretch, one can feel a novel forming. ⟨. . .⟩

What do her stories actually do? They take us into the private depths of lives about which we know almost nothing until the moment at which she chooses to begin her story. In "Point of Departure" we are not told the names

of the two characters, or anything about how they look or their private histories, nothing except the important thing: their intersecting fates and the
moment at which they meet. We enter her world willingly, because she has
shown us life, or the ashes of it, in her very small cup.

> —Doris Grumbach, *New York Times Book Review* (19 October 1975), in *The Chelsea House Library
> of Literary Criticism: Twentieth-Century American Literature*, Vol. 2, Harold Bloom, ed. (New York:
> Chelsea House Publishers, 1986), 656–57

ROBERT PHILLIPS

The title of one of Hortense Calisher's earlier collections, *Extreme Magic*, is an
apt description of her legerdemain with the short story genre. The *Collected
Stories* should regain readers for the author, readers who have found it difficult
to keep the faith after experiencing her recent novels. (This reviewer found it
difficult to praise Calisher from the advent of *Journey from Ellipsia*, that novel-
length work of speculative fiction; others I know hung in there until the seemingly endless novel *The New Yorkers*.) What *The Collected Stories* makes clear is that
Hortense Calisher not only is best at writing short stories, she is one of *the*
best. 〈. . .〉

〈. . .〉 Of all the things to praise, plot is not one. Her story lines often are
fragile, if not non-existent. This is because in her fiction incident is subordinate to insight. The landscape of her stories is more often than not a psy-
chescape of the protagonist. It is impossible to overpraise the psychological
acumen which the author brings to each story. She understands "the animal
self-possession of the very handsome"; the "malpractices of the rich and worn";
the regret of "a life spent among values despised"; "the shiny readiness" with
which we cover the segregation of Self; the ruses practiced by those "pre-
served in the amber of the status quo"; the narcissism of the analysand; the
frustration of those doomed always to exist on the fringe of things. She writes
with understanding of the persons who have "a homing instinct for the viti-
ated, the in-between," and of the persons who live alone and who come to feel
"that only one's own consciousness held up the world, and at the very same
time, that only an in to the world, or a recognition from it, made one continue
to exist at all."

One must also praise the beauty of Ms. Calisher's language. Not since
Elizabeth Bowen has such gorgeous prose been employed to spin a tale (and
Bowen, like Calisher, seems to have studied the figures in Henry James's car-
pet.) A pair of descriptions each for people and places demonstrates Calisher's
linguistic care: "her long hands lay in one's own like a length of suet just out
of the icebox and her upper teeth preceded her smile"; "she looked the way a
tired, pretty woman, of a certain age and responsibilities, might look at the
hour before dinner, at the moment when age and prettiness tussle for her face,

and age momentarily has won"; "the train creaked through the soft, heat-promising morning like an elderly, ambulatory sofa;" "It was that perilously soft hour of all great cities in the spring, when the evening rises to a sound like the tearing of silk and it is better not to be alone, to have some plan."

Ultimately one must praise Ms. Calisher's range. She writes of the urban and the suburban, the adult and the adolescent, the male and the female, the historical past and the hysterical present. Her most persistent theme is fail-ure—of love, of marriage, of communication, of identity. One of her singular abilities is to link or relate the individual defeats of her protagonists to the defeat of traditional social and moral values in the world at large, a world which has either progressed or regressed to the point of ignoring or defeating former standards of behavior or excellence.

—Robert Phillips, *Commonweal* (7 May 1976), in *The Chelsea House Library of Literary Criticism: Twentieth-Century American Literature*, Vol. 2, Harold Bloom, ed. (New York: Chelsea House Publishers, 1986), 649

ANATOLE BROYARD

I rather like a rich, even an overripe prose—or, at least, I like it better than the currently fashionable deadpan or phenomenological style. Writers such as Saul Bellow, John Updike, and, of course: Hortense Calisher—can always give you something to chew on, a bag of freshly buttered popcorn while you watch the movie. To go even further, I don't think you can do justice to a complex character without using a complex sentence once in a while. There is a sensu-ous—even a sensual—pleasure in the rise and fall of a sentence.

All too often, though, Miss Calisher's rhetoric seems to me to mire her characters as well as the movement of her book. Take this passage about a party: "The whole noble, fretful stream of human gossip that goes scalding along the glory-road, parroting the normal or murdering by proxy, or only sweet-talking with youth—sugar which'll drown in the morning—or seeing dog-blind." A passage like this one competes with the progression of the novel instead of encouraging it.

Miss Calisher's characters are "too conscious of too many things at once," in Wallace Stevens' phrase. They remind me of a striking observation made by Trigant Burrow more than 40 years ago: "It would appear that in his separa-tiveness man has inadvertently fallen a victim to the developmental exigencies of his own consciousness." ⟨. . .⟩

On the other hand, Miss Calisher's novel is rich in brilliant effects. When asked how she feels after making love, Lexie answers: "I feel loyal to the situ-ation." Her husband is "a man built up of other people's notations, even in his own mind." Lexie sees herself as "a woman damaged enough to be classical." *On Keeping Women* opens with Lexie lying naked, after a wild party next door, on a lawn on the banks of a river. She has been left there by a former lover who is defeated this time by too much drink and too much reflection, and she is determined to stay where she is until the commuter buses roll past on the road. She wants to make a statement, so to speak, naked to her enemies. I have everything and nothing to hide; something to that effect. Through sheer technical virtuosity, Miss Calisher sustains Lexie there, naked on that grassy bank, for 325 pages, even until her stilted husband returns from Spain, where he has been hospitalized with hepatitis. The two of them facing busloads of neighbors, hand in hand, clothed only in an ambiguous desire for a better life, make quite a picture.

> —Anatole Broyard, "Family Situations," *New York Times Book Review* (23 October 1977), in *The Chelsea House Library of Literary Criticism: Twentieth-Century American Literature*, Vol. 2, Harold Bloom, ed. (New York: Chelsea House Publishers, 1986), 653

B I B L I O G R A P H Y

In the Absence of Angels: Stories. 1951.

False Entry. 1962.

Tale for the Mirror: A Novella and Other Stories. 1962.

Textures of Life. 1963.

Extreme Magic: A Novella and Other Stories. 1964.

Journal from Ellipsia. 1965.

The Railway Police and the Last Trolley Ride. 1966.

The New Yorkers. 1969.

Queenie. 1971.

Herself: An Autobiographical Work. 1972.

Standard Dreaming. 1972.

Eagle Eye. 1973.

The Collected Stories. 1975.

On Keeping Women. 1977.

The Best American Short Stories of 1981 (ed., with Shannon Ravenel). 1982.

Mysteries of Motion. 1983.

The Collected Stories of Hortense Calisher. 1984.

Saratoga, Hot. 1985.

The Bobby-Soxer. 1986.

Age. 1987.

Kissing Cousins: A Memory. 1988.

In the Palace of the Movie King. 1994.
Age: A Love Story. 1996.
In the Slammer With Carol Smith. 1997.

EDNA FERBER

1887–1968

EDNA FERBER has been called the most popular Jewish American author in history. Born in Kalamazoo, Michigan, in 1887, Ferber was the second daughter of Julia and Jacob Charles Ferber. Her father was a Hungarian-born storekeeper. She grew up in urban Illinois, Iowa, and Wisconsin, where her experiences led her to believe that social and economic problems were the cause of anti-Semitism.

Ferber was the first female reporter for the *Appleton Daily Crescent* and later worked for the *Milwaukee Journal*. After suffering an emotional breakdown in 1909, she began writing fiction to keep her mind active. Her first published story, "The Homely Heroine," appeared the following year in *Everybody's Magazine*, and she published her first novel, *Dawn O'Hara: The Girl Who Laughed*, in 1911. Ferber's subsequent collections of short stories, including *Emma McChesney & Co.* (1915) and *Cheerful: By Request* (1918), earned her widespread popularity.

By 1912 Ferber resided chiefly in New York City and belonged to the famous Algonquin literary circle. A dedicated and disciplined writer, Ferber began, in 1917, to write 1,000 words a day. That same year her most autobiographical novel, *Fanny Herself*, was published.

Ferber's career as a best-selling novelist began in 1924 with *So Big*, which won her a Pulitzer Prize and sold well in America and Europe. *Show Boat* (1926) became the basis for the now classic musical of the same name, which opened in 1927, and coincided with the Broadway success of *The Royal Family*, the first of five plays Ferber wrote in collaboration with George S. Kaufman. By the time her novel *Cimarron* appeared in 1930, Ferber was enjoying extraordinary recognition and had become a leading figure in New York social circles.

A militant patriot, Ferber depicted life in various regions of the country in her well-researched novels, which continued with *American Beauty* (1931), *Come and Get It* (1935), and *Saratoga Trunk* (1941). The most notable of her post-war works are *Giant* (1952), set in Texas, and *Ice Palace* (1958), which celebrates life in Alaska. The many films based on her fiction provided starring roles for such actors as Gary Cooper, Ingrid Bergman, Rock Hudson, James Dean, and Elizabeth Taylor. She enjoyed two further Broadway successes with Kaufman, *Dinner at Eight* (1932) and *Stage Door* (1936).

Ferber's Jewishness was significant in her fiction, allowing her to both extol and censure attitudes expressed in the United States. Through fictional characters like Emma McChesney, she also emphasized the critical role that working women have played in America's development.

Ferber wrote two volumes of autobiography, *A Peculiar Treasure* (1939) and *A Kind of Magic* (1963). The latter was her last publication. Although her standing with literary critics was not always secure, she remained a best-selling author until her death on April 16, 1968.

CRITICAL   EXTRACTS

FREDERIC TABER COOPER

Dawn O'Hara, by Edna Ferber, is a book that does offer a problem and in a certain sense answers it in its own sub-title. The problem is this: supposing a girl, after a few months of mad happiness, finds that she is bound for life to a man who has suddenly broken down and whom the doctors pronounce incurably insane. The sub-title of the book is "The Girl Who Laughed;" and that is not a bad answer to a good many of life's most trying problems. At the opening of the story, however, Dawn is very far from being in a mood for laughter. Ten years of unrelieved strain on a New York daily paper, with the driving necessity of paying her husband's hospital bills ever at her heels, at last breaks her down; and her sister and her fairly well-to-do brother-in-law pick her up bodily and transfer her to the peace and quiet of their home somewhere not many miles from Milwaukee. At this point it is not surprising for the reviewer to discover that he has a story before him which he is simply going to spoil if he tries to retell it. Supposing, for instance, he should say bluntly: This is the story of a young woman who has no right to think of love and marriage, and to whom a perverse fate has sent the kindest, staunchest, most lovable young German doctor you can well imagine. He makes a well woman of her by the sheer magnetic force of his will to have her live. And then, when they both realise what they mean to each other and what the hopelessness of their case means to both, they try to bury themselves in hard work, he in his Milwaukee practice, she in newspaper reporting on a paper in the same city, where his influence has found an opening for her. And then, at an hour when it seems as though nothing worse could overtake them, fate does give one added twist of the screw and her husband is released from the asylum as cured and comes to Milwaukee to claim her. None of this begins to touch the real essence of the book because, although it deals in tragedy, it is a fabric woven from threads of sheer light heartedness, unquenchable courage, warm-hearted understanding of the things which go to make the essential joy of living. There are, for instance, certain chapters in the book picturing a delightful, unique, inimitable German boarding-house in Milwaukee that make one sigh while reading them, partly from a vague nostalgia for happy bygone days in German pensions, partly also from sheer envy of the subtle touch that penned them. And then, too, there is one portrait of a broken-down sporting editor, a man whose days are numbered, a man vulgar in speech and with many sins upon his conscience, but who, nevertheless, is rich in some of the rarest gifts that human nature knows and whose final tragedy leaves a vacant spot in the heart akin to that of a personal bereavement. For these reasons it seems the part of wisdom to inscribe the name of Edna Ferber in some easily accessible part of our memory whereby there shall be no danger in the future of missing anything that may come from her pen. It would seem that she is a young woman who has gone some distance already on the road of achievement and is likely to go much further.

—Frederic Taber Cooper, untitled *Bookman* review (June 1911), in *The Chelsea House Library of Literary Criticism: Twentieth-Century American Literature*, Vol. 3, Harold Bloom, ed. (New York: Chelsea House Publishers, 1986), 1369–70

EDNA FERBER

Most writers lie about the way in which they came to write this or that story. I know I do. Perhaps, though, this act can't quite be classified as lying. It is not deliberate falsifying. Usually we roll a retrospective eye while weaving a fantastic confession that we actually believe to be true. It is much as when a girl says to her sweetheart, "When did you begin to love me?" and he replies, "Oh, it was the very first time I saw you, when—" etc. Which probably isn't true at all. But he thinks it is, and she wants to think it is. And that makes it almost true.

It is almost impossible to tell just how a story was born. The process is such an intricate, painful, and complicated one. Often the idea that makes up a story is only a nucleus. The finished story may represent an accumulation of years. It was so in the case of the short story entitled "The Gay Old Dog."

I like "The Gay Old Dog" better than any other short story I've written (though I've a weakness for "Old Man Minick") because it is a human story without being a sentimental one; because it presents a picture of everyday American family life; because its characters are of the type known as commonplace, and I find the commonplace infinitely more romantic and fascinating than the bizarre, the spectacular, the rich, or the poor; it is a story about a man's life, and I like to write about men; because it is a steadily progressive thing; because its ending is inevitable.

It seems to me that I first thought of this character as short-story material (and my short stories are almost invariably founded on character, rather than on plot or situation) when I read in a Chicago newspaper that the old Windsor Hotel, a landmark, was to be torn down. The newspaper carried what is known as a feature story about this. The article told of a rather sporty old Chicago bachelor who had lived at this hotel for years. Its red plush interior represented home for him. Now he was to be turned out of his hotel refuge. The papers called him The Waif of the Loop. That part of Chicago's downtown which is encircled by the elevated tracks is known as the Loop. I thought, idly, that here was short-story material; the story of this middle-aged, well-to-do rounder whose only home was a hotel. Why had he lived there all these years? Was he happy? Why hadn't he married? I put it down in my note-book (yes, we have them)—The Waif of the Loop. Later I discarded that title as being too cumbersome and too difficult to grasp. Non-Chicagoans wouldn't know what the Loop meant.

So there it was in my note-book. A year or two went by. In all I think that story must have lain in my mind for five years before I actually wrote it. That usually is the way with a short story that is rich, deep, and true. The maturing process is slow. It ripens in the mind. In such cases the actual mechanical matter of writing is a brief business. It plumps into the hand like a juicy peach that has hung, all golden and luscious, on the tree in the sun.

From time to time I found myself setting down odd fragments related vaguely to this character. I noticed these overfed, gay-dog men of middle age whom one sees in restaurants, at the theater, accompanied, usually, by a woman younger than they—a hard, artificial, expensively gowned woman who wears a diamond bracelet so glittering that you scarcely notice the absence of ornament on the third finger of the left hand. Bits of characterization went into the note-book . . . "The kind of man who knows head waiters by name . . . the kind of man who insists on mixing his own salad dressing . . . he was always present on first nights, third row, aisle, right." I watched them. They were lonely, ponderous, pathetic, generous, wistful, drifting.

Why hadn't he married? Why hadn't he married? It's always interesting to know why people have missed such an almost universal experience as marriage. Well, he had had duties, responsibilities. Um-m-m—a mother, perhaps, and sisters. Unmarried sisters to support. The thing to do then was to ferret out some business that began to decline in about 1896 and that kept going steadily downhill. A business of the sort to pinch Jo's household and make the upkeep of two families impossible for him. It must, too, be a business that would boom suddenly, because of the War, when Jo was a middle-aged man. I heard of a man made suddenly rich in 1914 when there came a world-wide demand for leather—leather for harnesses, straps, men's wrist watches. Slowly, bit by bit, the story began to set—to solidify—to take shape.

Finally, that happened which always reassures me and makes me happy and confident. The last paragraph of the story came to me, complete. I set down that last paragraph, in lead pencil, before the first line of the story was written. That ending literally wrote itself. I had no power over it. People have said to me: "Why didn't you make Emily a widow when they met after years of separation? Then they could have married."

The thing simply hadn't written itself that way. It was unchangeable. The end of the story and the beginning both were by now inevitable. I knew then that no matter what happened in the middle, that story would be—perhaps not a pleasant story, not a happy one, though it might contain humor—but a story honest, truthful, courageous and human.

—Edna Ferber, "Foreword" to "The Gay Old Dog," *My Story That I Like Best* (1925), in *The Chelsea House Library of Literary Criticism: Twentieth-Century American Literature*, Vol. 3, Harold Bloom, ed. (New York: Chelsea House Publishers, 1986), 1368

LOUIS KRONENBERGER

At a time when realism is all but monopolizing literature, one experiences a sensation of delighted relief in encountering *Show Boat*. It is gorgeously romantic—not in the flamboyant and artificial manner of the historical romance which twenty-five years ago, under the titles of *Janice Meredith* and *Richard Carvel*, came definitely labeled before the American public; not staggering beneath a weight of costume and local color. *Show Boat* comes as a spirited, full-breasted, tireless story, romantic because it is too alive to be what the realists call real; because it bears within itself a spirit of life which we seek rather than have; because it makes a period and mode of existence live again, not actually different from what they were, but more alluring than they could have been. *Show Boat* is romantic not because its people and events violate any principle of possibility, but because they express a principle of selection. Miss Ferber has chosen the brightest colors and let the dull ones go. She has avoided the contrasts by which the brightness would fade into the common light of day. *Show Boat* is dominated by one tone as Hergesheimer's *Balisand* is dominated by another.

After the days of Mark Twain, the Mississippi holds small place in American literature. Now it reclaims its place, happily as the scene of later days than Mark Twain's. River travel such as he described had fallen off with the coming of railroads, and Captain Andy Hawks of *Show Boat*, facing the fact in the late '70s but satisfied by no life save that of the river, compromised with buying a show boat—one of those floating theatres which moved from town to town for a one or two night stand, by day approaching the town with calliope screaming and flags flying, by night shining with hundreds of lights above the river. On board with him was his wife Parthy, a hard, gaunt New Englander who should have been a spinster; his daughter Magnolia, at first a child, later on the ingenue of his troupe; the troupe itself, all "picked" characters for the purposes of the novel; and, when the time was ripe, that most engrossing and romantic character of all—Gaylord Ravenal.

Magnolia Hawks was as much in sympathy with her spry half-Gallic little father as his wife was out of it. Parthy Hawks mistrusted the show-boat existence, though in the end her repressions conquered her and made her the show boat's worst slave. She also mistrusted Gaylord Ravenal, who came aboard it to act, only because he fell in love with Magnolia. She found out all about him, but she could not keep Magnolia from marrying him. They stole off and were married in a small river town, Ravenal paying the minister with his last $10. How enjoyable a figure he is from start to finish and how flawlessly he comes up to every requirement of his romantic part! Exiled from New Orleans for killing a man in self-defense; aristocratic and nonchalant, perfectly groomed, a cool, inveterate gambler, leading Magnolia, in after years when Andy Hawks had been drowned, to a seesaw existence in Chicago, fluctuating with his gains and losses at faro—a delightful figure from start to finish, and a delightful finish, when he leaves Magnolia $600 and goes away forever. ⟨. . .⟩

All art is a luxury in the sense that it fills a place beyond the physical necessities of life, but some art there is which is entirely ornamental, which does not reveal life, or probe character, or feed the soul. *Show Boat* is such a piece of writing—a gorgeous thing to read for the reading's sake alone. Some, perhaps, will conscientiously refer to it as a document which reanimates a part of the American scene that once existed and does no more. But this writer cannot believe it is that; rather it is a glorification of that scene, a heightening, an expression of its full romantic possibilities. There was, no doubt, a gallant Andy Hawks in the old days, and a Magnolia, and more Gaylord Ravenals than one; there was such a scene as that recorded of Julie Dozier when she was discovered to have negro blood; there was a Parthy Hawks who ran a show boat down the river, an indomitable woman who formed an anomaly among show boat proprietors; but they were never the one group who lived on the *Cotton Blossom*. Plenty of prose intermingled with the poetry of the true scene, plenty of realism with the romance. And all these things, of course, Miss Ferber knew before and while and after she wrote *Show Boat*.

But Life, here, gives way unrestrainedly to Art. And Art functions in one tone—the romantic. Some will not submit to this, and will object to a piece of melodrama here, a wild coincidence there, an unconvincing character somewhere else. That will be an esthetic mistake. Let us accept the delightful lives these people lead. All in all, when you look back upon the story it is amazing how little that is exciting and complicated has happened; this is biography rather than "plot." Miss Ferber has told her story without stint, a long free-breathing story, safe from the careful selectiveness and lacunation of modern schools of writing. It never becomes sentimental; at times it is high romance, at times light romance, at times comedy; but it is never melancholy romance. There is no sighing after the snows of yesteryear. With *Show Boat* Miss Ferber establishes herself not as one of those who are inaugurating first-rate literature, but as one of those who are reviving first-rate storytelling. This is little else but an irresistible story; but that, surely, is enough.

> —Louis Kronenberger, "*Show Boat* Is High Romance," *New York Times Book Review* (August 1926), in *The Chelsea House Library of Literary Criticism: Twentieth-Century American Literature*, Vol. 3, Harold Bloom, ed. (New York: Chelsea House Publishers, 1986), 1370–71

WILLIAM MCFEE

Miss Ferber's talent, this reviewer is irrevocably convinced, does not lie in the way of the novel at all. She writes a novel as a modern athletic girl might wear a crinoline and a bustle. She manages the trick, but she is self-conscious and filled with secret amusement over the masquerade. Why so many words? Why such a portentous enclosure for a mere story? So I imagine Miss Ferber secretly regarding the novel form. Her forte, I humbly submit, is the short story. She has the gift, and it is my belief she has the predilection, for that form of literary art. But editors and publishers demand novels spun out to serial length and Miss Ferber, who can do it, supplies the demand. That does not vitiate the argument that her short stories are remarkably good stories, while her novels are only remarkably good short stories spun out to novel length and thereby largely spoiled.

Show Boat as an example. I am prepared to confess that I am inconsistent because I read the book with excitement, not over the story, which is negligible, but over the description of life on the Mississippi in a floating theatre. The reader can take it as a sign of ignorance and incompetence, but I didn't know anything about show boats. It is to me an inexplicable thing why George W. Cable did not write a book about them, and why Mark Twain (as far as I can remember) does not allude to them. In the case of *Show Boat*, one is yanked back to the fortunes of Magnolia and her daughter Kim—named after the states of Kentucky, Illinois and Missouri because she was born on the show boat at the confluence of the Ohio and Mississippi—one returns to the story with a sigh. But of course it is the story of Magnolia and Kim which will make *Show Boat* a best seller. They are in characteristic Edna Ferber vein.

If it be demanded outright what is the real trouble with *Show Boat* as a novel it is just this, that it is written in short story tempo. That, as already stated, is Edna Ferber's natural bent. Even though she writes a novel, it goes along at a speed which leaves the author out of breath and the reviewer out of patience. A novel is not a hundred-yard dash kept up mile after mile. It is something utterly different from a short story.

But *Show Boat* is enthusiastically recommended to the four out of five Americans who have no information on the subject. Miss Ferber "got up" that subject. If anything, the book is at times heavy with information. And certainly the information in the later chapters, telling us how certain well known and practicing dramatic critics, editors and column writers foregathered at the heroine's apartment, is a bad error of judgment and taste. It is cheap, and one very nearly adds, in irritation, nasty. It is lacking in dignity, which may be important after all. Because the first part of *Show Boat* is dominated by the Mississippi, and it is a drop indeed at the end to be fobbed off with anecdotes about Alexander Woollcott.

—William McFee, "Life on the Mississippi—New Style," *New Republic* (September 1926), in *The Chelsea House Library of Literary Criticism: Twentieth-Century American Literature*, Vol. 3, Harold Bloom, ed. (New York: Chelsea House Publishers, 1986), 1371

T. S. MATTHEWS

. . . ⟨Edna Ferber⟩ has no charm at all. Reading one of her books gives you the pleasant sense of toil vicariously accomplished. And her novels are always success stories, in spite of the threatening implications she turns up and pats neatly back into place—which makes her popular reading. She squares off at her job in workmanlike fashion and turns out a nationally advertised product that looks as sound as this year's model always does, until next year's model comes along. This time ⟨in *Come and Get It*⟩ she has elected to give the reader his money's worth by a report on the Wisconsin lumber industry. In fact, she gives double your money's worth, for the story not only ends but begins all over again, and finally peters out in a formless finish. The hero of the first part is a ruthless old self-crowned lumber king; at his death, halfway through the book, the girl whom he tried to get for himself but who had sense enough to snag his son instead becomes the centerpiece, and blossoms out into a rich vulgarian. The only point I could discover in the story was that Miss Ferber thought there was good stuff in the lass, because when the crash of the depression came, she had the gumption to cut the cackle and come home. In a pathetic attempt to justify Edna Ferber's national advertising, her publishers announce that she has now practically covered the mores of the entire United States. With what? may I ask. To paraphrase a famous disclaimer: "It's just an Edna Ferber, Mister; it don't mean nothing."

—T. S. Matthews, "Novels by Weight," *New Republic* (March 1935), in *The Chelsea House Library of Literary Criticism: Twentieth-Century American Literature*, Vol. 3, Harold Bloom, ed. (New York: Chelsea House Publishers, 1986), 1371

MARGARET LAWRENCE

Edna Ferber's first stories had to do with women who pushed their way into competition in business with men. She glorified the woman commercial traveler and the woman producer. They were case histories of actual go-getting women, and she related them by her astute journalistic sense to the subconscious opinion which all women were holding of themselves. The combination was excellent for her own bank account, and excellent stimulus for the progress of feminist enterprise, and excellent also for the increase of the primary documentary sources of the feminist movement. Unquestionably, future historians will turn to Edna Ferber for the gathering of vivid first-hand reporting of the time in fiction. She is, therefore, to an almost final extent, the supreme feminist.

Whether it was out of utter feminist conviction, or out of the accidental attraction of the keen journalist for good material, only Miss Ferber herself will know. But whatever the conscious, or subconscious, motivation might have been at the beginning, she stands now as the supreme fictional annalist of careerist women in the heyday of their careers. . . .

There is nothing in her stories borrowed from Europe. There is no shadow of sophisticated weariness. Sometimes there are touches of naïveté, but these touches come from the author's sense of the zest for living, which is the breath of any new civilization.

She writes as if none of the authors of Europe existed. From the classical standpoint she has no style whatever. But from the vital standpoint of how style is associated with the emotion of time and place, she has perfect style.

Apart entirely from her fidelity to the rhythm of primitive pioneer storytelling, and apart entirely from her absorption in the current of the American scene, Edna Ferber is of towering importance to the School of Femininity. She belongs to the great procession—Austen, the Brontës and Eliot—who presented the feminist picture.

Serena de Jong, the heroine of her greatest book, *So Big*, belongs with Elizabeth Bennett and Jane Eyre and Maggie Tulliver. Her other women are like the other women of Miss Austen, the Brontës and George Eliot. They are the Elizabeths and the Janes and the Maggies out in a new world on the make, selling lingerie, performing on show boats, running newspapers and raising prize asparagus, struggling with emotion and finding themselves relief in action. But there is one great difference, and it is the difference between the nineteenth-century lady and the twentieth-century woman—her women are not dependent upon men for the adequate conduct of their lives. Elizabeth Bennett, had she been disappointed in Mr. Darcy after marriage, would have been in an emotional whirlwind, and Miss Austen, had she tackled such a situation, would have been hard put to it to find a neat conclusion. Little Jane Eyre, if fate had not taken the wild and fascinating Mr. Rochester by the scruff of his unrighteous neck and handed him over to her, would have been a flattened out little mortal. Poor Maggie Tulliver had to be drowned after a purgatory of isolation because she had magnetism which she could not use to her own advantage. But Serena and all the women of Edna Ferber take erotic disappointment in their twentieth-century stride and do not expect anything from men. They say to themselves—men are like that—and find plenty to do besides looking around for another hero or getting drowned. And this in spite of the fact that they are women of deep emotions and strong passionate attachments. They observe their husbands; they mother their sons and their daughters, and expect no undue amount either of love or of great stature from any of them in return. Life to them is worth what it brings in experience. They live in the feminist era in the new world.

Serena de Jong, facing disappointment both in her husband and her son and raising the best asparagus in the State, is a symbol of the new woman. She is not a romantic figure in the old sense, yet she is a woman of new romance, courageous, real and vital.

In all Edna Ferber's work there is an undercurrent of dissatisfaction with men which is characteristic of all the general writing of the modern School of Femininity in its present phase. It may be a half-way phase. The woman of the next phase may come to the conclusion that her real work for the race is to maintain at all cost and with great creative effort the illusion of romance and greatness in men. But for the present she seems to be of the general opinion that men are weak, or that at least the men of this period are not strong enough for the women whose strength has been bred of the feminist pioneering era. Serena de Jong met no man who was as strong as herself, and this is true of all Edna Ferber's women. It is the plaint of all strong women, and women for the time are through with the nursing of an illusion. There is too much to do in the big impersonal world. It is the tragedy which Olive Schreiner foresaw when she wrote *The Story of an African Farm*. Men would inevitably be a step behind the new woman. But it is an even greater tragedy than Olive Schreiner foresaw. She believed in the race. She taught that strong women would breed strong sons. Edna Ferber shows her women disappointed in their sons; for the sons are never quite so rugged in fiber as their pioneering mothers; and the conclusion is that strength needs more than one parent. So has the feminist story reached one of its plateaux of experience, and what is to be done about it? For nature created women normally incapable of happiness in companionship with men weaker then themselves. Meanwhile there remains much of the world yet to be conquered for women, and this is the real love of the women she portrays in the height of their powers.

—Margaret Lawrence, "Go-Getters," *The School of Femininity* (1936), in *The Chelsea House Library of Literary Criticism: Twentieth-Century American Literature*, Vol. 3, Harold Bloom, ed. (New York: Chelsea House Publishers, 1986), 1368–69

JOHN BARKHAM

If you haven't read Edna Ferber's name on any new novel lately, it isn't (as you might have suspected) because she was relaxing on the royalties from *Show Boat, Cimarron, Saratoga Trunk* and other movie masterpieces made from her books. On the contrary, it was because Miss Ferber was brewing the biggest witch's broth of a book to hit the great Commonwealth of Texas since the revered Spindle blew its top. Miss Ferber makes it very clear that she doesn't like the Texas she writes about, and it's a cinch that when Texans read what she has written about them they won't like Miss Ferber either. Almost everyone else is going to revel in these pages.

For unsophisticated Easterners, *Giant* is going to be a guided tour to an incredible land unlike any they have ever seen before. (Texans, of course, have diligently fostered such a legend for years.) It outdoes anything our material culture has ever produced. Miss Ferber's Texas is the apotheosis of the grandiose, the culmination of that biggest-and-bestest cult peculiar to this side of the Atlantic. Whether it is recognizable to anyone inside of Texas is something else again. But *Giant* makes marvelous reading—wealth piled on wealth, wonder on wonder in a stunning, splendiferous pyramid of ostentation.

Her Texas was not altogether a surprise to this reviewer. Although he has not recently dallied at the Shamrock or shopped at Neiman-Marcus, he has run across oil aristocrats in the royal suites at the Savoy in London, the Grand in Stockholm and elsewhere, and had been suitably awed. And wasn't it Bob Ruark who recently told us in *Esquire* that in Texas even the midgets stood six feet high, and that you never met anybody there but rich millionaires and poor millionaires.

This is the Texas Miss Ferber has put into her bitter, brilliant, corrosive, excoriating novel. She refuses to genuflect to the lords of the oil wells or the barons of the ranches. Her Texas is a state where the skies are clamorous with four-engined DC-6's carrying alligator jewel cases and overbred furs, "where a mere Cadillac makes a fellow no better than a Mexican." An exaggeration? Perhaps, but one which Texans have put over.

It requires courage to take all this apart as scathingly as Miss Ferber has done; and in the process of so doing she paints a memorable portrait of that new American, *Texicanus vulgaris* which is all warts and wampum.

She does this by marrying her heroine, Leslie, an elegant Virginian, to Jordan Benedict 3d, head of the Reata Ranch, whose frontiers stretch into the middle of tomorrow. When "Bick" brings his lovely, naïve bride into his cattle empire, he also takes with him a host of curious readers whose prying eyes are to be dazzled by what they see. It's a world of its own, "all noise and heat, big men and bourbon, and elegantly dressed, shrill-voiced women who needed only three plumes to be presented as they stood at the court of St. James." Gradually Leslie becomes familiar with the gradations of Texas wealth: as cotton once snooted at the cattle rich, so now the cattle rich sneer at the oil rich—with Miss Ferber sneering at all of them.

For our author believes passionately that this glorification of wealth is a massive and dangerous symptom in our body politic. She makes Leslie say things like: "Here in Texas we have very high buildings on very broad prairies, but very little high thinking or broad concepts." Most of all she resents the treatment of the Mexican-American in his native Texas. To the monolithic men in cream-colored Stetsons and tooled boots whose daughters cost a heifer a day to keep in Swiss finishing schools, the Mexican is a sub-human to be used as a *vaquero* or ranch-hand but kept out of public places meant for white folks. To point her moral she makes one of the Benedict children marry a Mexican, and subjects one of them to a supreme insult at a four-motor party.

Admittedly, this novel presents the Texan larger and more chromatic than life, but life-size is large enough. And it's true that people in big empty places like to behave as the gods did on Olympus. As for bigness, says Miss Ferber militantly, it's time Texans stopped confusing it with greatness. "Are sunflowers necessarily better than violets?"

It's easy to spend hours debating the rights and wrongs of this red-hot novel. It all depends where you come from and what you think of Cadillac-cum-Dallas culture. But no one can deny the explosive impact of this story. For all the slickness of its writing (and Miss Ferber is a past mistress of best seller style), *Giant* carries the kind of message that seldom finds expression in such chromium-plated prose. What's more, Miss Ferber states it with a conviction that carries the ring of sincerity. All this may make it impossible for her to revisit the great Commonwealth without the law at her hip, but at least she has written a book that sets the seal on her career.

—John Barkham, "Where It's the Biggest and Bestest," *New York Times Book Review* (September 1952), in *The Chelsea House Library of Literary Criticism: Twentieth-Century American Literature*, Vol. 3, Harold Bloom, ed. (New York: Chelsea House Publishers, 1986), 1372

JAMES MACBRIDE

Miss Ferber's short stories (her blurbist informs us solemnly) are required reading in schools and colleges. For once, it is pleasant to agree with the publicity
department. Selected by the author herself from over a hundred published
items, the stories in ⟨One Basket⟩ will repay the closest study of the fledgling
who would go and do likewise. For the confirmed novel-reader who shuns
slick paper, they are vigorous examples of an author at the top of her form—
a virtuoso lightness of phrasing, a shrewd ear for dialogue, plus real understanding of the standard problems Americans have faced in the past and must
go on facing. Those who have found Miss Ferber's full-length output a bit
ciné-colored of late should take pleasure in rediscovering her at her best.
⟨. . .⟩
      As always, Miss Ferber is at her best when she stays closest to the milieu
of her formative years—when she was carving out the raw material of her art
as a reporter in the Middle West. Her back-street Chicago is more convincing
than her Riviera romances; her prairie mornings will stay in your memory long
after you've forgotten her station-wagon repartee. But even the most severely
hand-tailored of her stories is much more than merely entertaining: if her
matriarchs are terrifying and completely real, her star-crossed women execu-
tives, faded ingenues, and freshly lacquered adolescents are no less human
under their patter. Sometimes, as in her novels, Miss Ferber's sheer, exuberant
talent, her flair for the theatrical, outruns her material—with a consequent loss
of realism. But even here, the emotion is honest. Her effective range is much
narrower than these titles would indicate—yet every story is written from her
heart.
      —James MacBride, "Thirty-one by Ferber," *New York Times Book Review* (February 1947), in *The
      Chelsea House Library of Literary Criticism: Twentieth-Century American Literature*, Vol. 3, Harold
      Bloom, ed. (New York: Chelsea House Publishers, 1986), 1371–72

LOUIS HARAP

Edna Ferber was far more popular and versatile than Fannie Hurst. While the
detective story writer E. Phillips Oppenheim was in 1920 the first American
Jew to achieve a fiction best seller, *The Great Impersonation* (if one does not count
Bret Harte, one-quarter Jewish, with his best-selling *Luck of Roaring Camp* in
1870–1871), Edna Ferber's serious novel *So Big* became a best seller in 1924,
and she was often on the list thereafter. ⟨. . .⟩
      "All my life," she wrote in her autobiography, "I have been inordinately
proud of being a Jew, . . . something to wear with becoming modesty." She is
reputed never to have allowed an anti-Semitic slur to pass without response.
Vehemently anti-Zionist, even after the founding of the State of Israel, she
returned from a visit there with an unfavorable impression—she thought it "a

kind of Jewish Texas." She noted in her journal her growing "suspicion that the Jew himself is responsible" for his persecution, and that he "expects" and "even invites it."

However, her sense of Jewish identity was not expressed in her fiction, for only her second novel, *Fanny Herself* (1917), is concerned with Jewish characters. This novel has added interest today for its assertion of female independence. The story is in part autobiographical: it traces the growing up of a Jewish girl in the Middle West and her mother's able management of the family store. In the story, after the mother's death (Ferber's actual mother survived), her daughter gives promise of carrying the store on successfully, but decides to launch her own business in Chicago. The story thus projects two independent women, her mother and herself, who succeeded in careers then unusual for women. The milieu of the novel is Jewish, with its problems of coexistence with Gentile children (mild anti-Semitism is encountered), and a description of a Yom Kippur service. When Fanny applies for a job in a mail order house in Chicago, she hopes to evade discrimination by concealing her Jewish origin, but the personnel manager is not deceived. "You've decided to lop off the excrescences, eh?" In Chicago she renews her friendship with her non-Jewish schoolmate, Clarence Heyl. There she also develops her talent for drawing as she wanders over the city sketching, and for catching the feeling of deep trouble and sorrow in city folk. When she shows her sketches to Heyl, he tells her, "It's in your blood. It's the Jew in you." Of her drawings of the Chicago ghetto he says, "It took a thousand years of suffering and persecution and faith to stamp that look in his face, and it took a thousand years to breed in you the genius to see it and put it down on paper." In the end she quits business, marries Heyl, and turns to art.

With this novel Ferber ended her fictional treatment of Jews, and, except for the casual inclusion of Jewish characters in a few plays, did not return to them until her autobiographies. Her first autobiography, *A Peculiar Treasure* (1939), was dedicated "To Adolf Hitler, who made of me a better Jew and a more understanding and tolerant human being, as he has of millions of other Jews, this book is dedicated in loathing and contempt."

—Louis Harap, "The Apprentice Years: 1900–1919," *Creative Awakening: The Jewish Presence in Twentieth-Century American Literature, 1900–1940s* (New York: Greenwood Press, 1987), 20–22

DIANE LICHTENSTEIN

"All my life I have been inordinately proud of being a Jew. But I have felt that one should definitely not brag about it," proclaimed Edna Ferber in her 1939 autobiography *A Peculiar Treasure* (8). The ambivalence generated by the juxtaposition of these two sentences reminds us that the twentieth century had not resolved the dilemmas of the nineteenth; indeed, Hitler had made Jews more vulnerable than they had been for generations. Ferber's ironic use of "brag" dramatizes this vulnerability, this dilemma of the Jew: feel proud of your privileges, but do not call attention to yourself.

This tentative pronouncement of Jewish pride is one of the defining characteristics of the American Jewish women's tradition. As early as 1815 (Rachel Mordecai Lazarus) and as late as the 1890s (Emma Wolf), American Jewish women turned their attention to the theme of nationality through their questioning of the feasibility of living as American Jews. As the preceding discussion has revealed, often American Jewish women writers explored the meaning of their composite identities in segments. Toward the end of the nineteenth century, a growing number of American Jewish women sought ways to confirm, rather than simplify, the complexity of their amalgamated identities ⟨. . . .⟩

Edna Ferber (1887–1968), extremely popular and financially successful, fulfilled the tradition of the previous century's American Jewish women writers. Like many of those writers, she claimed to be proud of her heritage, yet she remained ambivalent about public declarations of her Jewish identity in her life as well as in her fiction. In *A Peculiar Treasure*, her first autobiography, Ferber explained, "It has been my privilege . . . to have been a human being on the planet Earth; and to have been an American, a writer, a Jew" (398). Although she gives equal weight to all three components of her identity, she separates American from Jewish and implies a scale of value through the order of the list. The fact that "woman" is not included raises the question of Ferber's response to her gender, although her fiction makes clear that that part of her identity was as important to her as the others; perhaps it was so obvious to her as to need no comment. ⟨. . .⟩

A Peculiar Treasure provides the most explicit revelation of Ferber's Jewish self. Very early in the volume, Ferber announces, "I should like, in this book, to write about being a Jew" (8). To Ferber, this meant being "especially privileged. Two thousand years of persecution have made the Jew quick to sympathy, quick-witted (he'd better be), tolerant, humanly understanding." But being a Jew "also makes life harder," she confessed (9). Ferber further probed the "riddle of the world's attitude toward the Jew" (61) by explaining that anti-Semitism has

> through the centuries, become a behavioristic habit, like stealing or arson or murder. It is a way of thinking that has been handed down from generation to generation, like tainted blood. It is a criminal weapon used against society by the unsuccessful, the bigoted, the depraved, the ignorant, the neurotic, the failures. It thrives on terror,

hunger, unemployment, hate, resentment. It is mob psychology
displayed at its lowest and most unreasoning. It is a thing to fill one
with a profound sadness and pity for the whole struggling human
race. (9–10)

In 1939, such an observation had immediate and chilling meaning. And it was
necessary for the same reasons that Alice Rhine's and Nina Morais's essays at
the time of the Russian pogroms were necessary: to try once again to explain
to America that it had a special mission both to uphold doctrines of freedom
and tolerance, and to welcome Jews when no one else would. ⟨. . .⟩

Also like many of the nineteenth-century writers, Ferber attempted to cast
her Jewish identity not only in an American, but also in a female, mold. Her
unique stamp on that mold was to transform the myths of True and Jewish
womanhood into the fearless, invincible pioneer woman who was appropriately female in being dedicated to her children and to beauty, but who
unabashedly used her abundant power. In the majority of Ferber's novels, it is
the women who direct the action of the plot as well as function as models of
correct values and behavior.

—Diane Lichtenstein, "American Jewish Women Themselves," *Writing Their Nations: The
Tradition of Nineteenth-Century American Jewish Women Writers* (Bloomington, IN: Indiana
University Press, 1992), 120, 129–31

B I B L I O G R A P H Y

Dawn O'Hara: The Girl Who Laughed. 1911.

Buttered Side Down. 1912.

Roast Beef, Medium: The Business Adventures of Emma McChesney and Her Son, Jock.
1913.

Personality Plus: Some Experiences of Emma McChesney and Her Son, Jock. 1914.

Emma McChesney & Co. 1915.

Fanny Herself. 1917.

Cheerful, by Request. 1918.

Half Portions. 1920.

$1200 a Year (with Newman Levy). 1920.

The Girls. 1921.

Gigolo. 1922.

So Big. 1924.

Minick (with George S. Kaufman). 1925.

The Eldest: A Drama of American Life. 1925.
Show Boat. 1926.
Mother Knows Best: A Fiction Book. 1927.
The Royal Family (with George S. Kaufman). 1928.
Cimarron. 1930.
American Beauty. 1931.
Dinner at Eight (with George S. Kaufman). 1932.
They Brought Their Women. 1933.
Come and Get It. 1935.
Stage Door (with George S. Kaufman). 1936.
Nobody's in Town. 1938.
A Peculiar Treasure. 1939.
No Room at the Inn. 1941.
The Land Is Bright (with George S. Kaufman). 1941.
Saratoga Trunk. 1941.
Great Son. 1945.
One Basket: Thirty-One Stories. 1947.
Your Town. 1948.
Bravo! (with George S. Kaufman). 1949.
Giant. 1952.
Ice Palace. 1958.
A Kind of Magic. 1963.

LILLIAN HELLMAN

1905–1984

LILLIAN HELLMAN was born in New Orleans on June 20, 1905, to Jewish parents, Max and Julia Newhouse Hellman, who were also native southerners. The family moved to New York City when Hellman was very young, but she returned frequently to New Orleans and attended school there. She studied at New York University and briefly at Columbia University, but did not receive a degree. She spent a year reading manuscripts for the publishing house of Horace Liveright in 1924.

The following year she married playwright Arthur Kober; they were divorced in 1932. She had been writing fiction for years before she began publishing her stories, articles, and reviews. In 1932 she began a relationship with detective novelist Dashiell Hammett, with whom she lived until his death. Hammett first encouraged Hellman to write what would become her first literary achievement, the play *The Children's Hour*, produced in 1934. *The Little Foxes* followed in 1939, continuing the theme of societal hypocrisy and corruption.

Hellman's left-wing political views led her to join the Communist Party, and she visited the Soviet Union as an honored guest in 1945. In the 1950s she was called before the House Un-American Activities Committee (HUAC). She denied being a Communist but refused to say whether she had ever been a member of the Communist party; nor would she testify about the political activities of her friends. Her dealings with the HUAC are described in her 1976 memoir, *Scoundrel Time*.

Hellman had stopped writing plays by the early 1960s, but in her last years she wrote three widely acclaimed memoirs: *An Unfinished Woman* (1969), *Pentimento* (1973), and *Scoundrel Time*. She died on June 30, 1984.

C R I T I C A L   E X T R A C T S

CARL ROLLYSON

Although there is a great deal of criticism of liberals in *Watch on the Rhine*, it is a crowd-pleaser because it suggests that ultimately liberals will do the right thing. Early drafts of the play were harsher. Kurt implies, for example, that he has to come to the United States illegally because "working anti-Fascists" are

33

not wanted; they are called "radicals" in America. Here Kurt expresses Hellman's feelings, which were published on December 10, 1940, in *The New Masses*. Along with Lion Feuchtwanger, a German-Jewish historical novelist, she was appealing for aid to the anti-Fascists who had fought for democracy in Spain but who now found themselves interned in French concentration camps. Thinking of men like Kurt Muller, Hellman noted that "there were days, not so long ago, when a political refugee was honored and welcomed by the liberals of every country in the world. But the places where he can be welcomed have each month grown fewer." The implication of Kurt's remarks and Sara's in the early drafts of the play is that American liberals *say* they are against fascism because it is the fashion to do so. They do not really want to support the anti-Hitler revolution in Germany. In the final draft, Fanny is given the pointed remarks and Kurt is circumspect:

> FANNY: Are you a radical?
>
> KURT: You would have to tell me what that word means to you, Madame.
>
> FANNY: (*after a slight pause*): That is just. We all have private definitions. We are all Anti-Fascists, for example—
>
> SARA: Yes. But Kurt works at it.

This is cunning revision. Everything Kurt says is measured and precisely spoken. It is up to Sara to deliver the rebuke to her mother (with a line originally given to Kurt). When Fanny forces Kurt to detail his political activity, he responds not with political opinions—sure to offend some members of the audience—but with an anecdote about Kirchweih, a gay holiday that gradually turns somber as the German economy deteriorates and the Nazis take control of the country. In this speech, Hellman manages to incorporate some of her extensive reading on post-World War I history and at the same time to make Kurt's antifascism spring entirely from his personal experience. ⟨. . .⟩

In *The New Masses* (April 15, 1941), Alvah Bessie handed down the party line on *Watch on the Rhine*. He admired Hellman's sincere and effective effort to get her audience's emotional consent to Kurt Muller's antifascism. But what was the basis of Kurt's politics? The play did not say. And what would be the "cure for this pestilence of our time"? Only a "world-wide organization by the working people against their separate home-grown brands of fascism." As a popular Broadway playwright, Hellman must have known that Bessie's line would prove to be much too controversial. She even deleted from an early draft Kurt's statement about an anti-Nazi organization's "attempt to teach the working mass of the German people." *Watch on the Rhine*, Bessie contended, "can be and has already been misused by those who would like to whip us or cajole us into imperialist war under the banner of fighting fascism in Germany." There it was: the implied rationale for supporting the pact. Because of Stalin's agreement with Hitler, the current war must be imperialist. After the Soviet Union was invaded, however, the war was no longer imperialist. Russia was now America's ally, and *Watch on the Rhine* was rehabilitated by American Communists.

Hellman's statements in the press during the production of *Watch on the Rhine* clearly show how much care she took to exclude many of her own political opinions from the play. As a dramatist, she came nowhere near her feelings about the persecution of the Jews or about home-grown fascism. At an authors' luncheon on January 9, 1941, sponsored by the American Booksellers Association and the *New York Herald Tribune*, she identified herself as a writer and a Jew. She wanted to be "quite sure" that she would be able to "say that greed is bad or persecution is worse . . . without being branded by the malice of people who make a living by that malice." She wanted to go on saying she was a Jew "without being afraid that I will be called names or end in a prison camp or be forbidden to walk down the street at night." Having been in Europe, she had returned "to see many of the same principles of propaganda and censorship apparently existing here," and she was particularly upset by the "private definitions" of terms like *Americanism* which she deemed especially "impertinent." She was already reacting to the campaign against so-called Communist subversives that would go into full swing after World War II.

    —Carl Rollyson, "Watch on the Rhine (1941)," *Lillian Hellman: Her Legend and Her Legacy* (New York: St. Martin's Press, 1988), 173–77

LILLIAN HELLMAN

It was with *Days to Come*, or perhaps it was with *The Little Foxes*—this forgetting has its cheery side—that I began to examine the two descriptions that some critics have found so handy for me: the plays are too well-made, the plays are melodramas. By the well-made play, I think is meant the play whose effects are contrived, whose threads are knit tighter than the threads in life and so do not convince.

Obviously, I can have no argument with those whom my plays do not convince. Something does not convince you. Very well, and that is all. But if they convince you, or partly convince you, then the dislike of their being well-made makes little sense. The theatre has limitations: it is a tight, unbending, unfluid, meager form in which to write. And for these reasons, compared to the novel, it is a second-rate form. (I speak of the form, not the content.) Let us admit that. Having admitted it—a step forward, since most of us are anxious to claim the medium by which we earn a living is a fine and fancy thing—we can stop the pretentious lie that the stage is unhampered. What the author has to say is unhampered: his means of saying it are not. He may do without scenery, he may use actors not as people but as animals or clouds, and he still must *pretend* the empty stage is a garden or an arena, and he still must *pretend* that living people are animals. He has three walls of a theatre and he has begun his pretense with the always rather comic notion that the audience is the fourth wall. He must pretend and he must represent. And if there is something vaguely awry, for me, about the pretense of representation—since by the nature of the stage it can never be done away with—it is not that I wish to deny to other writers their variations of the form, but that, for me, the realistic form has interested me most.

Within this form there must be tricks—the theatre is a trick—and they are, I think, only bad when they are used trickily and stop you short. But if they are there, simple, and come to hand, they are justified. In the last act of *Watch on the Rhine*, Kurt Müller is about to leave. He wants to say good-bye to his children who are upstairs. He asks his wife to bring them down. Now it is most probable that in real life a man would go upstairs, find the children in their room, say good-bye there. But it seemed to me, when this problem came up, that kind of un-well-madeness was not worth the candle. It seemed messy to ring in another set, to bring down the curtain, to interfere with a mood and a temper. The playwright, unlike the novelist, must—and here is where I think the charge of well-madeness should be made—trick up the scene. This is how he has to work. It is too bad, but it is not his fault. If he is good, and drives ahead, it will not matter much. If he is not good, the situation will worry him, and he will begin to pretend it doesn't exist and, by so pretending, fret and lengthen it.

I think the word melodrama, in our time, has come to be used in an almost illiterate manner. By definition it is a violent dramatic piece, with a happy ending. But I think we can add that it uses its violence for no purpose, to point no moral, to say nothing, in say-nothing's worse sense. (This, of course, does not mean, even by inference, that violence plus the *desire* to say something will raise the level of the work. A great many bad writers want to say something: their intention may make them fine men, but it does not make them fine writers. Winning the girl, getting the job, vanquishing the slight foe, are not enough.) But when violence is actually the needed stuff of the work and comes toward a large enough end, it has been and always will be in the good writer's field. George Moore said there was so much in *War and Peace* that Tolstoi must surely have awakened in the night frightened that he had left out a yacht race or a High Mass. There is a needed return to the correct use of the word melodrama. It is only then the critic will be able to find out whether a writer justifies his use of violence, and to scale him against those who have used it.

—Lillian Hellman, "Introduction," *Four Plays* (1942), in *The Chelsea House Library of Literary Criticism: Twentieth-Century American Literature*, Vol. 3, Harold Bloom, ed. (New York: Chelsea House Publishers, 1986), 1788–89

BARRETT H. CLARK

Watch on the Rhine, first produced in 1941, was probably even more popular than *The Little Foxes*. It is by all odds the most human of all the Hellman plays, the warmest and in some ways the most understanding. For one thing it has a full-length hero, again a man who "works for other men." He is articulate in a wholly winning manner, and he goes out of his way to stress his unimportance; besides, the enemy is not capitalism, or the privileged members of society, but fascism at its melodramatic worst. Kurt, the little German who gives up his work, his wife and children, and is ready to give up his life in order to crush what threatens all we believe in, could scarcely have been anything but sympathetic.

And again I call attention to the "villain" Teck, the Romanian aristocrat who blackmails his hosts into buying him off when he discovers who Kurt is and what he is trying to do. Teck is no lay figure; he does not even represent fascism: he is no more than a pitiful little rat, himself a victim. But the author wastes no hatred upon him; she even goes out of her way to make him understandable, and she likewise endows him with some remnants of human decency. In a word, she has learned that to symbolize a situation it is not necessary to assume the manner or dramatize the gestures of contempt. The fact speaks for itself when the fact is wholly and understandably embodied in speech and action. ⟨. . .⟩

⟨. . .⟩ The theme in *The Searching Wind* is neither so obvious nor so clearly stated as it was in *Watch on the Rhine*, because by its very nature it is hardly susceptible of perfect definition. When Moses finds himself in the midst of the *fait accompli* of Mussolini's capture of Rome, he says: "I knew most of this years ago. But I should have known before that, and I did. But I didn't know I did. All night long I've been trying to find out when I should have known." There is the heart of the problem Miss Hellman has sought to elucidate, if not to solve. Why have the men of good will and courage and intelligence allowed the destroyers of freedom and the dignity of man to get the upper hand, and how has it come about that little or nothing was attempted besides appeasement? How many of us knew what was happening, and what prevented our

killing the evil before it took root and spread? An episodic play of the ordinary kind could do little but remind us of twenty years' newspaper headlines,
and an episodic scene would have had to be added to point the moral. So the
ever seeking playwright, not content with spinning a little fable and tacking
an appendix onto it, conceived a dramatic structure which should combine a
personal knot of conflicting wills with a roughly parallel knot showing how a
world-wide situation was only an amplified personal drama on a large scale.
Cassie, Emily, and Alex, all seeking to understand their relationships one to
the other, are in the same sort of dilemma that the world faced twenty years
ago and about which the enemies of fascism were unable to do anything effective until a world war resulted.

> —Barrett H. Clark, "Lillian Hellman," *College English* (December 1944), in *The Chelsea House
> Library of Literary Criticism: Twentieth-Century American Literature*, Vol. 3, Harold Bloom, ed. (New
> York: Chelsea House Publishers, 1986), 1794

HAROLD CLURMAN

It is my belief that Lillian Hellman's *The Autumn Garden* is the most deftly constructed, the most maturely thought, the most scrupulously written play produced here in a long time; I do not think that, because I directed it, I should
refrain from saying this. Moreover, since Miss Hellman is one of the most
important American playwrights, I feel that criticism of her latest play should
attempt to confront it on the high level of its ambition.

The Autumn Garden has the density of a big novel. If this is a fault, to complain about it is like complaining, as a folk saying puts it, that the bride is too
beautiful. The play is dense because Miss Hellman has tried to construct it not
along the usual lines of a cumulatively progressive single story, but as a compact tissue of life unraveled with the apparent casualness of ordinary behavior.
Ten people's lives are disclosed, and what holds their interlocking stories
together is the author's theme and point of view.

To make a formula of it, what Miss Hellman is saying in *The Autumn Garden*
is that each of our lives constitutes a decisive act, and that when the chain of
these acts reaches a certain point—around the middle years—no sudden
movement of our will is likely to alter the shape and meaning of what we have
made. To hope, as most of us do, that though we dream one thing and do
another, it will come out all right in the end, come out satisfactorily according
to some abstract conception we have fuzzily projected in our imagination, is
to indulge in a lie that will finally rob us of pleasure, dignity and substance.

A play's ideology is not precisely the same thing as its content. What is
significant in *The Autumn Garden* is not so much its thematic emphasis as Miss
Hellman's approach, her feeling about most of us of the educated near-upper

class. We are earnest, we yearn, but we are not serious, we have no clear purpose. We have no binding commitments to ourselves or to others; we are attached to nothing. We allow ourselves to be deviated because we do not know exactly where we want to go.

This is not, as Miss Hellman suggests her thought in terms of her characters, simply a matter of high moral aims. The dilettante painter of her play, an intellectual lightweight and universal flirt, is actually less damaged than the intelligent Crossman whose words are always sounder than those of the others. The painter wants little more than what he does, while Crossman satisfies himself with "understanding" everything except that he is wasting his life and that his "honesty" has no object except to hide his own futility from himself.

The people of The Autumn Garden are ordinary, nice people, average to their class—but in this sense they are representative of far more of us than we care to believe. Miss Hellman finds none of them bad, but in the light of their own sweet earnestness, rather silly. They are unwittingly self-condemned, even before they are socially condemned, because they are not intelligent in relation to any total human objective. They are idealists whose ideals are conventions and chimeras rather than goals. They will wither and disappear in a mist of empty sighs.

Against these people, Miss Hellman pits the half-European Sophie, a normal girl who wants only to do an honest job back in the grim environment of her native land, where things are not pretty or "good," but concrete, unromanticized, real. Miss Hellman does not make a heroine of this girl; in fact she makes her rather sharp, shrewd, decently matter-of-fact and not above taking advantage—with a certain humor and pride that some might mistake for cynicism—of the folly of the sentimentalists around her.

The Autumn Garden is lucid, witty, incisive, dramatic, unquestionably the subtlest and most probing of Miss Hellman's plays. If it has a limitation, it is a philosophic or spiritual limitation which is part of her objectivity. The author is just with her characters; she sees them with a certain smiling asperity, an astringent, almost cruel, clarity. But she is unable to reveal in their weakness that which still makes them part of what is blessed and great in life. The blunderers in Chekhov are brothers in our nobility even as in our abjectness. The characters in The Autumn Garden are our equals only in what we do not respect about ourselves. Miss Hellman refuses to be "metaphysical," poetic or soft. She will not embrace her people; she does not believe they deserve her (or our) love. Love is present only through the ache of its absence. Miss Hellman is a fine artist; she will be a finer one when she melts.

—Harold Clurman, "Lillian Hellman's Garden," New Republic (26 March 1951), in The Chelsea House Library of Literary Criticism: Twentieth-Century American Literature, Vol. 3, Harold Bloom, ed. (New York: Chelsea House Publishers, 1986), 1790–91

W. DAVID SIEVERS

Miss Hellman's most recent play, *The Autumn Garden* (1951), is at the same time her most ineffectual, her most baffling and her most psychoanalytic. Although Freudian interpretation can help to explain it, it cannot give the play the dynamic plot development which it lacks. *The Autumn Garden* is a muted, obscure play with the characters moving through decadence, sterility and emptiness as in Chekhov's world, but without the Russian's warmth and affection for his characters. ⟨. . .⟩

The relationship of Nick and Nina is astutely depicted as that of a weak, passive-dependent man, destined always to be unfaithful and to return repentant to his wife, whose unconscious masochism requires just such a man-child. As Fred's old grandmother observes to Nick, shaking his hand off her shoulder, "You're a toucher. You constantly touch people or lean on them. Little moments of sensuality. One should have sensuality whole or not at all. Don't you find pecking at it ungratifying? There are many of you: the touchers and the leaners. All since the depression, is my theory." The grandmother's theory of the leaner or toucher suggests the psychiatric concepts of Harry Stack Sullivan.

The most sympathetic character up until now has been Sophie; but even she is doomed to betray a sour side of her nature. She would use Nick's attempted seduction as an excuse to blackmail him for $5000 with which to return to Germany. Miss Hellman seemed determined to remind us that the human personality is composed of sadistic and aggressive as well as tender and generous impulses in a subtle balance. With her back to the wall in a hostile, foreign land, Sophie uses her wits to advantage, a familiar trademark of Hellman's characters. ⟨. . .⟩

⟨. . .⟩ *The Autumn Garden* is a poignantly sad play of the discovery of the lies or rationalizations by which a group of people have lived—only to learn in the autumn of life that their ego-defenses were only excuses for not doing what they could not or would not will. With profound psychoanalytic perception, Miss Hellman has laid bare the dependency of humans upon each other and upon various rationalizations. If the material somehow eludes Miss Hellman's customarily tight dramaturgy, and if she gives us no single character with whom we can fully empathize, nevertheless *The Autumn Garden* is a masterful attempt to look deep into tragic, empty lives which lacked only self-awareness.

The Autumn Garden marks a step forward in psychology for Lillian Hellman, enlarging her grasp of unconscious motivation beyond the sado-masochism which permeated the Hubbard plays. The theme of latent inversion, too, is suggested in a number of her plays. The task of bringing together in one play the complex and deeply perceived motives of *The Autumn Garden* and the superbly structured theatrical tension of *The Little Foxes* remains the task which Miss Hellman's talents give promise of fulfilling.

—W. David Sievers, "Freudian Fraternity of the Thirties," *Freud on Broadway* (1955), in *The Chelsea House Library of Literary Criticism: Twentieth-Century American Literature*, Vol. 3, Harold Bloom, ed. (New York: Chelsea House Publishers, 1986), 1791–92

Marvin Felheim

Probably no play of the American theater (and I am including that feeble adaptation *The Wisteria Trees*) is more completely Chekhovian than Lillian Hellman's recent and most charming original drama, *The Autumn Garden*. Although the piece was only mildly successful when presented during the 1950–1951 season on Broadway, to the discerning (and here I quote Alan Downer) it is "Miss Hellman's most original play." ⟨. . .⟩

⟨. . .⟩ Without seeming to, in this play Miss Hellman organizes her materials in terms of artistic principles, dramatic principles (what Coleridge called "organic" principles). The realism is to the essence of human existence, not to the representation of life. There are many threads of action and of thought playing through *The Autumn Garden*. By the end of Act One, we have established the moral and artistic principle upon which the play is based: people must do the best they can; to do less is immoral. And Miss Hellman, as she hastens to admit, is "a moral writer." But the difference in *The Autumn Garden* is that the moral is within the situation and within the characters, not superimposed upon them by a skillful playwright. (This is the kind of thing David Magarshack refers to in his exciting study, *Chekhov the Dramatist*. Pointing out that "the chorus element" is "an indispensable feature of the play of indirect-action," he maintains that it is the characters themselves who perform the choral function, or moral judgment on the action. "Characters," he asserts, "assume the mantle of the chorus whenever their inner life bursts through the outer shell of their everyday appearance and overflows into a torrent of words." And when this occurs, the characters move from the world of realism into the world of art. For they are then not merely human beings but become also human symbols.) Nick Denery and Rose Griggs are both immoral and selfish people, but their immorality is a matter of degree inasmuch as all of the characters are to some extent tainted (or human). Perhaps one could say it in this way: in this play, Lillian Hellman lets her characters alone to act out their destinies, regarding them only with love and understanding; in her earlier play, she took sides; one can list the characters she admires and those whose behavior and beliefs she dislikes; in *Days to Come*, for example, she admits she even tried to balance characteristics: good against bad, well against sick, complex against simple. In *The Autumn Garden*, she does not make this kind of breakdown. The result is true complexity, both in dialectics and mechanics.

Mechanically, *The Autumn Garden* has Chekhovian grace. The characters all belong on the set: each has a legitimate reason for being at the Tuckerman house at this particular moment in history; each is searching for the meaning of life, and for love. Some are weak, some a little stronger, but one cannot make lists or easy judgments; this, in other words, is not melodrama; these are people, not puppets. 〈. . .〉

〈. . .〉 The kind of drama we have in *The Autumn Garden* is the only kind which makes for modern tragedy. It is not merely psychological (as in Tennessee Williams) nor sociological (as in Arthur Miller) but it is artistic (poetic) and moral—and all in the Chekhovian sense. And so Miss Hellman's movement in this direction is a movement toward seriousness. As one New York critic ironically put it, Miss Hellman is "our most promising playwright."

    —Marvin Felheim, "*The Autumn Garden*: Mechanics and Dialects," *Modern Drama* (September 1960), in *The Chelsea House Library of Literary Criticism: Twentieth-Century American Literature*, Vol. 3, Harold Bloom, ed. (New York: Chelsea House Publishers, 1986), 1795–96

ALLAN LEWIS

In *The Children's Hour* and *The Little Foxes* the forces of evil are clearly marked. Mary Tilford, the malicious brat, destroys good people in a world where evil is too prone to be accepted. In Regina, all human values have been destroyed by the lust for power and money. Mary confesses, but the harm has already been done. Regina triumphs, and her only defeat is her rejection by her daughter. In *Toys in the Attic*, Cyrus Warkins, the millionaire, is the one consciously malicious character, and he never appears. People who are outwardly good, who presumably sacrifice their lives for others, are now the instruments of human suffering. Misplaced or possessive love can destroy. Julian is beat up physically and his pride broken through the actions of a spinster sister who secretly prefers to keep him close to her, and by a silly, sex-hungry wife who mistakenly fears Julian will leave her. Both loves are selfish and devastating. The innocent are the tragic victims—Karen and Horace and Anna.

Hellman's dark world of those who triumph through a calculated disregard of moral values is as grim and full of pain as in the most extreme theatre of the absurd. Her dramas differ in that they are portraits of people and not of abstract symbols. Events are causative, and the individual the product of his environment. Her one effort to dramatize immediate social forces resulted in her weakest play, *Days to Come*, an obeisance to the times, in which workers and capitalists line up in opposing ranks. 〈. . .〉

Lillian Hellman's strength lies in the dramatic power she can extract from the realistic form. *The Little Foxes*, like *Ghosts*, is almost flawless in economy and structure, realization of character, and pertinence of dialogue. Characters generate events and in turn are influenced by them. *Toys in the Attic* has a weak first act with too much preparation for what follows, but its final resolution is explosive. Hellman's mastery of technique has led to the accusation that her plays are too contrived, too adroitly arranged by the author. Such charges are valid, but it is a pleasure to watch the work of a skilled craftsman. All writers rearrange life and impose their own will on the chaos of reality. The test in the realistic theatre is whether the characters appear to be self-propelled, as they do in *The Little Foxes*, a masterpiece of the Ibsen-influenced theatre. *Toys in the Attic* shows bits of the machinery, perhaps because family plays of psychological insight have become too familiar, but is so artfully contrived that it becomes compelling drama. Hellman does not use her skill to exhibit technical prowess, but to expose the extent to which greed and avarice have corrupted the human soul. She strives for a Chekhovian complex of frustrated and unhappy people, but her use of violence and sexuality brings her closer to Tennessee Williams. ⟨. . .⟩

Hellman's alert sensitivity is able to find varying means to express her major theme. Her problem is her loss of certainty. Her attacks have become negative and as impotent as Rona in *My Mother, My Father, and Me*. When she was stimulated by the social upheaval of the thirties she wrote a powerful drama in human terms, *The Little Foxes*, in which an entire society in decay is revealed. It ranks with Gorky's *Yegor Bulitchev* and Henry Becque's *Les Corbeaux*.

—Allan Lewis, "The Survivors of the Depression," *American Plays and Playwrights* (1965), in *The Chelsea House Library of Literary Criticism: Twentieth-Century American Literature*, Vol. 3, Harold Bloom, ed. (New York: Chelsea House Publishers, 1986), 1797–98

ROBERT BECHTOLD HEILMAN

As melodrama, *The Little Foxes* teeters between the slick and the substantial. By the slick I mean a skill in theatrical manipulations which make our responses too easy; Miss Hellman puts together a smooth succession of clichés and gimmicks to which we are vulnerable if we let slip that vigilance which is the price of freedom in the theater. By the substantial I mean a sense of reality which has some continuing power to gain assent. The slick predominates. Of the dramatic versions of "The love of money is the root of all evil" *The Little Foxes* has the most clear-cut division between bad guys (the brothers Ben and Oscar Hubbard, their sister Regina Giddens, and Oscar's son Leo) and good guys (Oscar's wife Birdie, Regina's husband Horace and her daughter Alexandra, and their black servants Addie and Cal). The Hubbards have got rich in business, and they have no scruples about getting richer; they scorn their less money-minded spouses. Their plots and counterplots, including robbing Horace and outsmarting each other, move ahead briskly, the over-all expectedness combined with entertaining unexpectedness of detail. (Surprise: Horace plans, by writing a new will, to turn their robbery of him into a punishment of his wife. Surprise: he dies (with help) before the will is written. Surprise: Regina uses her knowledge of the robbery to make her brothers toe the financial mark and cut her in for more profits than they intended. Surprise: Alexandra revolts against Regina, and brother Ben hints that he may still get the upper hand of Regina by learning a little more about Horace's death.) There are no surprises of character in the calculating Hubbards or in the nicer people, who are sensitive, musical, socially conscious, not very happy, and rather the worse for wear because of the Hubbards. There is pathos: Birdie drinks alone; Horace is at death's door because of a bad heart; Alexandra is pushed around by her scheming mother. Obviously we can do nothing but side with decent underdog Davids against tough-skinned Goliaths. Characters get new light on what others are up to, but none on themselves. Instead of the drama of divided personality we have the theater of duplicity in action; the clever deployment of single-track personalities invites numerous alternating responses rather than complex ones. The execution is strictly monopathic.

What is substantial is Miss Hellman's sense of the intensity of monetary self-seeking, of love of power, of how it works and what it leads to. She tries for the general validity that lies beyond stereotypes. Ben tells Regina that "the world is open . . . for people like you and me. . . . There are hundreds of Hubbards sitting in rooms like this throughout the country" (III). Insofar as this applies to the twentieth century or to the "new South," the realm is that of social documentation. A truth more general than historical appears in a common element in *The Little Foxes* and Jonson's *The Fox*: in both there is the foxiness of the acquisitive operating against each other—the persuasive irony of dishonor among thieves. This complexity crops up effectively in the final situation: as the Hubbards look ahead to a fatter world, they also face each other, and that means no final peace or certainty about advantages gained. This is a touch of the black comedy that we saw in Becque. But the divided-ness of appeal achieved by Becque is not produced by the final confrontation of the Hubbards; they simply make us wonder which of them will be cleverer in the next round.

Death appears, almost inevitably. In *Everyman*, death was an opportunity for spiritual reassessment, and in *The Vultures*, for the predators to move in on the vulnerable; in *The Little Foxes*, death is a made opportunity: Regina assists an ailing husband out of a troubled life. The action stays on the melodramatic level: Regina is untroubled by restraining imperatives.

—Robert Bechtold Heilman, "Dramas of Money," *The Iceman, the Arsonist and the Troubled Agent* (1973), in *The Chelsea House Library of Literary Criticism: Twentieth-Century American Literature*, Vol. 3, Harold Bloom, ed. (New York: Chelsea House Publishers, 1986), 1792–93

JAMES EATMAN

To assess *The Little Foxes* as merely a compelling struggle between the forces of good and evil is to underestimate the ambiguity of the moral positions implied by the play. The victims of the Hubbard machinations—represented by Birdie, Addie, Horace, and Alexandra—are appealingly sympathetic, but they are deficient as moral agents. Birdie quietly evades her painful environment by drinking and covert protest against the Hubbards. But at least she is willing to acknowledge her moral weakness in an attempt to spare her young niece Alexandra of a similar plight. In Birdie's last scene in the play, she confesses to Alexandra that she has been drinking privately for a long time. When Alexandra says she will still always love her, Birdie retorts:

> Well, don't. Don't love me. Because in twenty years you'll just be like
> me. They'll do all the same things to you. [. . .] You know what? In
> twenty-two years I haven't had a whole day of happiness.

Addie, also, does no more than quietly complain about the Hubbards. She says:

> Yeah, they got mighty well-off cheating niggers. Well, there are
> people who eat the earth and eat all the people on it like in the Bible
> with the locusts. And other people who stand around and watch
> them eat it. (*Softly*) Sometimes I think it ain't right to stand and watch
> them do it.

Edifying as this sentiment may be, Addie herself violates it, in a sense, by remaining a "loyal" servant to the Hubbards. She too "stands around and watches" while they despoil. Even though her chances for self-maintenance outside the Hubbard circle are probably limited, Addie has more freedom in choosing her circumstances than she had before the Emancipation Proclamation (1862). As for Horace, his decision to stand up against the Hubbards may be admirable, but it has taken him some twenty years to reach that decision. Moreover, his attempt to thwart Regina's financial hopes by using the Hubbard-like tactics of secrecy and evasion does not enhance his moral position. Alexandra experiences a moral awakening, but it would be premature to assume that she will carry out her stated intentions. Summarily, the morality that can be extrapolated from the actions of these four characters is humane but largely ineffectual.

As for the morality of the Hubbards themselves, special pleading cannot substantially justify their exploitation, which culminates in the death of Horace. Yet for all their excesses they are by no means anomalous to their moment in history. In a sense, their actions manifest the ethics of progress—namely, that traditional morality must be modified or set aside to accommodate the momentum of much needed economic progress. W. J. Cash and other historians have viewed the application of the ethics of progress as apparently necessary to the growth of Southern industry in this period. Thus, the Hubbards, whatever their methods or goals, were potentially contributors to the recovery of Southern economy by their promise of a cotton mill. 〈. . .〉

If *The Little Foxes* tests a historical era with a moral perspective rooted outside the era, then the play gains in its value as social history, in one important sense. Moral perspectives are, after all, as much a part of social history as economic pursuits. By examining an age of progress according to views from an age of skepticism, Miss Hellman reconstructs a crucial dilemma for American liberal democracy then and now: how to uphold both private freedom and public concern when the two are at odds.

—James Eatman, "The Image of American Destiny: *The Little Foxes*," *Players Magazine* (December–January 1973), in *The Chelsea House Library of Literary Criticism: Twentieth-Century American Literature*, Vol. 3, Harold Bloom, ed. (New York: Chelsea House Publishers, 1986), 1798–99

PHILIP M. ARMATO

The rancorous structure of interpersonal relationships in *The Children's Hour* is patterned after the structure of human association in the Venice of Shakespeare's *Merchant*. This can best be described as a victim-victimizer syndrome, the most concrete representation of which is the relationship between Antonio and Shylock. Antonio is convinced that his harsh treatment of Shylock is "just," because the Jew's interest rates are harsh. As victim, Shylock suffers from spiritual agony, feelings of persecution, and desires revenge. If he is able to consummate his wish, Shylock will become the victimizer of the man who originally victimized him. That the victim-victimizer syndrome is finally self-destructive is seen in the courtroom scene, when each victimizer in turn is reduced to the position of victim. Shylock's demand for Antonio's life is turned against him when Portia reminds the court that an alien Jew must suffer the death penalty if he plots against the life of a Venetian citizen. The Duke and Antonio destroy the vicious circle by showing mercy to Shylock.

In the first two acts of her play, Hellman develops three relationships which are characterized by the circular form and destructive content of the victim-victimizer syndrome; these pairs are; Karen Wright—Mary Tilford, Martha Dobie—Lily Mortar, and Amelia Tilford—Wright/Dobie. In *The Merchant*, a Jew who is socially inferior to a Christian is mistreated by the Christian and attempts to use the Duke—the land's highest authority—as a vehicle for his revenge. In *The Children's Hour*, an adolescent pupil who is socially inferior to an adult teacher is mistreated by the teacher and proceeds to use Lancet's most influential citizen—the powerful matron Amelia Tilford— as a vehicle for her revenge. Finally, in the much criticized third act, Hellman, like Shakespeare, posits mercy as the only solution to the moral dilemma which is created when we deal justly with each other. . . .

The two traditional criticisms of *The Children's Hour's* last act are that Mary Tilford is the central interest of the play and so should not be missing at its conclusion; and that the final "summing up" (Hellman's words) is tedious. However, Mary Tilford is not the central interest of the play; a certain perverse structure of human relationships is. Moreover, if critics paid more attention to what Hellman is "summing up," they would find that the conclusion of the play is a structurally necessary resolution, not a tedious reiteration of previous materials. Jacob H. Adler has noted that *The Children's Hour*, like *The Wild Duck*, "ends not with . . . [a] suicide but with a brief discussion pinning down the issues as a result of the suicide."

Works as diverse as Aeschylus' *Oresteia*, Shakespeare's *Measure for Measure*, and Melville's *Billy Budd* have dealt with the dichotomy between primitive justice and mercy. Although *The Children's Hour* is certainly a less monumental work of art than any of these, it is within its limits a wholly successful moral play. Hellman suggests that adults are too often "children." While infantile revenge is matter of course in men's dealings with each other, Hellman shows a last-act discovery—Karen Wright's discovery of a more mature concept of compassion.

—Philip M. Armato, "Good and Evil in Lillian Hellman's *The Children's Hour*," *Educational Theatre Journal* (December 1973), in *The Chelsea House Library of Literary Criticism: Twentieth-Century American Literature*, Vol. 3, Harold Bloom, ed. (New York: Chelsea House Publishers, 1986), 1792

ALFRED KAZIN

The success of *Scoundrel Time* is due in part to Hellman's long-standing grievance against government in America. This cannot but please a generation sickened by Vietnam, Watergate, governmental snooping, taxation on every civic level. The young, unlike old leftists and ex-leftists now in their seventies, have no interest in Russia but are understandably suspicious of their own government, so overgrown, unwieldy, secretive, demanding, hideously costly. . . . Lillian Hellman has been dramatizing herself ever since she stopped writing plays. She can dramatize anything about herself and she has done herself, Dashiell Hammett, her old retainers, the many people she hates, with a Broadway skill that is a mixture of social snottiness and glib liberalism. A large audience—if it includes many people who disagree with her if they ever think about it—finds her so-called memoirs irresistible.

If you wonder how a nonfiction book can have so much dialogue and why there should be so many baddies in her innocent life, the answer is that Broadway will rewrite anything. . . .

Hellman is easy on herself and Hammett, exquisitely nasty to those with whom she disagrees. Henry Wallace didn't seem to know that Communists were running his 1948 campaign until she told him. What she does then is mark him down for being dumb; pushes him down even more for being a stingy rube in restaurants; scorns his wife for serving a ridiculous supper of one egg on shredded wheat. She then caps the performance by explaining to Wallace that the Communists running him "'don't . . . mean any harm; they're stubborn men.' 'I see,' he said, and that was that." But it isn't. *Scoundrel Time* is historically a fraud, artistically a put-up job and emotionally packed with meanness. Oh, these ancient positions and position takers! These glib moral- ity plays about goodies and baddies in a world where millions have died, will go on dying, for not taking the correct "line"!

It cannot be said of Lillian Hellman, as was said of Henry James, that she has a mind so fine that "no idea can violate it." She is full of ideas. So, in another bad time, her book has pleased all those who think that Stalin lived in the time of Ivan the Terrible and that her taking the Fifth Amendment in 1952 gives political sanction and importance in the 1970's to her self-approval and her every dogged resentment.

—Alfred Kazin, "The Legend of Lillian Hellman," *Esquire* (August 1977), in *The Chelsea House Library of Literary Criticism: Twentieth-Century American Literature*, Vol. 3, Harold Bloom, ed. (New York: Chelsea House Publishers, 1986), 1793

KATHERINE LEDERER

A generation of theater-goers and theater students have been conditioned to associate the name Hellman with the terms "well-made play," "melodrama," "social protest." If this cultural reflex persists, then Hellman's metaphor of fash- ion in the theater will continue to describe her critical reputation.

An unnecessary stumbling block to a fresh perception of Hellman is the "political" label. Although, as Jacob Adler comments, "to one assessing her as an artist, politics—particularly her political problems in the Fifties—seems almost entirely beside the point," political partisanship is not likely to subside in the foreseeable future.

The Hellman vision is nonetheless moral, not political. Robert Corrigan and John Gassner arrived independently at the same judgment: Gassner said, "Miss Hellman concerns herself generally with damnation as a state of the soul, and a case might be made out for saying that her real theme, whether she knew it or not, is 'original sin' in a modern context, which brings her closer to such contemporary Catholic writers as Mauriac than to Bernard Shaw or Karl Marx." Corrigan concluded that "she cannot be considered, as she so often is, a social writer; rather, she is interested in showing damnation as a state of the soul, a condition that cannot be reformed out of existence or dissolved by sentimentality or easy optimism."

Murray Kempton said that Hellman's behavior before the House committee was partly determined by her sense of how things would look in due course. For "in due course" substitute the "days to come" of the Old Testament, days determined by human actions today. Engagement, commitment, self-knowledge, and self-acknowledgment of responsibility are the virtues Hellman urges on her audiences and readers. If the memoirs had never been written, the moral vision is clear in play after play.

As critics of the memoirs have pointed out, Hellman's moral vision is inseparable from the ironic vision and voice. Though obviously more overt in the memoirs, the voice is there in the plays. And "[a]s soon as an ironic voice has been used to any extent in any work of any kind," says Wayne Booth, "readers inevitably begin to take interest and pleasure in that voice—in the tasks it assigns and the qualities it provides; it thus becomes part of whatever is seen as the controlling context."

In *The Context and Craft of Drama*, James Rosenberg raises a pertinent question: "why must generic classification necessarily degenerate into a game of hierarchies? Is it not enough to perceive that there are various modes of perception . . . ?" What we should recognize is "a way of seeing, not a trick of writing."

Any final judgment must include a perception of Hellman as ironist, with a way of seeing, and seeing again. This is not to say that such an awareness will necessarily cause a reader to prefer Hellman to other major American playwrights. But it should prevent one's judging her by inapplicable criteria. To "rank" Hellman in a Williams-Odets-whoever list is, as she might put it, "a losing game." In the modern American theater Lillian Hellman is *sui generis*, and a careful reading of her plays reveals that those generally considered her best (*The Little Foxes*, *The Autumn Garden*, *Toys in the Attic*—to which list might be added *Watch on the Rhine* and *Another Part of the Forest*) are the most fully ironic (and novelistic). By the same criteria, *Pentimento*, in which Hellman most completely employs fictional techniques and a controlling ironic voice, is the superior memoir.

—Katherine Lederer, "An Ironic Vision," *Lillian Hellman* (1979), in *The Chelsea House Library of Literary Criticism: Twentieth-Century American Literature*, Vol. 3, Harold Bloom, ed. (New York: Chelsea House Publishers, 1986), 1790

ESTELLE C. JELINEK

In 1969, when Lillian Hellman (1905–84) published the first of her three life studies, she was already a successful playwright and not a controversial public figure. So, unlike Stanton and Stein (and, as we will see, Millett), she wrote neither to prove herself to the public nor to make herself famous. Also, she was neither a feminist nor a political activist. She was by temperament a woman of the twenties, that generation of women who believed they had won their freedom and needed only to prove by dint of talent and personality that they could make it in a man's world.

And, of course, she had. By 1969 all twelve of her plays, including adaptations, had been produced on Broadway—from 1934 to 1963. She was an independent woman, secure in the public's approval. The reason for undertaking her life study seems to have been primarily to try to make sense of the past for her own personal satisfaction.

However, when Hellman wrote *An Unfinished Woman* (1969), she seems to have had no preconceived idea of what her proper autobiographical mode would be. She wrote: "As I come now to write about them the memories skip about and make no pattern." There is no pattern in the first memoir either. In fact, it is a potpourri of styles, obviously a casual experiment to see which form most suited her personality and skills. Hellman starts with a chronological narrative of her early years. The first fourteen, untitled chapters follow one another chronologically, but internally all of them mix up the chronology with anecdotal flashbacks and flashforwards.

The first two chapters reveal painful and frank recollections of her family and her girlhood, recollections showing such a grasp of her materials that both chapters are capable of standing alone as independent vignettes. Once into young womanhood, however, her memories seem to wander as aimlessly as her own concept of herself. The middle ten chapters seem to have no purpose other than to record many anecdotes about friends and acquaintances. Two chapters on her experiences in the New York publishing world of the twenties (where she goes out of chronology to complete a profile of Horace Liveright) and two on her aimless years in Hollywood convey a sense of helpless torpor during a young womanhood spent waiting for something to happen. She presents a vague and quick vignette of her marriage to and divorce from Arthur Kober and an even more elusive sketch of her meeting and early life with Dashiell Hammett and their return to New York when her writing began in earnest. The reader is left with huge gaps in Hellman's life during the twenties and thirties, but the basic chronology is maintained.

In the next chapter, the eleventh, on her experiences in Spain during the Civil War and in the next five chapters on her trip to Russia during World War II, her narrative skips around. Unsure how to handle a historical panorama, she quotes long sections from her diaries, sometimes inserting in brackets her present reflections or hindsight on her experiences. In the last two chapters on Russia, she begins to get a grasp of her material. Looking back on her trip there in 1944 with the perspective of a return visit in 1967, she is much more capable of integrating the past and the present. Still, it must have become clear to Hellman that sketching an entire country was more difficult for her than writing about individual people. Finally, in the last three chapters of *An Unfinished Woman* she finds her style—in three portraits of people she cared about very dearly: Dorothy Parker, Dashiell Hammett, and Helen Jackson (along with a sketch of Sophronia Mason). None is a complete biography of its subject, but rather each consists of impressionistic and random anecdotes, mostly about the person's last years before death.

Thus, four years later, when Hellman wrote *Pentimento*, she was in complete control of her autobiographical mode. She had learned that her forte was in portraits and vignettes about people—the "silhouettes" that Frances Willard attached as afterthoughts to her life study have become the dominant mode. This second memoir, subtitled *A Book of Portraits*, contains seven skillfully shaped profiles of people she loved—all dead at the time of its writing. Hellman forgoes any attempt at a sustained chronological narrative though the portraits tend to follow one another progressively in time, with some over-lapping, and, of course, a great deal of selective omission. Instead of writing about herself directly as she had in one of the early chapters about her girl-hood in *An Unfinished Woman*, she presents herself indirectly by means of these miniature biographies. Within each portrait, the time sequence is interrupted constantly by flashbacks and flashforwards, as in the first book, but here she is in complete control of her material; there is no aimlessness but an artistic shaping of each profile. Even when she concentrates on one historical event, as she does in her third memoir, *Scoundrel Time*—her appearance before the House Un-American Activities Committee in 1952—Hellman disrupts the chronology by alluding to events as early as 1929 and as late as 1975, devel-ops cameo portraits of others and herself, and even successfully integrates diary notes with present reflections and insights.

Like other female autobiographers before her, Hellman discovered that the historical or chronological mode was insufficient for expressing her per-sonal vision, that her most comfortable autobiographical method was the vignette or portrait. By means of these entertaining profiles of others, Hellman orchestrates a portrait of herself, one that is never precise or sharp but always elliptical and impressionistic. In her psychologically sophisticated hands, the means of protecting one's vulnerable private self has progressed from Stanton's direct omission and Stein's camouflage to Hellman's subtle exposure.

—Estelle C. Jelinek, "Literary Autobiography Recast: The Oblique Heroism of Lillian Hellman," *The Tradition of Women's Autobiography: From Antiquity to the Present* (Boston: Twayne Publishers, 1986), 150–52

B I B L I O G R A P H Y

The Children's Hour. 1934.
Days to Come. 1936.
The Little Foxes. 1939.
Watch on the Rhine. 1941.
The North Star: A Motion Picture About Some Russian People. 1943.
The Searching Wind. 1944.
Another Part of the Forest. 1947.
Montserrat. 1950.
The Autumn Garden. 1951.
Selected Letters of Anton Chekhov (ed.). 1955.
The Lark (trans.). 1956.
Candide (adaptation; with Dorothy Parker and Richard Wilbur). 1957.
Toys in the Attic. 1960.
My Mother, My Father and Me. 1963.
The Big Knockover by Dashiell Hammett (ed.). 1966.
An Unfinished Woman: A Memoir. 1969.
The Collected Plays. 1972.
Pentimento. 1973.
Scoundrel Time. 1976.
Three. 1979.
Maybe. 1980.
Eating Together (with Peter Feibleman). 1984.

TILLIE OLSEN

1913–

TILLIE OLSEN was born in Nebraska on January 14, 1913, the second of six children. Her parents, Samuel and Ida Lerner, were Jewish immigrants who had fled Russia after the 1905 revolution. Her father, a manual laborer, later became secretary of the Nebraska Socialist Party.

Olsen left high school without graduating and worked in factories and warehouses. She joined the Young Communist League and was arrested in the early 1930s for trying to organize Kansas City packinghouse workers. By 1933 she had moved to California, where she settled permanently. As a union worker she took part in the San Francisco Warehouse Strike of 1934 and spent more time in jail. In 1936 she married Jack Olsen, a printer. To help support their three daughters Olsen worked as, among other things, a waitress, laundress, and secretary.

In 1956, a year after enrolling in a creative writing course at San Francisco State University, Olsen won a Stanford University fellowship. With the aid of several subsequent grants she embarked on a career as a writer and teacher. *Tell Me a Riddle*, her first book, was published in 1961, and the title story of this collection received the O. Henry Award for the best short story of that year. Between 1969 and 1972 Olsen taught at Amherst College, the University of Massachusetts, and Stanford University. After spending 1973 as a writer-in-residence at M.I.T., she returned to the University of Massachusetts as a visiting professor.

Olsen's writing has been influenced by her feminist concerns and by her working-class background; her major theme has been the waste of human potential that results from poverty, sexism, and racial prejudice. In addition to her collection of stories, she has published *Yonnondio* (1974), a novel about life in the 1930s, and *Silences*, a collection of essays.

CRITICAL   EXTRACTS

JOANNE S. FRYE

Motherhood as literary metaphor has long been a cliché for the creative process: the artist gives birth to a work of art which takes on a life of its own. Motherhood as literary experience has only rarely existed at all, except as perceived by a resentful or adoring son who is working through his own identity in separation from the power of a nurturant and/or threatening past. The uniqueness of Tillie Olsen's "I Stand Here Ironing" lies in its fusion of motherhood as both metaphor and experience: it shows us motherhood bared, stripped of romantic distortion, and reinfused with the power of genuine metaphorical insight into the problems of selfhood in the modern world. ⟨. . .⟩

The story is very fundamentally structured through the mother's present selfhood. It is her reality with which we are centrally concerned, her perception of the process of individuation to which the story gives us access. Her concerns with sorting through Emily's past are her concerns with defining the patterns of motherhood and of the limitations on her capacity to care for and support the growth of another human being. As she rethinks the past, she frames her perceptions through such interjections as "I did not know then what I know now" (p. 11) and "What in me demanded that goodness in her?" (p. 12)—gauges taken from the present self to try to assess her own past behavior. But throughout, she is assessing the larger pattern of interaction between her own needs and constraints and her daughter's needs and constraints. When she defines the hostilities between Emily and her sister Susan—"that terrible balancing of hurts and needs" (p. 16)—she asserts her own recognition not only of an extreme sibling rivalry but also of the inevitable conflict in the separate self-definitions of parent and child. Gauging the hurts and needs of one human being against the hurts and needs of another: this is the pattern of parenthood. But more, it is the pattern of a responsible self living in relationship. ⟨. . .⟩

One of the central defining premises for the working out of separate personal identity for both mother and daughter is the power of cultural circumstances. The narrative is laced with references to the depression, the war, the survival needs which dictate unsatisfactory child care arrangements and equally unsatisfactory work circumstances. Even the dictates of pediatric treatises on breast-feeding by the decree of the clock (p. 10) become a part of the general cultural pressure which operates to define and limit the power of individual choice. Over and over, we are told of the limitations on choice—"it was the only way" (p. 11); "They persuaded me" (p. 13)—and verbs of necessity recur for descriptions of both the mother's and Emily's behavior. In the attempt at summing up, the mother concludes: "She kept too much in herself, her life was such she had to keep too much in herself. My wisdom came too late. She has much to her and probably little will come of it. She is a child of her age, of depression, of war, of fear" ⟨. . .⟩

This claim to her own self-validation remains primarily a general premise of the story rather than a specific claim at points within the narrative. Her actual absolution—to the extent that she is seeking absolution from parental guilt—does not come in the particular recognition of past success or failure. Rather it comes in the growing emphasis upon Emily's separateness and Emily's right to make her own imprint upon the world in which she lives. The narrative's first interruption by immediate maternal necessity—the crying of the younger brother with wet diapers—marks the beginning of a clearer resistance to the forces of external necessities through this acceptance of Emily's separate selfhood. ⟨. . .⟩

Her efforts, then, "to gather together, to try and make coherent" (p. 18) are both inevitably doomed to failure and finally successful. There cannot be—either for parent or for story-teller—a final coherence, a final access to defined personality, or a full sense of individual control. There is only the enriched understanding of the separateness of all people—even parents from children—and the necessity to perceive and foster the value of each person's autonomous selfhood. Though that selfhood is always limited by the forces of external constraints, it is nonetheless defined and activated by the recognition of the "seal" each person sets on surrounding people and the acceptance of responsibility for one's own actions and capacities. At best, we can share in the efforts to resist the fatalism of life lived helplessly "before the iron"—never denying the power of the iron but never yielding to the iron in final helplessness either. We must trust the power of each to "find her way" even in the face of powerful external constraints on individual control.

—Joanne S. Frye, "'I Stand Here Ironing': Motherhood as Experience and Metaphor," *Studies in Short Fiction* (Summer 1971), in *The Chelsea House Library of Literary Criticism: Twentieth-Century American Literature*, Vol. 5, Harold Bloom, ed. (New York: Chelsea House Publishers, 1987), 2929–31

PETER ACKROYD

A great many American novels have concerned themselves with poverty and the Depression, but most of them have been very quickly smothered in that sentimental form known as 'documentary.' *Yonnondio* is written by a young girl who could never have heard of such a thing, since the book has that quality of innocence which comes from wonder rather than from knowledge: "'I am Maizie Holbrook,' she said softly, 'I am a knowen thing. I can diaper a baby. I can tell ghost stories. I know words and words'." Maizie is the child of one of those families which were slowly beaten into shape during the 'thirties when "words and words" were the merest palliative in the struggle to live. But Maizie's mother, a beautifully achieved character known as Anna, wants an "edjication" for her children and the whole family go on a long desolate wandering through America: they become tenant-farmers until their debts overtake them, and then they move into one of those restless American cities which were at that moment testing their strength. It is here that Tillie Olsen leaves them, to a fate which was not worth having.

It is a conventional story, as stories go, but the plot is in fact the least important element of the novel. This is not because it is incomplete (the book has only recently been recovered in a less than perfect form), but because the narrative is consumed by the effects of Miss Olsen's prose. A pattern of images is cast over the writing from the opening chapters, and there is a characteristic attention to description rather than analysis—it is a matter of dialogue rather than character, of situations rather then incidents. *Yonnondio* is a romantic novel, in the sense that Man and Nature are seen in a close and often destructive relationship, and its language becomes the space between them— instinctive with life, both mortal and at the same time capable of expressing certain permanent truths.

It is out of the mouths of children that this will come most naturally and there are some marvellously childish moments in this book. A young girl dreams of things which will not come:

> Luxuriously on her rug, pretend silk slinking and slithering on her
> body, turbanned, puffing her long pretend cigarette: Say vamp me,
> vamp me. I'm Nazimova. Take me to the roadhouse, I want to make
> whoopee. Hotcha. Never never never. O my gigolo, my gigolo. A
> moment of ecstacy, a lifetime of regret.

And the spell is broken by younger children who sing of things which certainly will come:

> Mother, Mother I am sick
> Call the doctor quick, quick, quick.
> Doctor, Doctor, will I die?
> Yes. You will. And so shall I.

Yonnondio is one of the most powerful statements to have emerged from the American 'thirties; a young woman has pulled out of that uneasy time a living document which is full of the wear and tear of the period, and she has done so without doctrinaire blues, and without falling into the trap of a sentimentality which is, at bottom, self-pity.

—Peter Ackroyd, "The Living Image," *Spectator* (14 December 1972), in *The Chelsea House Library of Literary Criticism: Twentieth-Century American Literature*, Vol. 5, Harold Bloom, ed. (New York: Chelsea House Publishers, 1987), 2927

FLORENCE HOWE

The current *possession* by women of literature by women writers is a phenomenon novel in my lifetime, and perhaps in general. I can remember when women students were annoyed with my syllabus because it contained mostly "lady writers." But now there are not enough Kate Chopins to satisfy. And when Tillie Olsen, whose stories we had read at the beginning of the year, was to visit the class, the anticipation was greater than anything I have known. Nor did the excitement abate when it was clear that Olsen was not very different in age, appearance, or speech from most of the members of the class. Indeed, the temperature rose.

Her visit inspired a communal supper, to which many of the women brought (unannounced) a daughter (one, a daughter-in-law). Several mothers introduced themselves and their daughters by saying, "This is my daughter. After I had read 'I Stand Here Ironing,' I gave it to her to read, and she wanted to meet you too." Again, for those of you who don't know this story, it is of working mother's reflections about her eldest daughter, now a high school student whose teacher has sent a worried note home about her. There are no men in the story. The themes—poverty, a young girl's life, and a mother's anxious love—are rare in literature. The language is simple and moves with the rhythms of the mundane ironing board. Yet its language is the poetry of speech perfectly caught.

I cannot describe that evening: the circle of chairs, the people on the floor, the quiet voice that read "Tell Me A Riddle," a story I won't describe but urge you to read. Like *Sons and Lovers*, which is the only story I know in English as good as "Tell Me A Riddle," the story contains the slow death of a strong woman. But unlike Lawrence's story, there is more here than pathos and waste. Surprisingly, there is both humor and courage in the life of an immigrant woman who might have been a revolutionary leader or a poet but was "only" a wife and mother. It was impossible to talk about the story that had moved us to tears. But we could ask about the writer, "Tell us, Tillie," the students asked, "how you came to be a writer." "Who encouraged you?" "What made you decide you could do it?" Some of the women asking the questions were her age. How could she not tell them about her life? Especially since her life was

like theirs. Indeed, her life, she said, was in stories. She had written "I Stand
Here Ironing" on the ironing board, in between chores. She knew that immigrant woman. Her life was in those stories and we must not be embarrassed to
announce that we recognize the life as our own.

> —Florence Howe, "Feminism and Literature," *Images of Women in Fiction Feminist Perspectives*,
> Susan Koppelman Cornillon, ed. (Bowling Green, OH: Bowling Green University Popular
> Press, 1972), 274–76

CATHERINE STIMPSON

Ostensibly, the action of *Yonnondio* occurs in the early 1920s. It concerns the
Holbrook family: Jim, the physically powerful father; Anna, the once ener-
getic and idealistic mother; the five children they have, within eight years,
conceived in genuine passion and she has borne in some pain. The Holbrooks
represent the people from whose toil a Tom Buchanan profits sufficiently to
buy a Daisy a string of pearls and himself a string of polo ponies. Jim works
in a mine, on a tenant farm, on a sewer construction crew, in a hellish meat-
packing plant. Anna struggles with the children in the houses in which Jim set-
tles them. When she can, she takes in laundry.

The Holbrooks are vital and decent. Their children, for whom they are
ambitious, justify their struggle to realize the American dream. Capable of
love in the present, they wish to exercise that love for the sake of the future.
Like Whitman at his most cheerful, Olsen believes that human nature, if per-
mitted to express itself freely and spontaneously, will be good. (She takes her
novel's title from a Whitman poem.) Physical nature is the most fertile setting
for such expression, although moments of human community, a family singing
or a picnic, can suggest a harmonious balance among people, animals, plants,
earth, water, fire, air. The Holbrooks are happiest on the farm, which they
lose. The industries Olsen despises most—mining, early agri-business, slaugh-
terhouses—spoil both human and physical nature for financial gain.

The "overwhelming, hostile forces" of modern capitalism bar the
Holbrooks from their Eden. The modesty, the simplicity of their hopes help
to make their failure poignantly grievous. ⟨. . .⟩

Olsen's compelling gift is her ability to render lyrically the rhythms of
consciousness of victims. Imaginative, affectionate, they are also alert to the
sensual promise of their surroundings. Harsh familial, social, political and economic conditions first cramp, then maim, and then seek to destroy them. The
fevers of poverty, dread and futility inflame their sensibilities. They risk reduc-
tion to defensive fantasy, pain, madness or cruelty. They remain, if in shadow,
heroes and heroic.

Olsen assumes that such victims cannot often speak for themselves. Their
dumbness is no fault of their own. Her self-imposed task is to become their

voice as well as their witness, their text as well as their mourner. She signifies her respect for their dignity in the exactitude and scrupulous effort of her work. She sardonically tells her reader that the received categories of culture, such as classicism and romanticism, also fit the citizens of a Wyoming town as they wait to hear how many men have died in a mine explosion that official cowardice, incompetence and corruption have caused. If she were to take part in that theological quarrel over whether an artist's primary commitment is to craft or to social change, she might say that an artist can work for change through writing about the oppressed with all the craft and tools at hand. She also comments on the economic basis of high culture. She writes of an adolescent boy forced into the mines:

> Earth take your dreams that a few may languidly lie on couches
> and trill "How exquisite" to paid dreamers.

Olsen's politics and anger are a part of a particular decade: her subtitle, "From the Thirties," is seriously meant. She notes that *Yonnondio* "bespeaks the consciousness and roots of that decade, if not its events." An anachronism or two betrays the gap between narrative setting and actual reference. Despite her nostalgia for rural ritual, she refuses to offer an exclusive vision of bucolic joy. She wants unions and solidarity among all workers, no matter what their race or ethnic heritage.

—Catherine Stimpson, "Three Women Work It Out," *Nation* (30 November 1974), in *The Chelsea House Library of Literary Criticism: Twentieth-Century American Literature*, Vol. 5, Harold Bloom, ed. (New York: Chelsea House Publishers, 1987), 2928

ROBERT COLES

In the prelude to *Middlemarch* (only three paragraphs long, but in them one of the most powerful and satisfactory statements about the predicament of women in our society) George Eliot refers to "blundering lives," to "a life of mistakes," to "a tragic failure which found no sacred poet and sank unwept into oblivion." She had in mind both masses of women and particular women, all of whom have suffered by virtue of what she describes as "meanness of opportunity," the general kind so many men and women alike faced in the 19th century, and the special kind women had to endure then, and still now. The novel is a masterful psychological presentation and analysis of rural, middle-class, early 19th-century England, but also, for the most part, a chronicle of loss, sadness, disappointment and failure. Characters endowed with intelligence and ambition, one after the other, fall upon bad times—not poverty, but the consequences of fate, that is, the world's accidents, incidents and circumstances which, in sum, exert their enormous, tellingly destructive influence.

The novel falls just short of tragedy: a village, a county, all of England's rising bourgeoisie had at least another half century or so to go. Yet, the story is littered with unfulfilled dreams.

So with Tillie Olsen's *Tell Me a Riddle*—four short stories which lack Eliot's extended, intricate dedication to character portrayal of the workings of historical change, but in which sensibility, point of view, and mood are spiritual kin of *Middlemarch*. The first, and briefest, "I Stand Here Ironing," introduces the reader to a woman who has known and suffered from the "meanness of opportunity" George Eliot mentions, a 20th-century American version of it. The title reveals the scene, tells of all the action to come—a mother reflecting upon the hard, curbed, sad life of her 19-year-old daughter, born in the Great Depression of the early 1930s. A social worker or guidance counselor or psychologist or psychiatrist (who knows which, and who cares—a substantial number of them all sound drearily alike) has told the mother that the young woman, her oldest child, "needs help." The mother is skeptical, and quietly, thoughtfully scornful. Not "defensive" or "guilty," not lacking in a capacity for psychological introspection, either—as might be said of her by the person who wants her to come in for one of those self-conscious "talks" that have become so much a part of so many lives in recent years—but determined to hold on to her dignity, to her right as an intelligent woman, however hard-pressed by life, to comprehend what it is that has happened to herself and her children, and just as important, to resist the interfering, gratuitous, self-serving or wrong-headed interpretations of others. "Let her be," the mother says to herself—a remark meant, also, for the one who, with the barely concealed arrogance and condescension of the clinic, had called and said, "I wish you would manage the time to come in and talk with me about your daughter." ⟨. . .⟩

"Let her be," the mother says, not defiantly and not out of escapist ignorance. "So all that is in her will not bloom," she continues, "but in how many does it? There is still enough left to live by." And in case the people at the unnamed clinic already have in response their various "interpretations," their "insight," the mother has a quiet request to make—that the young lady be accorded respect, be allowed her dignity, be regarded as and told she is "more than this dress on the ironing board, helpless before the iron."

That is all; the last words of the story bring the reader back to the first words, but not in a forced or contrived way—the all too clever and tidy work of a "literary" writer of short stories who has learned in school about rising action and falling action, and "structure," and the need for "impact" or "coherence." A working woman is making the best of *her* situation, even as she expects her daughter to do so. A mother shakes her fist at the universe, not excitedly, and with no great expectation of triumph, but out of a determination to assert her worth, her capabilities, however injured or curbed, her ability to see, to comprehend, to imagine; and too, her daughter's—everyone's.

—Robert Coles, "Tell Me a Riddle by Tillie Olsen," New Republic (6 December 1975), in The Chelsea House Library of Literary Criticism: Twentieth-Century American Literature, Vol. 5, Harold Bloom, ed. (New York: Chelsea House Publishers, 1987), 2931–32

MARGARET ATWOOD

Tillie Olsen's is a unique voice. Few writers have gained such wide respect based on such a small body of published work: one book of short stories, Tell Me a Riddle, and the unfinished novel, Yonnondio: From the Thirties. Among women writers in the United States, "respect" is too pale a word: "reverence" is more like it. This is presumably because women writers, even more than their male counterparts, recognize what a heroic feat it is to have held down a job, raised four children and still somehow managed to become and to remain a writer. The exactions of this multiple identity cost Tillie Olsen 20 years of her writing life. The applause that greets her is not only for the quality of her artistic performance but, as at a grueling obstacle race, for the near miracle of her survival.

Tillie Olsen's third book, Silences, is about this obstacle course, this ordeal, not only as she herself experienced it but as many writers have experienced it, in many forms. It begins with an account, first drafted in 1962, of her own long, circumstantially enforced silence. She did not write for a very simple reason: A day has 24 hours. For 20 years she had no time, no energy and none of the money that would have bought both. It may be comforting to believe that garrets are good for geniuses, that artists are made in Heaven and God will take care of them; but if you believe, as Tillie Olsen does, that writers are nurtured on Earth and nobody necessarily takes care of them, society cannot be absolved from the responsibility for what it produces or fails to produce in the way of literature.

Though Tillie Olsen begins with her own experience, she rapidly proceeds to that of others. The second part of the book is a grab bag of excerpts from the diaries, journals, letters and concealed autobiographical work of a wide range of writers, past and present, male and female. They are used to demonstrate, first, the ideal conditions for creation as perceived by the writers themselves, and second, almost every imaginable impediment to that creation. ⟨. . .⟩

Tillie Olsen's special concern is with how her general observations on silencings apply, more heavily and with additions, to women. Here, the obstacles may seem to be internal: the crippling effects of upbringing, the burdens of motherhood, the lack of confidence that may prevent women from writing at all; and, if they do write, their own male-determined view of women, the fear of competing, the fear of success. We've heard a lot of this before, but it's invigorating to see its first expressions by women coming new to the problems: Virginia Woolf worrying about her childlessness, Katherine Mansfield having to cope with all the domestic arrangements while John Middleton Murry nagged her about tea. And, in contrast, quotations from men whose wives dedicated their lives to sharpening pencils and filling the inkwell for them. As Tillie Olsen points out, almost all of the women in the 19th century who wrote were childless or had servants. ⟨. . .⟩

⟨. . .⟩ Despite the condensed and fragmentary quality of this book, the whole is powerful. Even the stylistic breathlessness—the elliptical prose, the footnotes blooming on every page as if the author, reading her own manuscript, belatedly thought of a dozen other things too important to leave out— is reminiscent of a biblical messenger, sole survivor of a relentless and obliterating catastrophe, a witness: "I only am escaped alone to tell thee." The tone is right: The catastrophes do occur, daily, though they may not be seen as such. What Tillie Olsen has to say about them is of primary importance to those who want to understand how art is generated or subverted and to those trying to create it themselves.

—Margaret Atwood, "Obstacle Course," *New York Times Book Review* (30 July 1979), in *The Chelsea House Library of Literary Criticism: Twentieth-Century American Literature*, Vol. 5, Harold Bloom, ed. (New York: Chelsea House Publishers, 1987), 2928–29

ELIZABETH JANEWAY

Tillie Olsen uses the minutiae of obscure lives to pose and reflect on major metaphysical questions. Such abstract questioning, as has been noted, is rare in women's writing of this period. When it occurs it is apt to be associated with the socialist or anarchist doctrines that were very much a part of working-class life among immigrants. Olsen goes far beyond ideology, however. What meaning can be found in life at the end of life? she asks, in the prose of *Tell Me a Riddle* (1961), as Yeats asked in his poems of old age. Here, these are questions put in a female voice, questions that value the high creeds of revolutionary self-sacrifice in terms of "one pound soupmeat, one soupbone . . . bread, day old" and "cheap thread." These cares are what an old woman remembers in her mortal agony, and they overwhelm memories of dedication to the Movement, marriage, children born and laboriously raised. Love, anger, frustration, hope, the fellowship that endured poverty—all fall away before the inescapable chores of living, relieved only by a sudden echo from music heard in childhood. To her husband the old woman becomes an astonishing, disturbing stranger: "It seemed to him that for seventy years she had hidden a tape recorder, infinitely microscopic, within her, that it had coiled infinite mile on mile, trapping every song, every melody, every word read, heard and spoken—and that maliciously she was playing back only what said nothing of him, of the children, of their intimate life together." He is right. What she had hoped for was a patch of life of her own, completely to herself; and then death intervened.

The full weight of consciousness is present and expressed in the simple events of life for Olsen's women. "I stand here ironing," begins a woman in the story of this title (in *Tell Me a Riddle*) and weighing out the inescapable failure of her care for her oldest child, raised without her father, passed to a neighbor in order that the mother could earn enough to keep them both, a little girl who had to be good and was; of whom too much was demanded. Reflection can find no cure, no solution, only note again how childhood loneliness was matched with adult anguish and balanced against what the other children needed, "that terrible balancing of hurts and needs I had to do . . . and did so badly, those earlier years." Awareness of what we owe each other and cannot give, of what humanity might become if love could be unrestricted, shapes this story, though "I will never total it all now," the mother tells herself. "My wisdom came too late . . . Let her be. So all that is in her will not bloom—but in how many does it? There is still enough left to live by. Only help her to believe—help make it so there is cause for her to believe that she is more than this dress on the ironing board, helpless before the iron."

—Elizabeth Janeway, "Women's Literature," *Harvard Guide to Contemporary American Writing*, ed. Daniel Hoffman (1979), in *The Chelsea House Library of Literary Criticism: Twentieth-Century American Literature*, Vol. 5, Harold Bloom, ed. (New York: Chelsea House Publishers, 1987), 2926

SALLY CUNNEEN

Her first book, the short stories collected in *Tell Me a Riddle*, was published when she was 50. Besides "I Stand Here Ironing" it contains three other fictional pieces of extraordinary intensity. "Hey, Sailor, What Ship?" is a character sketch of a seaman defeated by loss of belief in himself and his work, ruining his life and health with drink. The daughter of old friends he visits is now ashamed of one she used to show off to her friends. Yet love and loyalty warm even Whitey's bleak future. When the daughter first sees him sitting on the sofa with her parents, she thinks:

> Never saw so many peaceful wrecks in my life . . . That's what I want to be when I grow up, just a peaceful wreck holding hands with other peaceful wrecks.

(As I grow older, I have come to see this as no mean ambition in life.)

"Oh, Yes!" is an introduction to racism and the class system as experienced by two young girls, one black, one white, who have been close friends but are now parted involuntarily into separate worlds. The initiation begins with the white girl's attendance at a black religious service, where the intense emotionalism causes her to faint. It continues by means of a rigid high school tracking system until the white girl asks: "Oh why is it like it is? And why do I have to care?" The mothers are as involved as the girls, and at the end the white mother muses silently: "Caring asks doing. It is a long baptism into the seas of humankind, my daughter. Better immersion than to live untouched. . . . Yet how will you sustain?"

The great title story of the volume, "Tell Me a Riddle," while it recounts the quarrel between an aged grandfather (who wants to retire to the Happy Haven, play cards and watch TV) and an obdurate grandmother, eventually seen to have cancer (who wants silence, selfness, and reconnection with the revolutionary humanist ideals of their Russian youth), also conveys the larger dimensions of America's own loss of contact with its idealistic, hardworking, communal roots. Before her death, the old woman awakens these memories in the old man:

> "Aaah, children. . . . how we believed, how we belonged." And he yearned to pack for each of the children, the grandchildren, for everyone, *that joyous certainty, that sense of mattering, of moving and being moved, of being one and indivisible with the great of the past, with all that freed, ennobled.* Package it, stand on corners, in front of stadiums and on crowded beaches, knock on doors, give it as fabled gift.

⟨. . .⟩ "Tell Me a Riddle" was about her own mother and dedicated to her, Olsen said, in a clear, mid-western, ladylike voice that quavered slightly. Like the grandmother in the story, her mother had been part of a movement to effect change in the Russia of 1905 before she came to this country. Since in that repressive regime religion had allied itself with power, in the name of human possibility and freedom she had become an incorruptible atheist. All her life she had been silent, hardworking, yet—like so many mothers—wise, loving and creative.

Just before her death, Tillie Olsen's mother had a dream in which someone knocked on her bedroom door. She smelled a marvelous smell, heard a neighing sound, and saw three wise men in gold, blue and crimson robes, embroidered as in her old village. "We've come to talk to you," the first one said. When she replied, "I'm not a believer," he assured her, "We don't want to talk about that. We want to talk about wisdom."

"Come in," her mother said. Then she saw that country. ⟨. . .⟩ They were worn out, but they had come to worship a universal human infant who was going to be crucified into sex, race and class divisions. In her dream, Tillie Olsen's mother joined them in this worship.

This memory, linked with personal inspiration, is undoubtedly close to the source of Olsen's vocation as storyteller of the silent, hardworking men and women who find their voice in her fiction. Its vision is the root of its force. Olsen's art helps us to make sense out of the pain and defeat that life inflicts on ordinary people by pointing to the dignity and wonder still present there. On fire as she is with this sense of human possibility, her stories call out to their readers to be responsible for serving this potentiality in every person they encounter in the tarnished yet real miracle of everyday existence. Heir to a vital prophetic tradition of humanism, Tillie Olsen expends her energies to pass that tradition on to us. In reading her stories, we encounter the ambivalence of the human condition itself.

—Sally Cunneen, "Tillie Olsen: Storyteller of Working America," *Christian Century* (21 May 1980), in *The Chelsea House Library of Literary Criticism: Twentieth-Century American Literature*, Vol. 5, Harold Bloom, ed. (New York: Chelsea House Publishers, 1987), 2926–27

DEBORAH ROSENFELT

Olsen's importance to contemporary women who read and write or who write about literature is widely acknowledged. Yet although her work has been vital for feminists today, and although one article does discuss her background in some depth, few of Olsen's contemporary admirers realize the extent to which her consciousness, vision and choice of subject are rooted in an earlier heritage of social struggle—the communist Old Left of the 1930s and the tradition of radical political thought and action, mostly socialist and anarchist, that dominated the left in the second and third decades of the century. Not that we can explain the eloquence of her work in terms of its sociopolitical origins, not even that left-wing politics and culture were the single most important influences on it, but that its informing consciousness, its profound understanding of class and sex and race as shaping influences on people's lives, owes much to that earlier tradition. Olsen's work, in fact, may be seen as part of a literary lineage so far unacknowledged by most contemporary critics: a socialist-feminist literary tradition.

Critics such as Ellen Moers and Elaine Showalter have identified a literary tradition of women writers who read one another's work, corresponded with one another about everything from domestic irritations to the major issues of the day, and looked to one another for strength, encouragement and insight.

Literary historians like Walter Rideout and Daniel Aaron have traced the outlines of a radical literary tradition in America, composed of two waves of twentieth-century writers influenced by socialism in the early years, by communism in the thirties, who had in common 'an attempt to express a predominantly Marxist view toward society'. At the intersections of these larger traditions is a line of women writers, associated with the American left, who unite a class consciousness and a feminist consciousness in their lives and creative work, who are concerned with the material circumstances of people's lives, who articulate the experiences and grievances of women and of other oppressed groups—workers, national minorities, the colonized and the exploited—and who speak out of a defining commitment to social change.

In fiction this tradition extends from turn-of-the-century socialists like Charlotte Perkins Gilman, Vida Scudder and Susan Glaspell, through such thirties Old Left women, as Meridel Le Sueur, Tess Slesinger, Josephine Herbst, Grace Lumpkin and Ruth McKenney, to contemporary writers with early ties to the civil rights and antiwar movements and the New Left: Marge Piercy, Grace Paley, Alice Walker and others. Although the specific political affiliations of these writers have varied from era to era and from individual to individual, the questions they raise have been surprisingly consistent. These range from basic questions about how to survive economically to more complex ones, such as how to understand the connections and contradictions between women's struggles and those struggles based on other categories and issues, or how to find a measure of emotional and sexual fulfillment in a world where egalitarian relationships are more ideal than real. Sometimes, as in Gilman's *Herland*, published serially in *The Forerunner*, or Piercy's *Woman on the Edge of Time*, these writers try to imagine socialist-feminist utopias. More often, as with the women writers associated with the left, especially the Communist Party, in the 1930s, their work constitutes a sharp critique of the present. Sometimes, as in Agnes Smedley's *Daughter of Earth*, Slesinger's *The Unpossessed*, Piercy's *Small Changes*, much of Alice Walker's fiction and, implicitly, Olsen's *Tell Me a Riddle*, that critique includes a sharp look from a woman's point of view at the sexual politics of daily life in the political milieus with which these authors were associated. ⟨. . .⟩

As Elinor Langer has remarked, when Olsen began to write again in the 1950s, it was not as a woman who had lived her life as an artist but as an artist who had lived her life as a woman. Yet in those turbulent years of the early to mid-1930s, Olsen lived fully as artist, as activist, as worker and as woman/wife/mother, though often suffering from the conflicting demands, always having to give primacy to one part of her being at the expense of another. ⟨. . .⟩

First, the left required great commitments of time and energy for political work, on the whole valuing action over thought, deed over word; yet it also validated the study and production of literature and art, providing a first exposure to literature for many working-class people, fostering an appreciation of a wide range of socially conscious literature, and offering important outlets for publication and literary exchange. Second, although much left-wing criticism, especially by Communist Party writers, was narrowly prescriptive about the kind of literature contemporary writers should be producing, it also inspired—along with the times themselves—social consciousness in writers that deepened their art. Third, for a woman in the 1930s, the left was a profoundly masculinist world in many of its human relationships, in the orientation of its literature, and even in the language used to articulate its cultural criticism; simultaneously, the left gave serious attention to women's issues, valued women's contributions to public as well as to private life, and generated an important body of theory on the woman question.

> —Deborah Rosenfelt, "From the Thirties: Tillie Olsen and the Radical Tradition," *Feminist Criticism and Social Change: Sex, Class and Race in Literature and Culture,* Judith Newton and Deborah Rosenfelt, eds. (New York: Methuen, Inc., 1985), 218–19, 224–25

TILLIE OLSEN

The power and the need to create, over and beyond reproduction, is native in both women and men. Where the gifted among women (*and men*) have remained mute, or have never attained full capacity, it is because of circumstances, inner or outer, which oppose the needs of creation.

Wholly surrendered and dedicated lives; time as needed for the work; totality of self. But women are traditionally trained to place others' needs first, to feel these needs as their own (the "infinite capacity"); their sphere, their satisfaction to be in making it possible for others to use their abilities. This is what Virginia Woolf meant when, already a writer of achievement, she wrote in her diary:

> Father's birthday. He would have been 96, 96, yes, today; and could have been 96, like other people one has known; but mercifully was not. His life would have entirely ended mine. What would have happened? No writing, no books;—inconceivable. . . .

If I talk now quickly of my own silences—almost presumptuous after what has been told here—it is that the individual experience may add.

In the twenty years I bore and reared my children, usually had to work on a paid job as well, the simplest circumstances for creation did not exist.

Nevertheless writing, the hope of it, was "the air I breathed, so long as I shall breathe at all." In that hope, there was conscious storing, snatched reading, beginnings of writing, and always "the secret rootlets of reconnaissance."

When the youngest of our four was in school, the beginnings struggled toward endings. This was a time, in Kafka's words, "like a squirrel in a cage: bliss of movement, desperation about constriction, craziness of endurance."

Bliss of movement. A full extended family life; the world of my job (transcriber in a dairy-equipment company); and the writing, which I was somehow able to carry around within me through work, through home. Time on the bus, even when I had to stand, was enough; the stolen moments at work, enough; the deep night hours for as long as I could stay awake, after the kids were in bed, after the household tasks were done, sometimes during. It is no accident that the first work I considered publishable began: "I stand here ironing, and what you asked me moves tormented back and forth with the iron."

In such snatches of time I wrote what I did in those years, but there came a time when this triple life was no longer possible. The fifteen hours of daily realities became too much distraction for the writing. I lost craziness of endurance. ⟨. . .⟩

My work died. What demanded to be written, did not. It seethed, bubbled, clamored, peopled me. At last moved into the hours meant for sleeping. I worked now full time on temporary jobs, a Kelly, a Western Agency girl (girl!), wandering from office to office, always hoping to manage two, three writing months ahead. Eventually there was time.

I had said: always roused by the writing, always denied. Now, like a woman made frigid, I had to learn response, to trust this possibility for fruition that had not been before. Any interruption dazed and silenced me. It took a long while of surrendering to what I was trying to write, of invoking Henry James's "passion, piety, patience," before I was able to re-establish work.

When again I had to leave the writing, I lost consciousness. A time of anesthesia. There was still an automatic noting that did not stop, but it was as if writing had never been. No fever, no congestion, no festering. I ceased being peopled, slept well and dreamlessly, took a "permanent" job. The few pieces that had been published seemed to have vanished like the not-yet-written. ⟨. . .⟩

More and more women writers in our century, primarily in the last two decades, are assuming as their right fullness of work *and* family life. Their emergence is evidence of changing circumstances making possible for them what (with rarest exception) was not possible in the generations of women before. I hope and I fear for what will result. I hope (and believe) that complex new richness will come into literature; I fear because almost certainly their work will be impeded, lessened, partial. For the fundamental situation remains unchanged. Unlike men writers who marry, most will not have the societal equivalent of a wife—nor (in a society hostile to growing life) anyone but themselves to mother their children. ⟨. . .⟩

As for myself, who did not publish a book until I was fifty, who raised children without household help or the help of the "technological sublime" (the atom bomb was in manufacture before the first automatic washing machine); who worked outside the house on everyday jobs as well (as nearly half of all women do now, though a woman with a paid job, except as a maid or prostitute, is still rarest of any in literature); who could not kill the essential angel (there was no one else to do her work); would not—if I could—have killed the caring part of the Woolf angel, as distant from the world of literature most of my life as literature is distant (in content too) from my world:

The years when I should have been writing, my hands and being were at other (inescapable) tasks. Now, lightened as they are, when I must do those tasks into which most of my life went, like the old mother, grandmother in my *Tell Me a Riddle* who could not make herself touch a baby, I pay a psychic cost: "the sweat beads, the long shudder begins." The habits of a lifetime when everything else had to come before writing are not easily broken, even when circumstances now often make it possible for writing to be first; habits of years—response to others, distractibility, responsibility for daily matters—stay with you, mark you, become you. The cost of "discontinuity" (that pattern still imposed on women) is such a weight of things unsaid, an accumulation of material so great, that everything starts up something else in me; what should take weeks, takes me sometimes months to write; what should take months, takes years.

—Tillie Olsen, "From *Silences*," *Writing Women's Lives: An Anthology of Autobiographical Narratives by Twentieth-Century American Women Writers*, Susan Cahill, ed. (New York: HarperPerennial, 1994), 148–150, 153–55

B I B L I O G R A P H Y

Tell Me a Riddle: A Collection. 1961.
Yonnondio: From the Thirties. 1974.
Mother to Daughter, Daughter to Mother: Mothers on Mothering (ed.). 1984.
Allegra Maud Goldman (with Edith Konecky). 1987.
Mothers & Daughters: That Special Quality: An Exploration in Photographs (with Julie Olsen Edwards and Estelle Jussim). 1995.

CYNTHIA OZICK

1928–

CYNTHIA OZICK, novelist, short-story writer, and essayist, was born in New York City on April 17, 1928. Her father, William Ozick, owned a drugstore in the Bronx. Ozick earned a B.A. from New York University in 1949 and an M.A. from Ohio State University in 1950. While in school she read voraciously, Henry James being a particular favorite. Ozick began to write after college, and she spent seven years on a long philosophical novel she never finished, although two excerpts have appeared as "The Butterfly and the Traffic Light," which is included in *The Pagan Rabbi and Other Stories* (1971), and "The Sense of Europe," published in *Prairie Schooner* in 1956. From 1952 to 1953 Ozick worked as an advertising copywriter at Filene's Department Store in Boston. In 1952 she married Bernard Hallote; they have one daughter.

Ozick has said that she began her first novel as an American writer and ended it six and a half years later as a Jewish writer. In the early 1950s she began an intensive study of the literature, history, and philosophy of Judaism, and since then her writing has been mostly concerned with religious issues. Her first novel, *Trust*, appeared in 1966 and received generally favorable reviews. In this novel, as in many stories that followed, Ozick examines the conflict between the pagan and the sacred. The stories in *The Pagan Rabbi* focus on dislocated Jewish immigrants and their loss of the Yiddish language and of religious traditions. *Bloodshed and Three Novellas* (1976) centers on a woman artist and introduces the idea that storytelling is a divine and magical act and therefore upstages God.

Although Ozick has written two other novels, *The Cannibal Galaxy* (1983) and *The Puttermesser Papers* (1997), and published dozens of essays, she is best known for her three collections of short stories: *The Pagan Rabbi and Other Stories; Bloodshed and Three Novellas;* and *Levitation: Five Fictions* (1982). *A Treasury of Yiddish Poetry* (1969) is a collection of her translations edited by Irving Howe and Eliezer Greenberg.

C R I T I C A L   E X T R A C T S

DAVID L. STEVENSON

Cynthia Ozick's *Trust* is that extraordinary literary entity, a first novel that is a genuine novel, wholly self-contained and produced by a rich, creative imagination, not an imitation of someone else's work or thinly disguised autobiography. Moreover, it stands boldly apart from the two types of serious fiction that have dominated the postwar years in America: the activist-existential novel of Saul Bellow, William Styron and Walker Percy; and the realistic novel of information, the novel of "what it was like," of J. D. Salinger, Reynolds Price and John Updike. The tradition of narrative to which *Trust* returns, I think, is that of James, Conrad and Lawrence. It is the tradition that explores and reveals the inward man.

Trust deals with events in the life of Allegra Vand, a very rich, very spoiled, twice-married woman who has "alertness without form, energy without a cause." She had recklessly flirted with communism and free-love in the thirties, and at the time of the novel, 1957, wishes to regularize her affairs so that her present husband may be appointed to an ambassadorship. Part of the necessary tidying up includes a forced meeting between a daughter and her actual father, Allegra's one-time lover from the thirties.

These events, interesting in themselves, exist to reveal the sensibility of the narrator, Allegra's daughter. She is never given a name. Hers is the only voice we hear directly, whether scene and event occur in New York in the summer of 1957, or whether they occur in Germany after World War II when she was 10, or in England just before the war.

The narrator begins at the moment of her graduation from college, when she finds herself simmering in envy over the coming marriages of her acquaintances. She longs to play some simple, easy feminine role herself. But she faces the fact that she is both appallingly intellectual and an emotional recluse. She has cultivated her wit, but has been unable to define her role as a woman. As she prepares to confront her father, we are made aware that the mother's wish to protect her own reputation has stunted and twisted the daughter's emotional life. We also learn that Enoch Vand, who married Allegra for her money and is an adjunct to her self-esteem, has always refused to acknowledge his stepdaughter as anything but a minor curiosity. Thus the daughter, at the age of 22, is eager for the prerequisites that should be hers as a woman, but is floundering badly in their pursuit.

The main body of the novel, then, is a revelation of the narrator's inner, turbulent, psychic drama, which ends with her reprieve. Her father has performed this small but believable miracle, naturally and inadvertently, by being for her what he has been for her mother and for all of his women: the sly, sexually provocative male animal.

There is an occasional, irritating marring of the novel's carefully wrought prose. In the midst of setting forth perceptions and emotional states delicately balanced, Miss Ozick sometimes gives us weedy passages of exposition that must be got through. These may serve as verbal equivalents of the narrator's feelings, but for me they impede communication. Take, for instance, the description of a thunderstorm which occurs when the narrator is in a state of erotic excitement. The storm "sailed like a woman in long silky hems across a brush-hard lawn; at uneven intervals she stoops and we hear the burred movement of her gloves across the ears of the grass—all that is left of the thunder is this sly caress, and all that is left of the lighting are those erratic senile imbecile winks and licks."

If the flow of images occasionally gets out of hand, this is at worst only a minor blemish. In ordering the difficult interplay of elements, characters observed simultaneously by the narrator and by the reader in somewhat different ways, the author is wholly successful. More important, she succeeds because her protagonist insists upon coming to terms with the recalcitrant sexual elements in her life and, by fictional extension, in ours. Because *Trust* is the product of a highly perceptive intelligence, one responds to its substance from the deepest recesses of self-knowledge.

—David L. Stevenson, "Daughter's Reprieve," *New York Times Book Review* (17 July 1966), in *The Chelsea House Library of Literary Criticism: Twentieth-Century American Literature*, Vol. 5, Harold Bloom, ed. (New York: Chelsea House Publishers, 1987), 3012–13

Eugene Goodheart

The source of the trouble with *Trust* is its heroine. From the very beginning she speaks as if she has the taste of ash in her mouth. She is not disillusioned, because she was never illusioned. In the first chapter, we are told that "the world does not exist." "And I reflected mournfully how bitter it was to wear the face of youth, to be rooted among jubilants, to feign delights, and all the while to keep close that clandestine disenchantment, that private corrosion of illusion, which belongs to the very old." Her impertinence, unredeemed by wit, is rampant throughout the novel. Everyone she deals with remarks this of her. Since she is the narrator and voyeur of the novel, the effect is to sully every character she presents. It is a case of reverse sentimentality: not the false roseate glow of a sentimental narrator, but the fog of chronic dyspepsia in the narrator. The source of her misery is that she is the unprepossessing offspring of a moment of passion between two beautiful people. So repugnant is the heroine to everyone in the novel (including herself) that she is never even named. Her real father gets about as close to affection as possible, when he addresses her as "girlie"—with condescension, of course.

How often the reader revolts against the novelist who creates for his "hero" (the character in whom he has made a special investment) an aura which distinguishes him from other characters. Like God, the novelist arrogates to himself the power to bestow grace, which by definition is unmerited. Mrs. Ozick (as if to anticipate the reader's revolt) seems concerned to do the opposite: she deprives the heroine of every grace a woman can have. But it is precisely her ungraced condition that compromises the gift of perception and expression that she must possess as narrator. The climactic moment in the novel (the visionary account of lovemaking between her discovered father and a young woman) is simply observed by the heroine, who has no other privileges in the world of experience than to observe the lives of others. Brilliant as this passage is, it seems unmotivated. One might say that the general condition of the novel is a discontinuity between language and reality or between expression and feeling. The language expands and develops like a tumor or a wild growth that quickly conceals its roots in feeling. So that the lyric passages, for instance, appear as gratuitous flowerings on the barren ground of the heroine's sullennesses.

The sense of gratuitousness extends to the very existence of the characters. For instance, for all the detail in the rendering and the energy with which she is invested, the heroine's mother seems more like an hallucinated projection of the heroine's resentment than a credible mother or wife or woman. Mrs. Ozick, on the other hand, is successful in creating her arch-conservative first stepfather, particularly in the long episode in which he reveals to the heroine the truth of her past.

One wants to mitigate the harshness of the judgment of the novel, because the novel shows symptoms of power and talent. But the inescapable impression that the novel makes, despite every desire to wish it well, is that the book is a performance from ambition, that if Mrs. Ozick is to write a successful novel she must achieve a more authentic accommodation between her language and her feeling.

—Eugene Goodheart, "Trust," Critique: Studies in Modern Fiction 9, No. 2 (Winter 1967–68), in Cynthia Ozick, Harold Bloom, ed. (New York: Chelsea House Publishers, 1986), 13–14

ARTHUR A. COHEN

Cynthia Ozick comes forward in this masterful collection, not as a Jewish writer, but as a Jewish visionary—something more. All of her characters are, to begin with, distraught, distended by the world, trapped by misunderstanding, incommunicativeness, loneliness, exhaustion. But their distraction is only a starting-point. The stories are never simply descriptive or evocative. Isaac

Kornfeld, the pagan rabbi, who surrenders to his lust for a mythological dryad he has conjured and in his passion to enforce upon her pure spirit the vividness of his flesh, loses her and in grief is hung (hangs himself) by his trailing prayer shawl. The great public scholar of the Law, husband of Sheindel who has survived the death camps, father of children, an upright and grave young scholar has pressed beyond the restricted order of the Jewish security system of girdles and fences and wandering free has found only madness and death. "The Dock Witch," another mythological extrusion, is the Gentile counterpoint to "The Pagan Rabbi," for the young shipping executive from Ohio, obsessed with the sea and the ships that bear people away from their flat worlds encounters an omnipresent sea nymph, aged, ageless Undine, who is all immediacy of flesh and sensational violence and through his love and terror loses all contact with ordinary days. One death, two transfigurations.

"Envy; or Yiddish in America," one of the funniest stories ever written—funny, mordant, miserable—chronicles the infinite frustrations and bitterness of a Yiddish writer who is dying with his language. Offsetting Edelshtein of "Envy" is "Virility," a story narrated by a desiccated *Wasp* journalist named Edmund Gate who is depredated by a greenhorn who pilfers his name (he is born Elia Gatoff from Glusk-, Russia, via Liverpool, to New York). Young Elia/Edmund insists upon becoming an English poet and despite no talent manages—and that is the mystery of the story—to become the most celebrated poet of his day, vaunted for his masculinity, his energy, his potency. Edelshtein collapses under the weight of his frustration before universal anti-Semitism and Edmund Gate, the bogus, is last seen by Edmund Gate, the real, masqueraded as a quasi-transvestite, his virility hopelessly compromised by the revelation that his masculine power was all copped from his old Jewish aunt who stayed behind in Liverpool.

Cynthia Ozick is always refining and winnowing obsessions and for the projection and substantiation of obsessions, thought is indispensable. A writer has to mind the language when obsession is at stake. It isn't enough to record the experience, because the experience is not given. It is wrested free from the encumbrance of normal perception and wrenched apart, examined like the entrails of a haruspex, and sewn up again differently. For this work all of the literature, philosophic, moral, mythological, and all of the language, its unfamiliar words and its delicious words have to be used. And Cynthia Ozick does all this, the language textured by a network of associations, reminiscences, allusions to the vast intellectual tradition of the West which has tried to crack the hard nut of thought with its bare teeth.

—Arthur A. Cohen, *Commonweal* (3 September 1971), in *The Chelsea House Library of Literary Criticism: Twentieth-Century American Literature*, Vol. 5, Harold Bloom, ed. (New York: Chelsea House Publishers, 1987), 3013–14

JOHANNA KAPLAN

When Cynthia Ozick's novella "Envy; or, Yiddish in America" was first published, I had never read anything of hers before, and having no particular expectations or preconceptions about her work, I found myself overwhelmed by the story itself and was amazed at its effect on me. I read it, reread it and lent it to friends, all as in a fever; it brought back for me those early years in adolescence when reading is obsessive, when all literature is new and opens itself out before you with the sensuous and exploding hypnotic draw that real life cannot begin to compete with. After adolescence, there are probably relatively few writers who are able to overtake and own one in this way—Borges, Kawabata and García Márquez come to mind. With the publication of this collection of stories, I think Cynthia Ozick can lay claim to being one of them.

Miss Ozick's first book, the novel *Trust*—rich, convoluted, even virtuosic—revealed a rare quality of mind and a joy and a facility in language that was almost literally staggering but, because of its very complexity, tended at times to be opaque. In this new book of seven stories, all that was best in the novel—that relentless, passionate discovering and uncovering intelligence—is present and instantly recognizable, but there is now a difference in the prose. It is sharpened, clarified, controlled and above all beautifully, unceasingly welcoming.

From the very first opening sentences, we are immediately drawn in. "When I heard that Isaac Kornfeld, a man of piety and brains, had hanged himself in the public park, I put a token in the subway stile and journeyed out to see the tree." Who is this man? Quick! We have to know: in one sentence alone, we are at the end of a life and in the middle of a world—a world, as it happens (because it is Cynthia Ozick's), about which all our guesses, as rapidly as they come, will be wrong.

Or the beginning of "Envy": "Edelshtein, an American for forty years, was a ravenous reader of novels by writers 'of'—he said this with a snarl—'Jewish extraction.' He found them puerile, vicious, pitiable, contemptible, above all stupid. . . . Also, many of them were still young, and had black eyes, black hair, and red beards. A few were blue-eyed like the *cheder-yinglach* of his youth. Schoolboys. He was certain that he did not envy them, but he read them like a sickness."

Instantaneously, we are right in the center of a mind, in the swirl of a world. *People* live here and people with ideas: who they are, how they think, what they do, matter. Accomplices, voyeurs, we quickly want to draw up the shades and find out.

What we find out is that these people live as much in a real country, a real place (the brilliantly evoked smells and textures of streets in Manhattan, of a rich man's house in Kiev in "Envy," of a close, muggy summer night in a suburban town in "The Doctor's Wife") as much as in a confused and adamantly uncompromsing country of the spirit. They puzzle how to live not only within the confines of daily life as it's given to all of us, but with the gnawing agony of the unsleeping, merciless past that carries them into no country that exists: the supernatural.

It is not the familiar science-fiction, super-technology land that they are teased into inhabiting. Rather, because America—what Edelshtein, the embittered, untranslated Yiddish poet calls "America the bride, under her fancy gown nothing"—is so severe a disappointment to them, a lie they cannot forge a compromise with, they push out the boundaries of their imaginations and reach into territories that they know in their hearts, in their history, are forbidden. They cannot make peace with or take part in human life as it goes on: husbands, wives, babies, are so much endless, purposeless repetition seen as ugliness, a species of unalterable decay, sickness and stupidity. What comes upon them—they are forced to it, it's not within their control—is a lust for the supernatural, for God's earthly form in fantastic, inadmissible, demonic creatures. This lust, torturously pursued and grappled with, blinds them, overwhelms them; in frenzy and passion, they feel themselves freed, and at the very same time know that their punishment is not concealed, but in fact embedded in their ecstatic, maddened liberation.

Miss Ozick seems to be constantly struggling with this theme, which is of course a variant of the question: what is holy? Is it the extraordinary, that which is beyond possible human experience—dryads ("The Pagan Rabbi") or seanymphs ("The Dock-Witch")? Or is the holiness in life to be discovered, to be seen in what is ordinarily, blindly, unthinkingly discounted? "The disciples of Reb Moshe of Kobryn . . . disregarded feats in opposition to nature—they had no awe for their master when he hung in air, but when he slept—the miracle of his lung, his breath, his heartbeat!"

This tension runs through all the stories and all the characters. Yet they are never characters who, as in some fiction, exist primarily to represent attitudes. From their smallest idiosyncratic gestures—their ways of eating, dressing, moving and arguing—to their largest concerns, they are people whom one knows, and not because we have met them before, but because we are meeting them, getting to know them *now*.

Cynthia Ozick is a kind of narrative hypnotist. Her range is extraordinary; there is seemingly nothing she cannot do. Her stories contain passages of intense lyricism and brilliant, hilarious, uncontainable inventiveness—jokes, lists, letters, poems, parodies, satires. In the last story, "Virility," a young, immigrant, would-be poet tries to learn English and write poetry at the same time by scrawling his poems on the torn-out pages of a dictionary. When asked why he doesn't use "regular paper," he says, "I like words . . . I wouldn't get that just from a blank sheet."

This book has no blank sheets. It reminds us that literature is not a luxury or diversion or anachronism, but an awakening and a restorative for the center of our lives.

—Johanna Kaplan, "The Pagan Rabbi and Other Stories," New York Times Book Review (13 June 1971), in Cynthia Ozick, Harold Bloom, ed. (New York: Chelsea House Publishers, 1986), 15–17

PAUL THEROUX

The characters in Cynthia Ozick's first collection of stories, The Pagan Rabbi, are uncommon, and though there is a category of fiction known as "the American Jewish novel", Mrs Ozick's Jewish characters would not be at ease in the company of the people who appear in the work of Malamud, Bellow, Roth and Co. This is to her credit, and it might go some way toward reviving what must be by now a flagging interest in a literary form made up exclusively of extended ethnic jokes and backhanded compliments. She writes of people and situations who are rarely if ever seen in American novels, and one is interested to know whether her own novel Trust had the same imaginative daring.

Isaac Kornfeld, the pagan rabbi of the title story, has hanged himself in a New York park. The narrator, his old friend, visits Kornfeld's widow, who produces her dead husband's notebook. She is upset—understandably: it emerges from the gouts of script on the pages that Kornfeld has been communing with nature—or rather, Nature—and, more than that, has had a number of nocturnal meetings with a charming little dryad. The rabbi is torn between scripture and sensuality, and his body, made light and airy under Pan's influence, regards his soul (personified by a dusty old man with his nose stuck in a book) as something futile. It can be seen as a serious philosophic effort, but ultimately it fails, partly because it depends so much upon classical fantasy, and mainly because it is insufficiently dramatized and unpersuasive as a story. "The Dock-Witch" has the same result: a beautiful idea which an excess of fantasy deflates. ⟨. . .⟩

Yet two of the stories are excellent in all ways. The first of these, "Envy; or, Yiddish in America", is a portrait of Edelshtein, a Yiddish poet whose special curse is to remain without a translator in a country where the only glory is in being translated into English. He is tenacious in his struggle to be recognised, but he is unknown and unwanted: people giggle and mutter at his lectures and are bewildered by his recitations. "He was a rabbi who survived his whole congregation," and he is, credibly, the supreme Yiddishist, the last Jew. Mrs. Ozick is at her best in describing Edelshtein's maniacal, self-consuming envy for Yankel Ostrover (who bears a passing resemblance to I. B. Singer), a short story writer who, ably translated from Yiddish to English, has won the admiration of everyone. ⟨. . .⟩ At one of Ostrover's hugely successful readings Edelshtein meets Hannah, and later in an epistolary dialogue with the young girl sums up his dilemma, which is the dilemma of "Jewish writing." He tries to persuade Hannah to be his translator and implies that in doing so she will redeem her generation. Hannah refuses for the understandable reason that she doesn't like the old man very much. Edelshtein's delirium at the end is amply justified, but not a wholly satisfactory conclusion to what is otherwise a wonderful and pointed tale. "Virility", her other superb story—this one about an internationally acclaimed poet who is a determined plagiarist (but with a twist: like turning Nabokov's story "A Forgotten Poet" inside-out)—confirms Mrs. Ozick's skill and shows her to be a vigorous, sly and accomplished writer, who deserves a very wide audience.

> —Paul Theroux, "Miseries and Splendours of the Short Story," *Encounter* (September 1972), in *The Chelsea House Library of Literary Criticism: Twentieth-Century American Literature*, Vol. 5, Harold Bloom, ed. (New York: Chelsea House Publishers, 1987), 3014–15

RUTH R. WISSE

The struggle against the assaults and seductions of the Gentile world continues to absorb Cynthia Ozick in her latest collection of fiction, *Bloodshed and Three Novellas*. Three of the four novellas here are directly about that confrontation, and though free of the actual "bloodshed" promised by the book's title, do throb with ominous intensity.

The first story. "A Mercenary," introduces Lushinski, a Polish Jew by birth, now a citizen and the UN representative of a tiny African nation, and a permanent resident of New York. Lushinski's prodigious services and warm attachments to other cultures, African and American, are stimulated by the stark fear of his own Jewish identity, but his mistress, whom he calls a German countess, and his UN assistant, a true African by the name of Morris Ngambe, have little difficulty penetrating the ironic mask of the intellectual and exposing the vulnerable Jew, the potential victim, beneath. In the title story, "Bloodshed," a Jewish fund-raiser visits his distant relative in a newly established hasidic community outside New York. Suspicious of fraudulence in others, he is forced, during the course of an interview with the *rebbe*, to acknowledge his own deceit and his own demonic capacities. "An Education," the earliest and the least successful of the four novellas, is a heavily ironic treatment of a prize student who tries, and fails, to understand life by the same ideal systems of grammar and definition that can be used in Latin declension. In the last novella, "Usurpation," the protagonist-narrator is a Jewish writer identifiable with the author herself. With disturbing unreserve, the writer-narrator covets, appropriates, and then corrupts the work of others in her own need to make a perfect story and to win the "magic crown" of fame and immortality.

The unsettling effect of both action and style in this last story is deliberate. The novella blurs the normal lines of demarcation between fact and fiction: the narrator tells us that she attended a public reading by a famous author and heard him read a story that she felt to be "hers"; then gives us the plot of a recently published story by Bernard Malamud that the knowledgeable reader would recognize as *his*; then changes the ending of the Malamud story and proceeds to find the "real persons" on whom the story was presumably based, as well as the unpublished manuscripts of its main character. In questionable taste, Miss Ozick also incorporates into her novella another story, which she uses as a literary foil, an actual work that she had seen in manuscript (it was subsequently published in *Response* magazine) by a young writer with a less secure reputation than Malamud's. On this story too she builds her own, in a candid act of plagiarism.

The novella, which freely reworks and passes comment on the works of other writers, is intended to undermine the act of fiction as process and as product. To deflate the mystique of the artist, Miss Ozick presents "herself" as a selfish and somewhat nasty finagler. In place of the grand notions of creativity, she gives us the petty emotions and treacherous techniques, the false bottoms and promises that produce the illusion of fictional magic.

But this act, the "Usurpation" of "Other Peoples' Stories," to use the double title of the novella, is only the lower manifestation of a higher, more significant act of false appropriation to which Miss Ozick wishes to draw attention. The thoroughly Jewish concern of this work is the writing of fiction itself, in Miss Ozick's view an inheritance from the Gentiles and by nature an idolatrous activity. Art—in the Western tradition of truth to fiction as its own end—is against the Second Commandment, she says, and anti-Jewish in its very impulse. As a Jewish artist, Miss Ozick undertakes to subvert the aesthetic ideal by demonstrating its corrupting and arrogant presumption to truth. Thus, the Hebrew poet Saul Tchernikhowsky, one of those who worshipped at the shrine of pagan freedom and natural beauty, finds himself, at the end of the novella, caged in Paradise before a motto that teaches: "All that is not Law is levity." ⟨. . .⟩

The preface betrays the insecurities of both the artist and the Jew. Though she admires the transforming, magical kind of art, Miss Ozick is, in fact, an intellectual writer whose works are the fictional realization of ideas. Her reader is expected, at the conclusion of her stories, to have an insight, to understand the point of events rather than to respond to their affective power. Miss Ozick has publicly regretted this quality of hers, and accused herself of lacking what George Eliot calls "truth of feeling." It is true that, marvelously imaginative as she is with words and ideas, Miss Ozick is not on the whole successful at creating autonomous characters whose destiny will tantalize or move the reader.

—Ruth R. Wisse, "American Jewish Writing, Act II," *Commentary* (June 1976), in *The Chelsea House Library of Literary Criticism: Twentieth-Century American Literature*, Vol. 5, Harold Bloom, ed. (New York: Chelsea House Publishers, 1987), 3015–16

SARAH BLACHER COHEN

Satiric indictment and sympathetic acquittal of petty Yiddish writers is not Ozick's primary concern in "Envy." The story allows her to express her affection for Yiddish, the *mamaloshen*, the mother tongue, in which childhood endearments, *shtetl* solidarity, and a closeness with God are conveyed. Moreover, she laments the American Jews' abandonment of Yiddish for English, a language they consider more secular and thus more aesthetic. Abandonment of the Jewish sources for creativity in pursuit of more worldly fame is also the theme of "Virility," the next short story Ozick wrote after "Envy." On the surface, "Virility" appears to be a feminist comedy of literary manners revealing the double standard in the world of letters. Edmund Gate, born Elia Gatoff, has come to America from Czarist Russia via Liverpool to make his literary fortune. His first attempts at poetry are marred by contrived alliteration and polysyllabic diction. Though his work is continually rejected, he is a confident male and still believes in his talent. After several years of persistence, his poems miraculously improve and appear in the best magazines. Promoted by a married woman with whom he has had two illegitimate children, he publishes five volumes of poetry, each entitled *Virility*. The critics, more impressed with the title of the poetry than with its substance, single out what they consider its masculine virtues and overpraise them: "If Teddy Roosevelt's Rough Riders had been poets, they would have written poems like that. If Genghis Khan and Napoleon had been poets, they would have written poems like that. They were masculine . . . poems . . . [like] superbly controlled muscle . . ." (p. 257).

It turns out, however, that Edmund Gate is not the author of these poems. They have been written by Tante Rivka, his spinster aunt who cared for him in Liverpool. Soon after his arrival in America, he has been passing off as his own the eloquent poems she sent him in her letters. Three years after her death, he has nearly exhausted the supply of her poetry and faces artistic sterility. A Jamesian mentor convinces him to confess his plagiarism and do right by Tante Rivka. Her remaining poems, which were to comprise Gate's *Virility VI*, are published under her own name as *Flowers from Liverpool*. This collection contains Tante Rivka's finest poetry, yet the reviewers are unimpressed. Employing phallic criticism, they find her book to be "Thin feminine art," "Limited as all domestic verse must be. A spinster's one-dimensional vision" (p. 266). Yet Gate's poetry they acclaimed as "Seminal and hard," "Robust, lusty, male" (p. 254).

This flagrant example of male critical bias which Cynthia Ozick describes with bitter humor could be straight out of Victorian England. Elaine Showalter mentions a similar occurrence concerning the publication of George Eliot's *Adam Bede*. Since the book was thought to be too good for a woman's work, the critics hastily found the male whom they assumed to be the author, a clergyman named Joseph Liggins, who readily accepted credit for the book. When the real George Eliot could not abide the homage paid to the fraudulent author and revealed her identity, the reviews changed. "Where critics had previously seen the powerful mind of the male George Eliot . . . they now discovered feminine delicacy . . . a disturbing unladylike coarseness."

"Virility," however, is not exclusively an attack upon male parasites and male supremacists. Ozick includes an element of the ludicrous within Edmund Gate's treachery for the purpose of jest and symbolic import. Since he has appropriated a woman's talents, Ozick has him fear he has acquired a female's gender as well. Clutching his genitals to confirm his sex, his last words to the narrator are: "I'm a man" (p. 266).

Gate's uneasiness about his anatomy is symptomatic of his uneasiness about being a Jew. He readily saps the creativity of Tante Rivka, Ozick's allegorical figure representing Judaism, but he is reluctant to acknowledge his indebtedness to her. Once in America he ceases to communicate with her and lets her starve to death. If he had provided nourishment for her, she would have survived many more years and prolonged Gate's poetic career. Instead, Tante Rivka, productive until the end, died with dignity, whereas Edmund Gate, disaffected Jew and poet manqué, committed suicide.

—Sarah Blacher Cohen, "Jewish Literary Comediennes," *Comic Relief: Humor in Contemporary American Literature* (1978), in *The Chelsea House Library of Literary Criticism: Twentieth-Century American Literature*, Vol. 5, Harold Bloom, ed. (New York: Chelsea House Publishers, 1987), 3017–18

A. ALVAREZ

Ezra Pound once divided writers into carvers and molders. The molders—Balzac, Lawrence, Whitman—work fast, not much worried by detail or repetition or precision, impatient to get down the shape and flow of their inspiration, while the carvers—Flaubert, Eliot, Beckett—work with infinite slowness, painstakingly writing and rewriting, unable to go ahead until each phrase is balanced, each detail perfect.

Cynthia Ozick is a carver, a stylist in the best and most complete sense: in language, in wit, in her apprehension of reality and her curious, crooked flights of imagination. She once described an early work of hers, rather sniffily, as "both 'mandarin' and 'lapidary,' every paragraph a poem." Although there is nothing stiff or overcompacted about her writing now, she still has the poet's perfectionist habit of mind and obsession with language, as though one word out of place would undo the whole fabric.

She has, in fact, published poems, but the handful I have read seem a good deal less persuasive and subtly timed than her prose. Listen, for example, to the narrator of "Shots," the best story in her new collection. She is a professional photographer, hovering on the edge of infatuation with gloomy Sam, who is an expert on South American affairs, heavily but uneasily married to a paragon. She and Sam have been brought suddenly together when a simultaneous translator at a symposium Sam is addressing and she is photographing is murdered by a terrorist who can't shoot straight:

> The little trick was this: whatever he said that was vast and public and South American, I would simultaneously translate (I hoped I wouldn't be gunned down for it) into everything private and personal and secret. This required me to listen shrewdly to the moan behind the words—I had to blot out the words for the sake of the tune. Sometimes the tune would be civil or sweet or almost jolly— especially if he happened to get a look at me before he ascended to his lectern—but mainly it would be narrow and drab and resigned. I knew he had a wife, but I was already thirty-six, and who didn't have a wife by then? I wasn't likely to run into them if they didn't. Bachelors wouldn't be where I had to go, particularly not in public halls gaping at the per capita income of the interior villages of the Andes, or the future of Venezuelan oil, or the fortunes of the last Paraguayan bean crop, or the differences between the centrist parties in Bolivia and Colombia, or whatever it was that kept Sam ladling away at his tedious stew. I drilled through all these sober-shelled facts into their echoing gloomy melodies: and the sorrowful sounds I unlocked from their casings—it was like breaking open a stone and finding the music of the earth's wild core boiling inside—came down to the wife, the wife, the wife. That was the tune Sam was moaning all the while: wife wife wife. He didn't like her. He wasn't happy with her. His whole life was wrong. He was a dead man. If I thought I'd seen a dead man when they took that poor fellow out on that stretcher, I was stupidly mistaken; *he* was ten times deader than that. If the terrorist who couldn't shoot straight had shot *him* instead, he couldn't be more riddled with gunshot than he was this minute—he was smoking with his own death.

The writing is intricate and immaculate: a poet's ear and precision and gift for disturbing image—"it was like breaking open a stone and finding the music of the earth's wild core boiling inside"—combined with the storyteller's sense of timing and flow, the effortless shift between the colloquial and the allusive, the changes of pace and changes of tone—her subtle, passionate ironies, his nagging self-pity—the paragraph balancing gradually, logically, to its climax.

—A. Alvarez, "Flushed with Ideas: *Levitation*," *New York Review of Books* (13 May 1982), in *Cynthia Ozick*, Harold Bloom, ed. (New York: Chelsea House Publishers, 1986), 53–54

ADAM MARS-JONES

"You have no feelings", one character accuses another in one of Cynthia Ozick's new stories, but the accusation is immediately modified: "he meant that she had the habit of flushing with ideas as if they were passions." And the whole book ⟨*Levitation*⟩ flushes likewise, with passionate learning and with passionate phrasing. Cynthia Ozick is a woman, and Jewish; and a New Yorker; these conditions in combination might be expected to produce a narrow art, if any at all. And certainly there are few men in these stories, fewer gentiles, and hardly a single out-of-towner, but the result is anything but narrow; the absentees are hardly noticed.

Cynthia Ozick has the enviable knack of moving, with impressive speed, in opposite directions at the same time; her specialities are prose poetry, intellectual slapstick, meticulous detail, and wild rhetorical fantasy. The result at its best is an audacious and unorthodox balancing of forces, both within the story and within the sentence. Within the story, there is tension between a carefully rendered milieu and the wildly elaborated fantasy which arrives to transform it. Within the sentence, there is a running battle between a realism that describes things as they are, and a rhetoric that takes constant liberties with the appearances. ⟨. . .⟩

When the materials are properly combined, the results are formidable: the text flushes with the idea of Jewishness and the idea of New York. The sense of history and the sense of place become resources of fact and feeling for an entirely new enterprise, and the whole unlikely rocket takes off, trailing sparks and coloured rain. After a vivid and exhilarating flight, admittedly, all that comes clattering down through the trees is a scorched stick; but with very little more discipline and expertise Cynthia Ozick will produce fireworks that can carry passengers.

—Adam Mars-Jones, "Fantastic Flushes," *Times Literary Supplement* (23 April 1982), in *The Chelsea House Library of Literary Criticism: Twentieth-Century American Literature*, Vol. 5, Harold Bloom, ed. (New York: Chelsea House Publishers, 1987), 3016

KATHA POLLIT

⟨Art & Ardor⟩ is not your typical collection of essays by an eminent middle-aged writer of fiction. You know the sort of book I mean—a graceful miscellany of book reviews, introductions and speeches, all wrapped up and offered to the public less as a book, really, then as a kind of laurel, a tribute to the author's literary importance. The magazine articles collected here do more than stand on their own. They jump up and down, they grab the reader by the shirt-front. We may be living in "an era when the notion of belles-lettres is profoundly dead," as Miss Ozick says in her foreword, but it's thriving in Art & Ardor, which is by turns quarrelsome, quirky, unfair, funny and brilliant.

Looked at one way, these essays, though originally published in magazines as divergent as Ms. and Commentary, are a unified and magisterial continuation of Miss Ozick's short stories by other means. Admirers of her three story collections (her one novel, Trust, is, sadly, out of print) will recognize at once her yeasty, extravagant prose, her intellectual preoccupations (jeremiads against violations of the Second Commandment, for instance—that's the one about worshiping idols) and some of her characters too. ⟨. . .⟩

Looked at another way, though, Art & Ardor is the work not of one Cynthia Ozick but three: a rabbi, a feminist and a disciple of Henry James. Among them, this trio—old classmates, perhaps, or relatives, but hardly friends—have co-authored a fascinating and very odd anthology of essays about Judaism, women and literature.

As rabbi, Miss Ozick's chief target is idol worship, whose ramifications, she argues, include the Holocaust, Jewish assimilation and much modern literature, all of which are the result of substituting "aesthetic paganism" for moral seriousness. "When a Jew becomes a secular person he is no longer a Jew," she writes in "Toward a New Yiddish"; he's merely a neuter, an "envious ape" of gentile culture. It follows that Miss Ozick regards most of the writers we think of as Jewish—Proust, Kafka, Heine, not to mention Philip Roth and Norman Mailer—as Christians manqués, the main exception being Saul Bellow, for reasons I couldn't quite catch. (Actually, the writer who best fits Miss Ozick's criteria is Miss Ozick herself, whose fiction does indeed answer her call for "a new Yiddish," that is, a culturally Jewish-American literature informed by a "sacral imagination" and an engagement with history.) ⟨. . .⟩

The feminist Ozick, a more cheerful sort, takes on Anatomy as Destiny. "If anatomy were destiny, the wheel could not have been invented; we would have been limited by legs," she snaps in "The Hole/Birth Catalogue," a masterly demolition of Freud on women. She's outraged by sentimentalists who patronize women by comparing housekeeping or pregnancy to artistic creation: "It is insulting to a poet to compare his titanic and agonized strivings with the so-called 'creativity' of childbearing, where—consciously—nothing happens. One does not will the development of the fetus . . . the process itself is as involuntary, and unaware as the beating of one's own heart."

Miss Ozick reserves particular scorn for the "Ovarian Theory of Literature," whose proponents include feminist literary scholars, the author's own college students (who decided Flannery O'Connor was "sentimental" when they learned she was not a man) and most book reviewers: "I think I can say in good conscience that I have never—repeat, *never*—read a review of a novel or, especially, of a collection of poetry by a woman that did not include somewhere in its columns a gratuitous allusion to the writer's sex and its supposed effects," she wrote in 1971. ⟨. . .⟩

At this point, the Jamesian Ozick takes over. For her, the imagination is a holy mystery and the writing of fiction the only thing that matters. The Jamesian knows precisely what was wrong with R. W. B. Lewis's biography of Edith Wharton—it left out her life as a writer. She's devastating on Truman Capote's arch early novels—perhaps too devastating, for she denounces "Other Voices, Other Rooms" like someone going after a hummingbird with a chain saw. The Jamesian even knows that worshiping James is a trap: Art may be all that matters, but one can't be an artist if one lives as though that were true. As I'm trying to indicate, Cynthia Ozick has a complicated mind. ⟨. . .⟩

I suspect that Cynthia Ozick's three selves do not try harder to make peace with each other because they sense it can't be done. The secular drift she castigates as a religious Jew is, after all, exactly what gives her the freedom to reexamine traditional notions of women, and to posit the imagination as sovereign. All the same, it would be interesting to see what she would come up with if she set herself the task of synthesis. For now, though, it's enough that she has given us this wonderful, if sometimes frustrating book.

—Katha Pollit, "The Three Selves of Cynthia Ozick," *New York Times Book Review* (23 May 1983), in *The Chelsea House Library of Literary Criticism: Twentieth-Century American Literature*, Vol. 5, Harold Bloom, ed. (New York: Chelsea House Publishers, 1987), 3019–20

PETER S. PRESCOTT

Ozick's first novel, *Trust*, was an exercise in Henry James. Three collections of short stories followed—*The Pagan Rabbi, Bloodshed* and *Levitation*—and it is on these that her reputation principally rests. Now after 17 years she returns to the novel form. James's mannerisms have been abandoned, but a vestige remains: the clash of the old world with the new.

The hero of *The Cannibal Galaxy*, Joseph Brill, is the principal of an ambitious, dismal, private elementary school somewhere in Middle America. Brill is a French Jew, a refugee from the Holocaust. It is his conceit that a school might develop what he calls a "Dual Curriculum": half Talmudic studies, half European culture. Such an education would embrace a passion for the ideal and a passion for sardonic detail: "Two such separated tonalities . . . could between them describe the true map of life." Brill is a bachelor, a failed astronomer, "a melancholic, a counter of losses. . . . used to consorting with the Middle." His students are middling and so is his faculty, which is given to assigning long lists for memorization. Ozick picks him up at age 58, confronting the mother of a dull student. The mother, Hester Lilt, is European, too, a formidable philosopher: "an imagistic linguistic logician." Ozick has modeled her, I suspect, on Hannah Arendt. Brill is at first sycophantic, but Lilt rebukes him: she's too good for a man who quit trying to be great too soon. She taunts him by sending him her writings—until Brill unexpectedly discovers that the guiding principle behind her thinking is a sham. ⟨. . .⟩

⟨. . .⟩ Ozick's imagery may offend some of her women readers, but it's nonetheless tough-minded and in the highest sense comical. And so is her novel: tough, sad, funny, beautiful in its design.

—Peter S. Prescott, "Vision and Design," *Newsweek* (12 September 1983), in *The Chelsea House Library of Literary Criticism: Twentieth-Century American Literature*, Vol. 5, Harold Bloom, ed. (New York: Chelsea House Publishers, 1987), 3016

EDMUND WHITE

Some writers are so enthralled by ideas (one thinks of Doris Lessing) that their characters become debaters, and their fables approach allegory. Other writers are pretty but dumb; their prose may beautifully render the physical world but it is contentedly mindless, as though to entertain an idea were a gaffe in literary propriety, a descent into the essayistic. Miss Ozick falls between these two extremes. Ideas interest her, but only as they force decisions, determine actions, lead to self-deception and ruin or spawn strange feats.

In her celebrated (and very funny) novella "Puttermesser and Xanthippe," in *Levitation: Five Fictions*, a lawyer working for New York City, Ruth Puttermesser, becomes obsessed with a vision of a better community. This idea eventually leads her, almost unconsciously, to create a golem, a big and steadily-getting-bigger demon-servant named Xanthippe, who reforms New York—and then destroys it with her rampant sexual appetites. But this horrible outcome derives from Puttermesser's initial utopian idea:

"Every day, inside the wide bleak corridors of the Municipal Building, Puttermesser dreamed an ideal Civil Service: devotion to polity, the citizen's sweet love of the citizenry, the light rule of reason and common sense, the City as a miniature country crowded with patriots—not fools and jingoists, but patriots true and serene; humorous affection for the idiosyncrasies of one's distinctive little homeland, each borough itself another little homeland, joy in the Bronx, elation in Queens, O happy Richmond! Children on roller skates, and over the Brooklyn Bridge the long patchwork-colored line of joggers, breathing hard above the homeland-hugging green waters."

This passage reveals the Gogolian side of Miss Ozick's style: her robust zest for details that never sink a sentence but rather spurt out of it, her vivid rendering of an inspired but cracked dream that issues forth from the brain of a minor functionary, a sleight-of-hand within a single paragraph that transforms naturalist detail ("wide bleak corridors") into an imagined glimpse of the sublime ("homeland-hugging green waters") and a seemingly childlike but actually artful snatching after expression that makes the syntax hard to diagram but thrilling to read ("joy in the Bronx"). Here one detects all the energy and drive of Miss Ozick's style and the tricky transitions it can negotiate from one level of narrative reality to another. ⟨. . .⟩

Precisely on account of her style, Miss Ozick strikes me as the best American writer to have emerged in recent years. Her artistic strength derives from her moral energy, for Miss Ozick is not an esthete. Judaism has given to her what Catholicism gave to Flannery O'Connor—authority, penetration and indignation.

    —Edmund White, "Images of a Mind Thinking," *New York Times Book Review* (11 September 1983), in *The Chelsea House Library of Literary Criticism: Twentieth-Century American Literature*, Vol. 5, Harold Bloom, ed. (New York: Chelsea House Publishers, 1987), 3012

B I B L I O G R A P H Y

Trust. 1966.
The Pagan Rabbi and Other Stories. 1971.
Bloodshed and Three Novellas. 1976.
Levitation: Five Fictions. 1982.
Art and Ardor. 1983.
The Cannibal Galaxy. 1983.
The Messiah of Stockholm. 1987.
The Shawl. 1989.
Metaphor and Memory. 1991.
What Henry James Knew. 1993.
A Cynthia Ozick Reader (Elaine M. Kauvar, ed.). 1996.
Fame and Folly: Essays. 1996.
The Puttermesser Papers: A Novel. 1997.

GRACE PALEY

1922–

GRACE PALEY was born in the Bronx, New York City, on December 11, 1922. The daughter of Mary and Isaac Goodside, a doctor and part-time painter, Paley grew up in a socialist Russian-Jewish family and was surrounded by enthusiastic storytellers. She attended Evander Childs High School and, in 1938 and 1939, Hunter College. Although she later took courses at New York University and studied poetry with W. H. Auden at the New School for Social Research, she never received a college degree.

In 1942, at the age of 19, she married Jess Paley, a motion-picture cameraman. They had two children and were divorced more than 20 years later.

Paley began writing in the mid-1950s. She has been praised for the warm, comic tone of her stories and for her sophisticated technique. Her stories are usually set in middle-class, Jewish neighborhoods of New York and focus on the ordinary lives of the characters. Paley has been criticized for sacrificing her writing to her political views; she is particularly active in feminist and anti-war causes.

Paley has also been a teacher since the early 1960s, when she taught at Columbia and Syracuse Universities; she has also taught at Sarah Lawrence College in New York and at City College, New York, since 1983. Paley received a Guggenheim grant in 1961; a National Endowment for the Arts grant in 1966; and an American Academy Award in 1970. She lives in New York City with her second husband, Robert Nichols.

C R I T I C A L   E X T R A C T S

PATRICIA MACMANUS
The glad tidings from this reviewer's corner are of the appearance of a new-comer possessed of an all-too-infrequent literary virtue—the comic vision. Grace Paley is the writer, and heretofore, apparently, her light has been confined to some of the smaller quarterlies. Now, however, *The Little Disturbances of Man* brings together ten of her short stories, and a welcome event it is. While they may not, to be sure, fully satisfy confirmed plot-watchers, they are by no means simply "mood" stories—rather, they are marked throughout by a well-

defined and artfully guileless form of narrative progression. But the heart of the matter in these tales is their serio-comic stance: character revealed through the wry devices that man contrives, consciously and unconsciously, to shore up his uncertain existence and, sometimes, to salvage laughter from lamentation.

In "The Loudest Voice" for example, the Paley approach is glimpsed in the reaction of a Jewish immigrant to his wife's horrified announcement that their child is to be in a Christmas—a *Christian*—play. "You're in America," the husband retorts. "In Palestine the Arabs would be eating you alive. Europe you had pogroms. Argentina is full of Indians. Here you got Christmas." Or in the lyrically risible opening of "The Contest"—"Up early or late, it never matters, the day gets away from me. Summer or winter, the shade of trees or their hard shadow, I never get into my Rice Krispies till noon."

The people in these tales exist on the far periphery of the Important world; and the themes are as the title states: the little disturbances of man— "little" vis-à-vis cosmic catastrophes, but major to the personal business of daily living. A middle-aging, sanguine-spirited "bachelor girl" recollects an amorous past on the eve of her marriage to a long-ago beau; a determined teen-ager cons a bemused young soldier into a thoroughly entangling alliance; a husband-abandoned wife and mother wait out the idolized prodigal's return, imperturably confident; a pixilated youth who lives in a philodendron-decorated automobile and functions as a kind of curb-service problem consultant; a girl's long, frustrated need for love is examined from her own viewpoint—and from the viewpoint of the man she wants. These are a few of the characters who move through the oblique human comedy of Mrs. Paley's stories. Small-time people, in terms of the world worldly, they none the less reflect the perdurable instinct of most people everywhere to improvise ways and means of accepting the indifferent universe.

—Patricia MacManus, "Laughter from Tears," *New York Times Book Review* (19 April 1959), in *The Chelsea House Library of Literary Criticism: Twentieth-Century American Literature*, Vol. 5, Harold Bloom, ed. (New York: Chelsea House Publishers, 1987), 3027

IVAN GOLD

The ten stories in *The Little Disturbances of Man* explore the levels of feeling and turmoil beneath the "little disturbances" of our lives in a variety of ways, from many points of view. By turns, often at once, the stories give quirky, anguished, funny, loving, deep and antic glimpses into the hearts and lives of children, mothers, lovers, spouses divorced and abandoned, the ageing and the old, in a prose as resilient and unpredictable as one imagines the fate of her characters to be at any story's end, no matter how often one has read it.

Yet when I asked the author not long ago, in connection with the reissue of her book and the piece I might do about this glad event, to say a word about her fiction, or about the impulse which led her to write the kind of thing she does after her beginnings as a poet, she could say, "I felt bad about men and women," and with that profoundly simple remark, worthy of a number of the living, bleeding humans who inhabit her pages, she could illumine the connection I have been trying to describe: that she lived precisely where she worked, wrote out of the heart of her perplexity and sense of wonder at the countless ways we have for dealing with each other, her grief that it so often turns out so badly, joy all the greater because less often found.

It is a sticky painful way to write, and the very excellence of the result, the moving, honest, somehow *unbreakable* quality of her stories, seemed, to some, sufficient explanation of why, in the years following the book's first appearance, Grace Paley produced so little else. She was known to be "working on a novel," and, indeed, sections of it would appear in magazines from time to time—in the defunct *noble savage*, in the first issue of *New American Review*—but of shorter pieces there were few, and these very short, and rather playful. Those whose task this is began to mourn her as one of the mysterious casualties of the literary life—writers who give us a brilliant first work of fiction and then falter, or are heard from no more. ⟨. . .⟩

But during her literary lean years, Grace Paley's life was fat. She gave to the roles of wife and mother the profound, existential attention her readers would have been able to predict. She was among the earliest and fiercest agitators against the grisly treatment afforded inmates of Greenwich Village's Women's House of Detention, her human and political involvement in this and other "community" matters widening along with the war in Vietnam to the point where she was and remains in the thick of resistance to that bizarre, bloody conflict, and to the Administration which continues to wage it. Operating out of the Greenwich Village Peace Center, she is an indefatigable pamphleteer and hander-out of leaflets, was among the signers of the Writers and Editors War Tax Protest, is an active member of both the local and national committees of *Resist*, in which connection she was arrested, not for the first time, during the pre-dawn gathering at the induction center on Whitehall Street last December, for voicing particularly vociferous objection to the tactics of the police, and she saved a few young heads from being broken in the process.

For the past several years she has been giving courses in the short story, at Columbia, at Syracuse, and at Sarah Lawrence (where she teaches still). Her classes at Columbia, when I was there, were always oversubscribed, her students full of praise of her and an eagerness to work. Whatever the often justifiable criticisms made of "creative writing" courses, it was easy to see that something was being transmitted during that particular once-weekly two-hour stretch which was not listed in the catalogue: that Grace Paley was able—probably, she had no choice—to gift her students with herself.

And what of her novel? The signs are that it will be along. Lately, in the midst of all busyness, she has begun to publish again. In the past several months, first-rate short fiction has appeared in the *Atlantic* and in *Esquire*, as well as the aforementioned excerpt from her novel in *New American Review*. One wants to exhort the pundits to fight back the crocodile tears, and have a little patience.

Meanwhile, as we wait, the Viking edition of *The Little Disturbances of Man* has come out to tide us over.

—Ivan Gold, "On Having Grace Paley Once More Among Us," *Commonweal* (25 October 1968), in *The Chelsea House Library of Literary Criticism: Twentieth-Century American Literature*, Vol. 5, Harold Bloom, ed. (New York: Chelsea House Publishers, 1987), 3027–28

CHARLES SUGNET

⟨Interviewer⟩ Q: Does your reading influence your writing a lot?

⟨Paley⟩ A: I used to read a lot more than I read. For years I was what was called a big reader. Now I read a lot less. I think that everything I ever read is very influential on my writing and by that I mean the stuff you read from a very early age. The poets I read had a strong influence on me. But I think when we talk about influences we omit some of the most important influences on our writing, and they're never discussed really, and they're not literary at all. It may be why I feel close to Russian writers. It's because that's the language of my father and mother. So one of the major influences on my writing, I feel, is the street in which I grew up. I was out in it all the time. And the language of my family which was English and Russian and some Yiddish running back and forth a lot at great speed, and the life they talked about, the life they led. That language that I heard, and the language of the street, of the kids and also of the grown ups, who hung out in the street a lot in those days, that was as great an influence on my writing as anything I've read. As for form, that's another thing. I'm just like anyone my age. I read a lot of Joyce when I was a kid and those stories probably had a lot to do with my first ideas of form. I read a lot of Chekhov. I think those old things have influence. I don't think that anything you read . . . now, can strongly influence you, it can superficially do so but not really deeply.

Q: Can you talk about the writing process in terms of your thinking? Do you "think on the page"? Do you do a lot of thinking about something before you begin to write? Or do you discover it as you write?

A: Well, I begin by writing something, and I just write it, and I may not even look at it for the next two years. So I have a lot of pages lying around. When I finish a story I start going through all my pages. I have all these pages. Some of them, I'm amazed to see, are part of what I'm thinking about. We have this one head, so everything is just in there all the time. You write a few pages and then you . . . go away. . . . Which is, again, the distractable way that I work and it's not to be construed as a decent or honourable way of doing things [laughter] but I do think about things a long long time. When I'm really into a story I work very very hard on it. People ask me, How do you know when it's at an end? I just thought last week what was the answer: I know I'm at the end when I say to myself, How'm I going to end this thing? When I think I've finished it I then begin to go over it and I go over it for falsity mostly, and for lies. I just revise. I just think of it in those terms. I don't want anybody to think I just write when I feel like it, especially who are going to go into that line of work. You write also when you don't feel like it. It really is such hard work that if you are naturally lazy, like I am, you often feel like it, so you have to keep that in mind.

Q: What do you think are the most commonly encountered lies that come up in your work?

A: Wanting certain characters to be something, or pushing them around. You get stuck with your own examples of things. The example I always use is how I got stuck giving some guy the wrong job. I was working on this story for a very long time and I just couldn't move ahead on it, and the reason was I'd given him the wrong job. He really was a taxi-driver and I think I gave him some sort of administrative responsibility somewhere. [Laughter] It really was bad, but until I realized that . . . I'd call that a lie. I wanted him in an office, you know? But once I'd got him out of the office, because he didn't belong there, then a lot of other things changed. There are other kinds of lies too. There are lies of language where you exaggerate, or put in a lot of adjectives, or you try to be high styled, or you try to be up-to-the-minute with what's being done. Those are lies. You can go through a story again and again and again until you can't change it any more, and then at the end . . . don't think in terms, is this story good or bad, you know? Because you never will know. What you can think about is whether it's true as you can make it. And then even if you think it's bad, you're probably wrong. "Oh, this lousy story I just finished." But it's what I had to say, and it's what I said, and everything in it is truly invented and true . . . then you probably have a good story.

Q: Could you say something about humour in short stories?

A: The only thing I can say about humour is that if you're not funny you can't be. [*Laughter*] But did you want me to say something more serious about it? [*Laughter*] Humour I think by its very nature is out of place. I mean that. You have humour when you have great disparity.

> —Charles Sugnet (interview by Alan Burns), *The Imagination on Trial* (1971), in *The Chelsea House Library of Literary Criticism: Twentieth-Century American Literature*, Vol. 5, Harold Bloom, ed. (New York: Chelsea House Publishers, 1987), 3026

MICHELLE MURRAY

When Grace Paley's first collection of stories, *The Little Disturbances of Man*, appeared in 1959, it was clear at once that a fresh writing talent had presented itself. While her subject matter—the frantic life of urban men and women, mostly Jews, in and around the West Village—was hardly new, her style was very much her own. She wrote like the ultimate *yenta*, Molly Goldberg raised to a fine art without losing her roots in oral speech, and the stories she told were splendidly suited to her style, being mostly tales of feminine woe of the kind that would set Molly Goldberg's tongue wagging—women abandoned by husbands, women caring for small kids in airless flats, and in the best of the tales in that first book, "Goodbye and Good Luck," a woman kept by a celebrated actor of the Yiddish theater. In this triumph of style, a conventional story of a young girl and an older man is turned into a comic routine with a happy ending.

But a comic routine isn't even a three-act Neil Simon play, and a virtuoso style has its own pitfalls, more obvious in Paley's new collection, *Enormous Changes at the Last Minute*, which reprints a generous selection of her work from the past 15 years. The setting is the same—the increasingly grimy and decaying streets of Manhattan and Brooklyn—and many of the same characters appear for a second turn, most notably Johnny Raftery and Ginny, and piecemeal Faith with her boys Richard and Tonto—while the style is, if anything, more dazzling than ever.

The question is: to what purpose so much bedazzlement? And the answer, I think, is: to keep the stories from sinking into the quicksands of their own misery. For even with the glitter of its style, over which Paley skates like some Olympic champion of language, *Enormous Changes* is a book of losses and failures that add up to one of the most depressing works of fiction to be published in the last decade, hardly a time noted for the prevalence of upbeat writing.

First there's the setting. Paley knows what travel writers and eager young things don't want to see, that New York is a city of failures. Of course there are successful ones, more than a handful, dwellers in certain East Side blocks, luxury apartments and Fifth Avenue cooperatives, but they're the cream,

500,000 skimmed off the 6.5 million others huddled in cramped tenements, clustered in Lefrak City's human hive, or wiping the venetian blinds in antique brick semidetached houses clinging to the edges of the city in Canarsie or Staten Island.

These failures are Paley's people and the inhabitants of her stories, especially the mothers who sit lumpily on park benches so that their pasty-faced children will get as much of the sun as the smog-ridden parks can attract. And they are going nowhere but home to kitchens of sour milk and roaches, a fact they try to disguise with all the jauntiness they can muster, a true New York salesman's jauntiness, like the diamond pinky ring flashed to conceal the too-shiny suit and the shirt with a frayed collar.

But beneath that jauntiness, which is Paley's style, the stories sag into consistent failure. ⟨. . .⟩

Death and old age are, in fact, the leitmotifs of this collection, even when young people are featured. Paley can't imagine any public stage for them to act upon and she has lost confidence in the ability of private passions to assure happiness. Nor is it a dilemma imagined for the sake of plot—put 'em in a box and watch 'em get out again. Most of Paley's stories are too short for any plot. They're quick sketches, blackouts, comic monologues spoken in a theater bereft of audience by a voice increasingly desperate for coherence.

Finally though, there isn't any coherence, or nothing more substantial than the style, to which we return in the absence of anything else that will reward our attention. One of her characters exclaims, "Tragedy! . . . When will you look it in the face?" But it's not tragedy that weighs down these stories, it's no more than despair and repetition. Tragedy suggests depths and alternatives and is built into a world of choices. Paley's world, while a plausible look at the way we live now, is severely limited, the world as given, without any imagined alternatives, only endless vistas of crumbling buildings, bedrooms opening onto air shafts, and a phalanx of old people's homes running the boardwalk where young people frolicked so long ago that even the memory of such happy days can barely be clutched from the darkening air.

—Michelle Murray, *New Republic* (16 March 1974), in *The Chelsea House Library of Literary Criticism: Twentieth-Century American Literature*, Vol. 5, Harold Bloom, ed. (New York: Chelsea House Publishers, 1987), 3028

CLARA CLAIBORNE PARK

Rereading ⟨*Enormous Changes*⟩ it's easy to see that Paley has never encouraged us in the shallow notion that if things are going well for our heroine they are tipping toward sunshine for everybody. But we like thinking that, and though four of the stories in *Enormous Changes* dealt directly and piercingly with death, our minds gravitated to the title's assertion of continuing possibility, and the upbeat ending. In *Later the Same Day* things are still going well for Faith—she's with Jack still, the boys are doing ok, she even has a car. Eight of the seventeen stories, and three-quarters of the pages, belong to her in one way or another. But she is no longer the center. "I am trying to curb my cultivated individualism," she begins one story (in which only two proper names distinguish the speaker from Paley herself), individualism "which seemed for years so sweet. It was my own song in my own world, and of course it may not be useful in the hard time to come." It is that individualism that the new stories decisively curb. The reader's commitment to Faith, to her parents, to her children, now young men, need not dissipate, but it must expand, with Faith's, to a wider embrace. The new stories offer even more focuses of attention. Never conventionally organized, they are more discontinuous than ever. Form follows function. Paley has always despised plot, she has told us. And why? "Not for literary reasons, but because it takes all hope away," because it denies the possibility of those enormous changes, because "everyone, real or invented, deserves the open destiny of life." But the lack of plot no longer asks us to believe that everything is possible ("Oh, Pa," I said. "She could change [*Enormous Changes at the Last Minute*]). We owe it to the young and to ourselves not to put on a gloomy face, but this novel by accretion now makes another statement. It is, as Paley has said elsewhere, not the "I" but the "we" that is important.

Novel? Paley will not present it as such. Loose ends and inconsistencies are left from story to story and volume to volume as if to mock our conviction that her inventions are solider than our wraithlike lives. Why does Arthur Mazzano become Phillip, as he definitely does in Volume Three? Did Faith grow up in Coney Island or the Bronx? The stories are a web, a tapestry, something woven, or embroidered, or a patchwork—feminine handiwork anyway, extensive enough that irregularities don't matter and threads and bits and snippets in all colors can be greeted and made welcome.

The form for such an entertainment will not be linear. In the same story in which she repudiates individualism (in the most individual of voices) Faith— Paley—identifies the habit of beginning a story at the beginning as something men love and do. Middles, she implies, are for the untidy world of women, whose work and webs are never done. It is in middles that life is woven close. Paley's work will take its meanings, not from a beginning artificially charged with the significance of a climactic ending, but from the daily, seemingly inconsequential maintenance-work of the enduring and expanding middle.

—Clara Claiborne Park, "Faith, Grace, and Love," *Hudson Review* (Autumn 1975), in *The Chelsea House Library of Literary Criticism: Twentieth-Century American Literature*, Vol. 5, Harold Bloom, ed. (New York: Chelsea House Publishers, 1987), 3034

JONATHAN BAUMBACH

In *Enormous Changes*, as in the first collection, Paley writes about families, about lost and found love, about divorce, death, ongoing life—the most risky and important themes—in a style in which words count for much, sometimes for almost all. The stories—in some cases, the same stories—deal on the one hand with their own invention and, on the other, profoundly (and comically) with felt experience. In this sense, and in a wholly unschematic way, Paley combines what has been called the "tradition of new fiction" in America with the abiding concerns of the old.

Grace Paley's stories resist the intrusion of critical language about them, make it seem, no matter what, irrelevant and excessive. The stories are hard to write about because what they translate into has little relation, less than most explication, to what they are: themselves, transformed events of the imagination. The voice of Paley's fiction—quirky, tough, wiseass, vulnerable, bruised into wisdom by the knocks of experience—is the triumph and defining characteristic of her art.

"An Interest in Life," probably the best piece in *The Little Disturbances of Man*, and one of the best American stories of the past twenty-five years, illustrates Paley's mode. A story initially about a husband's desertion of a wife and four children, it opens: "My husband gave me a broom one Christmas. This wasn't right. No one can tell me it was meant kindly." The matter-of-fact, ironic voice of the protagonist, Ginny, distances the reader from the conventions of her pathos, makes light of easy sentiment, only to bring us, unburdened by melodrama, to an awareness of the character as if someone known to us intimately for a long time. Ginny, in a desperate moment, writes out a list of her troubles to get on the radio show, "Strike it Rich." When she shows the list to John Raftery, a returned former suitor unhappily married to someone else, he points out to her that her troubles are insufficient, merely "the little disturbances of man." Paley's comic stories deal in exaggerated understatement, disguise their considerable ambition in the modesty of wit. ⟨. . .⟩

Paley is a major writer working in what passes in our time as a minor form. Her short fiction has continually deceived media, that system of mirrors that tends to discover the very things it advertises to itself, into taking it for less than it is. "A Conversation with My Father," my favorite of the second collection, concerns itself in part with the making of fiction. The narrator's father asks her why she doesn't write simple stories like de Maupassant or Chekhov. "Just recognizable people and then write down what happened to them next." To please her father, to prove the task hopeless, she offers him (and us) in abbreviated form a plain story, a self-fulfilling failure since the narrator holds that "Everyone, real or imagined, deserves the open destiny of life." The father complains that she leaves everything out, and Paley's narrator invents another, more elaborate version of the same story. The longer version is no closer to the kind of story the father wants, and he berates her for making jokes out of "Tragedy." "A Conversation with My Father" is by implication a self-criticism, a limiting and defining of mode, yet, symptomatic of Paley's best work, it illustrates by example the large and complex seriousness she affects (as if placating the gods) to deny herself.

—Jonathan Baumbach, "Life-Size," *Partisan Review* (1975), in *The Chelsea House Library of Literary Criticism: Twentieth-Century American Literature*, Vol. 5, Harold Bloom, ed. (New York: Chelsea House Publishers, 1987), 3029–30

Marianne DeKoven

Though Paley has published only two collections of stories, *The Little Disturbances of Man* and *Enormous Changes at the Last Minute*, she is nonetheless an important writer—important in the significance of the fictional possibilities she realizes rather than in the uniform merit of her published work. She is not always at her best. But when she is, Paley reconciles the demands of avant-garde or postmodern form for structural openness and the primacy of the surface with the seemingly incompatible demands of traditional realist material for orchestrated meaning and cathartic emotion.

"A Conversation with My Father," in *Enormous Changes*, makes of this seeming incompatibility an argument between father and daughter, from which emerges the statement, crucial to Paley's work, that traditional themes can no longer be treated *truthfully* by formally traditional fiction: formal inventiveness and structural open-endedness not only make fiction interesting, they make it "true-to-life." Paley's concern is not mimesis or verisimilitude, but rather the problem of creating a literary form which does not strike one as artificial; which is adequate to the complexity of what we know. Her narrator in "A Conversation with My Father" calls traditional plot "the absolute line between two points which I've always despised. Not for literary reasons, but because it takes away all hope. Everyone, real or invented, deserves the open destiny of life." Her father, arguing that plot is the truth of tragedy, wants her to write like Chekhov or Maupassant: "Tragedy! Plain tragedy! Historical tragedy! No hope. The end." Paley's narrator-surrogate, arguing for open-ended hope and change, clearly bests her father in the conversation. But in the story, Paley gives him the last word: the setting is his hospital room, and he speaks from what we may assume is his deathbed. His lecture on writing is "last-minute advice," and the closing speech, from father's pain to daughter's guilt, is his: "'How long will it be?' he asked. 'Tragedy! You too. When will you look it in the face?'"

The assertion of hope through change and open-endedness is therefore neither easy nor unambiguous. As the literary father sees, an inevitable component of optimistic belief in saving the situation through "enormous changes at the last minute" is evasion of genuine and unavoidable horror, the father's tragedy. As Faith herself says in "Living" (*Enormous Changes*), "You have to be cockeyed to love, and blind in order to look out the window at your own ice-cold street." ⟨. . .⟩

Though linear storytelling is attractive to Paley's moral-political sensibility, and she feels guilty that she doesn't write that way, the marrow of her fictions remains "enormous changes at the last minute." Her narrator in "A Conversation with My Father" claims that she does not hate plot "for literary reasons." But Paley's narrator is either misrepresenting or misunderstanding the "literary reasons" of Paley's fiction. Traditional plot does not necessarily preclude the possibility of hope; or, in cruder terms, the possibility of a happy ending. The narrator confuses the closure of traditional plot with the closure of despair, and once we acknowledge her mistake, we can go on to see her very "literary" reason for making it: it is the "enormous change" *as a phenomenon of literature* that is life-giving and hope-giving. In "Life" (the conversation between father and daughter), the father in his hospital room not only propounds but represents the tragic vision: he is dying testimony to the inevitability of what the narrator, meaning hopelessness, calls plot. In "Literature" (the story-within-a-story the narrator invents about a redeemed junkie), the narrator insists not so much on a happy ending for her character but on sudden and total change interrupting what would be a tragic trajectory toward doom in the kind of traditional fiction her father wants her to write. Life, unlike the narrator, has no pity: it is about to deprive her of her beloved father. The locus of the "open destiny of life," where hope and "enormous changes at the last minute" are possible, is fiction itself.

Paley places the tragic material which interests and moves her within an antitragic structure of sudden, abrupt transformations, "enormous changes," but the tragic material is nonetheless left intact. There is none of the hollow laughter, the mocking, alienated distance from pathos that is characteristic of serious modern fiction. But transformation undercuts tragic inevitability—fictional structure becomes tragedy's antidote rather than either its vehicle or its negation—and, equally important, as we will see, transformation undercuts the sentimentality that so easily trivializes pathos.

—Marianne DeKoven, "Mrs. Hegel-Shtein's Tears," *Partisan Review* (1981), in *The Chelsea House Library of Literary Criticism: Twentieth-Century American Literature*, Vol. 5, Harold Bloom, ed. (New York: Chelsea House Publishers, 1987), 3030–31

JEROME KLINKOWITZ

More than one of Grace Paley's stories feature a writer reflecting on her art, asking herself why she writes. Her narrator is often named "Faith," whose children are always named "Richard" and "Tonto" (short for Anthony), and whose mother and father play similar roles from story to story. In her second collection, *Enormous Changes at the Last Minute* (New York: Farrar, Straus & Giroux, 1974), everybody is just about a decade older than in her first, *The Little Disturbances of Man* (New York: Doubleday, 1959). "It was possible that I did owe something to my own family and the families of my friends," her narrator suspects. "That is, to tell their stories as simply as possible, in order, you might say, to save a few lives" (*EC*, p. 10). Such has been the traditionally moral role for the fictionist, which here becomes a metafictional concern. But for all her friendships and stylistic allegiances with innovators such as Donald Barthelme, Mark Mirsky, and others of this manner, Paley holds fast to several older, sociological concerns. For one, she is a woman writing; and secondly, of even more importance, she is an older woman, divorced and remarried, mothering two nearly-raised children while coping with the economic and social difficulties of life in a not-too-fancy neighborhood of New York City. Thirdly, she is a writer concerned with the viability of her occupation, particularly from the posture of the woman that she is. Hence for Grace Paley, metafiction—fiction which explores the conditions of its own making—is a peculiarly social matter, filled with the stuff of realism other metafictionists have discarded. For them, realistic conventions have been obstacles to or distractions from self-consciously artistic expression. Only Grace Paley finds them to be the materials of metafiction itself.

"A Conversation with My Father" is Paley's metafictional model and at the same time pledge of allegiance to the traditions of storytelling. First of all, the convention of character is made experimental by an interesting enhancement. "Everyone in this book is imagined into life except the father," Paley states in the book's opening disclaimer. "No matter what story he has to live in, he's my father, I. Goodside, M.D., artist, and storyteller." This unconventionally "real" character, whose existence in the story is due to the most innovative of techniques, then argues with his daughter that her fiction be more conventionally realistic. She resists a simple causal plot, "The absolute line between two points which I've always despised. Not for literary reasons, but because it takes all hope away. Everyone, real or invented, deserves the open destiny of life" (*EC*, p. 162). At her father's prompting, she tells and retells a story, fleshing out character and adding narrative detail. But in typical Paley fashion, the ending remains open. "I'm not going to leave her there in that house crying," she protests. "Jokes, jokes again," the father complains, but the daughter is profi-

cient in the ways of metafiction and of the new style of life which has spawned
it. "No, Pa," she argues, "it could really happen that way, it's a funny world
nowadays" (EC, p. 167). Rejecting his argument for tragedy as unrealistic, she
practices her own storytelling art with a more experimental sense of realism—
here as those conventions are debated with a superrealistically portrayed character. ⟨. . .⟩

By making the most of these small offerings, Paley throws the conventions
of narrative art into high relief. Her narrators speak with a peculiar sense of
animation: "It is something like I am a crazy construction worker in conversation with cement," one of them admits (EC, p. 25). In another story, a drunk
and enraged husband holds a pistol "and waved it before his eyes as though it
could clear fogs and smogs" (EC, pp. 113–14). With so little apparent action
to work with, Paley cannot simply let the sun set; instead, it must assume the
graphic dimensions of a Saul Steinberg cartoon to become "a red ball falling
hopelessly west, just missing the Hudson River, Jersey City, Chicago, the
Great Plains, the Golden Gate—falling, falling" (EC, p. 121). To articulate the
real is not just to describe it; Paley's motive is to create, to find a language
which takes the most familiar affairs and gives them fictional (that is, imaginative) life.

> —Jerome Klinkowitz, "Grace Paley: The Sociology of Metafiction," *Literary Subversions: New
> American Fiction and the Practice of Criticism* (Carbondale, IL: Southern Illinois University Press,
> 1985), 70–73

ALIX KATES SHULMAN

In *Later the Same Day*, her third collection of stories, Grace Paley plunges us
back into the lives of a group of Greenwich Village characters (in both senses)
who entered literature in her 1959 collection, *The Little Disturbances of Man*. Here
they all are: Faith, the protagonist or narrator of many of the stories; her
neighbors; the local shopkeepers; Faith's pals from the antiwar movement,
playground, and PTA; their children, lovers, ex-lovers, husbands, ex-husbands
(who sometimes switch roles within the group), aging parents, and even a
reappearing grandparent (whom the reader recognizes by the frozen herring
he carries in his pocket). The settings too are familiar. By now some of the
characters, most of them good leftists, have visited the People's Republic of
China (the focus of two stories in this collection), and sometimes they go back
to Brooklyn to relive the past or visit the Children of Judea Home for the
Golden Ages, Coney Island Branch; but despite what Faith calls "my wide geographical love of mankind," we seldom see them north of 14th Street. There
are newcomers to the scene—friends of the original crew, visitors from China,
a younger playground crowd, shtetl ancestors—but they enter the book as

naturally as new people enter our lives: they're political comrades, neighbors, relatives, friends, friends of friends. All are rendered with that wildly comic Paley charm, her generous politics, her perfect ear-hand coordination. Again she tells her sad/funny stories and wry parables, in a wisecracking, ironic New York voice that sounds like no other—except, amazingly, Isaac Babel.

Going from *Little Disturbances* to *Later the Same Day* we hardly notice that time has passed. True, the kids we saw in the playground in earlier stories may have grown up, some swallowed by "history" (living underground, dead of an overdose, mad, gone to California, or off "in different boroughs trying to find the right tune for their lives"); the married couples memorialized by having sandwiches named after them at the Art Foods Deli may have gotten divorced; and some of the sandbox mothers of 20 years before are turning 50 or starting to die. But Paley can do for time what astrophysicists do for space: whether stretching or shrinking it, they deepen the mystery with every advance in describing it. As her narrator comments, "the brain at work pays no attention to time and speedily connects and chooses." Knowing this, Paley blithely sprinkles her stories with lines like, "Hello, my life, I said. We had once been married for twenty-seven years, so I felt justified" or, "What did you do today with your year off?" In a Paley story connections are forged—between generations, eras, cultures, continents—to show how different worlds are essentially the same, thus *Later the Same Day* might be 40 years later—as in the story "Ruthy and Edie," which begins when Ruthy and Edie are children, then halfway through rushes ahead to Ruthy's 50th birthday party—or it might be a century earlier, when Faith's ancestors (activists like Faith and her friends) opposed the tyranny of the Tsar. With its vision of universal reconciliation, Paley's sensibility simply cannot be restricted by the ordinary boundaries of space or time.

Paley has sometimes been criticized for allowing her passionate commitment to politics to "interfere" with her art, but the two feed each other, are in fact one. Paley is as political as García Marquez or Camus. In story after story she demonstrates the inseparability of "private" and "public" passions—especially the passion to save the children, which she implicitly equates with saving the world. In Paley's universe children ("babies, those round, staring, day-in-day-out companions of her youth"), the ever-precarious next generation, are the raison d'être of political action. When Faith asks herself, recalling the PTA struggles of a bygone time, "Now what did we learn that year?" her answer is "The following: Though the world cannot be changed by talking to one child at a time, it may at least be known."

—Alix Kates Shulman, "The Children's Hour," *Voice Literary Supplement* (June 1985), in *The Chelsea House Library of Literary Criticism: Twentieth-Century American Literature*, Vol. 5, Harold Bloom, ed. (New York: Chelsea House Publishers, 1987), 3030

LOUIS HARAP

The unprecedented unleashing of creative energies by Jewish writers by the 1950s, both quantitatively and qualitatively was so abundant that this outpouring, together with unprecedented receptivity to their writing by the general American public, justifies calling the 1950s the "Jewish Decade." ⟨. . .⟩

Although the Jewish theme was problematic for publishers until mid-century, anti-Semitism was far less often encountered in fiction after the 1920s. If the Jew had been a sensitive subject before the 1930s, he became more so with the growth of Nazism and its influence even in this country. Pre-World War II agitation of pro-fascist demagogues, which included anti-Semitic incitement, sensitized the subject, and this sensitivity endured not only through the war but afterward. The popular media tended to avoid "controversial" issues in popular entertainment so as not to jeopardize, as they believed, their investments. In 1944 the newly awakened Jewishness of Ben Hecht led him to complain, "the greatest single Jewish phenomenon in the last twenty years has been the almost complete disappearance of the Jew from American fiction, stage, radio, and movies." Hecht was exaggerating, of course but there was limited validity to his charge, at least as far as popular culture was concerned. The Jew certainly did not "disappear" from literature, as is obvious from our account. But the entrepreneurs of the mass arts were unwilling to risk "controversy" and did at least soft-pedal the Jewish presence in their products. ⟨. . .⟩

A highly individual, sophisticated note was sounded in the short stories of Grace Paley, well known as a peace activist, in *The Little Disturbances of Man* (1959) and later in several stories in *Enormous Changes at the Last Minute* (1974). The style is peculiarly "modern" in its mood and economy, compact, and replete with unexpected and whimsical turns of meaning. Many of her stories convey a bittersweet attitude to the life of everyday Jews in the sense that she combines a hard realism with a sensitive appreciation of human fallibility. The Jewishness of her characters is social rather than religious and sharply outlines a person, child, or adult. A wry preoccupation with human weakness rather than Jewishness is her primary interest.

Eleven years later she published a third volume of stories, *Later the Same Day* (1985), in a more somber mood that reflected the disappointment of many hopes, aftermath of the 1960s counterculture, especially in its effect upon activists and their young, too-soon adult children. The prose is far more compact than the earlier stories; they have lost their pervasively light touch. It is elliptical and at times fragmentary. Many of the characters are Jewish in a Jewish milieu.

—Louis Harap, "The Jewish Decade: The 1950s," *In the Mainstream: The Jewish Presence in Twentieth-Century American Literature, 1950s–1980s* (New York: Greenwood Press, 1987), 21–23, 36–37

B I B L I O G R A P H Y

The Little Disturbances of Man: Stories of Men and Women in Love. 1959.

Enormous Changes at the Last Minute. 1974.

Later the Same Day. 1985.

Leaning Forward. 1985.

A Dream Compels Us: Voices of Salvadoran Women. 1989.

365 Reasons Not to Have Another War. 1989.

The Safe Deposit and Other Stories About Grandparents, Old Lovers, and Crazy Old Men. 1989.

Long Walks and Intimate Talks. 1991.

Ergo: The Bumbershoot Literary Magazine. 1992.

What We Know So Far: Wisdom Among Women (Beth Benatovich, ed., with Billie Jean King and Matilda Cuomo). 1995.

Conversations with Grace Paley (Gerhard Bach and Blaine Hall, eds.). 1997.

DOROTHY PARKER
1893–1967

DOROTHY PARKER, poet, short-story writer, and critic, was born Dorothy Rothschild in West End, New Jersey, on August 22, 1893. Her mother, a Scottish Presbyterian, died while Dorothy was a child. Dorothy was raised by her father, who was Jewish, and by her step-mother, who was also Scottish Presbyterian. Parker was sent to a Catholic convent school and to Miss Dana's School in Morristown, New Jersey, from which she graduated in 1911.

Parker began writing poetry while in convent school, and in 1915 one of her verses was accepted by *Vogue* magazine. The magazine later hired Parker to write captions for fashion illustrations. In 1917 she became a drama critic for *Vanity Fair*, and that year she married Edwin Pond Parker II. Famous for her quick wit and low wisecracks, Parker became part of what came to be known as the Algonquin Round Table, a group of writers that included, at that time, Alexander Woollcott, Heywood Broun, Robert Benchley, and George S. Kaufman.

Parker's first book of poetry appeared in 1926 under the title *Enough Rope*. This volume and the two that followed, *Sunset Gun* (1928) and *Death and Taxes* (1931), were collected in *Not So Deep as a Well* (1936). Her short stories and sketches were published in *Laments for the Living* (1930) and *After Such Pleasures* (1933), and later collected in *Here Lies* (1939).

After leaving *Vanity Fair* Parker had her poems, reviews, and short stories printed in a variety of journals, most notably the *New Yorker*, with which she has been particularly identified. She was a newspaper correspondent in Spain during the Spanish Civil War, and later in Hollywood she wrote scenarios and screenplays with her second husband, Alan Campbell, for many well-known films, including *A Star Is Born* (1937) and Alfred Hitchcock's *Saboteur* (1942). She died on June 7, 1967.

In 1944 the Viking Portable Library issued a popular edition of her work, and a revised edition was issued in 1973.

CRITICAL EXTRACTS

ALEXANDER WOOLLCOTT

Mrs. Parker's published work does not bulk large. But most of it has been pure gold and the five winnowed volumes on her shelf—three of poetry, two of prose—are so potent a distillation of nectar and wormwood, of ambrosia and deadly nightshade, as might suggest to the rest of us that we all write far too much. ⟨. . .⟩

I think it not unlikely that the best of it will be conned a hundred years from now. If so, I can foresee the plight of some undergraduate in those days being maddened by an assignment to write a theme on what manner of woman this dead and gone Dorothy Parker really was. Was she a real woman at all? he will naturally want to know. And even if summoned from our tombs, we will not be sure how we should answer that question.

Indeed, I do not envy him his assignment, and in a sudden spasm of sympathy for him, herewith submit a few miscellaneous notes, though, mark you, he will rake these yellowing files in vain for any report on her most salient aspects. Being averse to painting the lily, I would scarcely attempt a complete likeness of Mrs. Parker when there is in existence, and open to the public, an incomparable portrait of her done by herself. From the nine matchless stanzas of "The Dark Girl's Rhyme"—one of them runs:

> There I was, that came of
> Folk of mud and flame—
> I that had my name of
> Them without a name—

to the mulish lyric which ends thus:

> But I, despite expert advice,
> Keep doing things I think are nice,
> And though to good I never come—
> Inseparable my nose and thumb!

her every lyric line is autobiographical.

From the verses in *Enough Rope, Sunset Gun,* and *Death and Taxes,* the toiling student of the year 2033 will be able to gather, unaided by me, that she was, for instance, one who thought often and enthusiastically of death, and one whose most frequently and most intensely felt emotion was the pang of unrequited love. From the verses alone he might even construct, as the paleontologist constructs a dinosaur, a picture of our Mrs. Parker wringing her hands at sundown beside an open grave and looking pensively into the middle-distance at the receding figure of some golden lad—perhaps some personable longshoreman—disappearing over the hill with a doxy on his arm.

Our Twenty-First Century student may possibly be moved to say of her, deplorably enough, that, like Patience, our Mrs. Parker yearned her living, and he may even be astute enough to guess that the moment the aforesaid golden lad wrecked her favorite pose by showing some sign of interest, it would be the turn of the sorrowing lady herself to disappear in the other direction just as fast as she could travel. To this shrewd guess, I can only add for his information that it would be characteristic of the sorrowing lady to stoop first by that waiting grave, and with her finger trace her own epitaph: "Excuse my dust."

—Alexander Woollcott, "Our Mrs. Parker," *While Rome Burns* (1934), in *The Chelsea House Library of Literary Criticism: Twentieth-Century American Literature*, Vol. 5, Harold Bloom, ed. (New York: Chelsea House Publishers, 1987), 3036–37

JAMES GRAY

It is a little startling to realize that Dorothy Parker, even while she lives and continues to write (now and then), has achieved the kind of celebrity that belongs only to a few very great writers, like the contributors to the Bible, Shakespeare, and Alexander Pope. That is to say, Mrs. Parker is the sort of person who is always suspected of being the author of a famous, but elusive, quotation.

Whenever one is asked to identify a ringing line notable for its frightening sagacity, one automatically risks the guess that it must be from the Bible. When such a quotation bowls along competently in iambic pentameter, the ear whispers to the mind that surely this must be Shakespeare. If the point of a saying tinkles out its passage in a rhyming couplet, one draws a deep breath of relief and says, Alexander Pope. But if wisdom puts on a wry-lipped smile and expresses itself with a startling aptitude that rocks the mind momentarily out of its usual mood of somnolent acceptance, one blinks and says, Dorothy Parker.

There cannot be much doubt about it now. Dorothy Parker is one of the few writers of our time who is destined for immortality. It is nice for us who have always cherished her gift to know that in centuries to come she will represent the sad, cocky, impudent mood of our tragic era. Waking from our graves five hundred years from now, we shall be pleased to see Dorothy Parker strolling Olympus, perhaps in the company of Marguerite of Navarre and

Madame de Sévigné. Proudly we shall say, "We knew her when she was just a quick-witted girl who kidded around with Robert Benchley and wrote pieces for the *New Yorker*.

> —James Gray, "A Dream of Unfair Women," *On Second Thought* (1946), in *The Chelsea House Library of Literary Criticism: Twentieth-Century American Literature*, Vol. 5, Harold Bloom, ed. (New York: Chelsea House Publishers, 1987), 3036

BRENDAN GILL

Readers coming to Mrs. Parker for the first time may find it as hard to understand the high place she held in the literary world of forty or fifty years ago as to understand the critical disregard into which she subsequently fell. The first precaution for such readers is to bear in mind the fact that the so-called world that gave her her reputation was really only a province, and, like all provinces, it considered itself much bigger and more important than it was. Its arbiters did well to praise Mrs. Parker, but she was a better writer than they took her for, and the difference between who she was and who they supposed she was held considerable risks for her. ⟨. . .⟩

Mrs. Parker's reputation suffered from the literary company she kept; it suffered also from the fact that the milieu that was her natural subject matter— the narrow section of American society that could be summed up as Eastern, urban, intellectual, and middle class—underwent a sudden and overwhelming change during the Depression. The people Mrs. Parker had kept under close scrutiny and about whom she had written with authority seemed so remote from the realities of the post-Depression period as to be stamped, for a time, with a kind of retroactive invalidity. In the forties and fifties they simply did not matter any more, and the reading public was tempted to conclude, mistakenly, that they ought never to have mattered. Little by little over the years, the period and the people who gave it its character have recovered importance. By now we find it worth while to make an effort to apprehend them fairly, according to the tone and temper of their day, and in order to do so we turn with relish to Mrs. Parker. ⟨. . .⟩

The most popular woman poet of the twentieth century, prior to Mrs. Parker, was Edna St. Vincent Millay, who was often thought to have served as a literary model for her. It was not altogether so; for one thing, Miss Millay was a much more skillful prosodist than Mrs. Parker, with a mastery of many forms of verse that Mrs. Parker never attempted, and, for another, Miss Millay enjoyed a far wider range of expressible feelings, which she spent a lifetime of hard intellectual effort exploring. She struggled to achieve greatness, and if the effort failed, it produced a number of sufficiently remarkable volumes of poems. Mrs. Parker worked less hard and less steadily, and she flinched from thorough self-examination: the depths were there, and she would glance into them from time to time, but she was not prepared to descend into them and walk their bounds. Her true literary mentor was that forbidding male spinster, A. E. Housman, who with the help of high intelligence, classical learning, and an exquisite ear, contrived to turn a reiterated whining into superior poetry.⟨. . .⟩

⟨. . .⟩ Mrs. Parker wrote what was essentially light verse; it was not Housman's perennial ruefulness that she ought to have imitated, but the witty aplomb of her contemporary, Ogden Nash. Along with, in her sunnier moods, Miss Millay, Nash broke up the old forms and fashioned new ones that accommodated to perfection the spoken language of the period. Nevertheless, Mrs. Parker was someone to be taken seriously. Edmund Wilson wrote at the time that he had been "sometimes accused of overrating the more popular irony of Mrs. Dorothy Parker. It is true that Mrs. Parker's epigrams have the accent of the Hotel Algonquin rather than that of the coffee houses of the eighteenth century. But I believe that, if we admire, as it is fashionable to do, the light verse of Prior and Gay, we should admire Mrs. Parker also. She writes well: her wit is the wit of her particular time and place, but it is often as cleanly economic at the same time that it is flatly brutal as the wit of the age of Pope; and, within its small scope, it is a criticism of life. It has its roots in contemporary reality, and that is what I am pleading for in poetry."

Wilson expressed that opinion of Mrs. Parker nearly fifty years ago; it continues to be a sound one, and the poems that we admire today are those that most ably sum up her particular time and place. It is a world that has grown very distant from ours, but because she was true to its nature it remains, with certain attendant risks, visitable. In 1944, in the course of reviewing the first edition of this book, Wilson wrote in *The New Yorker* that, while he found Mrs. Parker's poems a little dated, her prose seemed to him as sharp and funny as in the years when it was first coming out. Again, a sensible judgment, worth quoting after almost thirty years. If it is easier to visit the world of the twenties and thirties through Mrs. Parker's short stories and soliloquies than through her verse, it is also more rewarding; to a startling degree, they have a substance, a solidity, that the poems do little to prepare us for. Not the least hint of the Round Table is detectable in the stories—no sassy showing off, no making a leg at the reader. The author keeps her distance, and sometimes it is a distance great enough to remind one of Flaubert.

—Brendan Gill, "Introduction," *The Portable Dorothy Parker* (1973), in *The Chelsea House Library of Literary Criticism: Twentieth-Century American Literature*, Vol. 5, Harold Bloom, ed. (New York: Chelsea House Publishers, 1987), 3039–40

ARTHUR F. KINNEY

Certain clues to ⟨Parker's⟩ life and work both can be found in two of her obsessions and in a memory from childhood. One obsession was being half-Jewish.
Her father was a Rothschild, and although she dropped the name as soon as
she married Edwin Pond Parker II, doubtless it is significant that she chose in
Parker a successful businessman from an established Hartford family that
reminded others of the father she hated. Her first book was a collaboration
with the Jewish Franklin P. Adams, her first play with Elmer Rice, the subject
she chose for her first book review in *The New Yorker* a novel about the intolerance shown Jews. Many of her friends at the Algonquin Round Table were
Jewish (Hart, Kaufman, Ferber) as well as her Long Island host Herbert Bayard
Swope and many of her associates in Hollywood (Hellman, Hecht, Herman
Mankiewicz, Edwin Mayer) where, in her early days, she worked for Irving
Thalberg and Sam Goldwyn. Her later marriages were to Alan Campbell, son
of a Jewish mother but possessing a Gentile name. Sheilah Graham recalls that
she "used to announce that she was half Jewish," and only six weeks before her
death, Lillian Hellman interrupted a story in a letter to Dorothy Parker to
remark, "so O.K., for the fiftieth time don't tell me you're half Jewish."

In many ways, her life follows the paradigm of the second and third generation Jew from New York traced by Irving Howe: well educated in private
schools, she respected education and high culture; she combined a personal
self-consciousness in her writing with set pieces in the formulas of the ladies'
magazines; she was attracted to the world of entertainment but distanced herself by an easygoing cynicism; she worked long and hard at her writing,
although she wanted it to seem casual and spontaneous; she combined bitter
(if subtle) satire of others with a running self-condemnation (both light-
hearted and serious). Although her work is softer and more sentimental than,
say, the stories of Bernard Malamud, there is still present some of the hardness
and pity Howe finds in *The Magic Barrel*. Howe's description of the work of the
New York Jewish intellectual does, in one way or another, help characterize a
portion of everything she wrote. Yet only once, in *The New Yorker*, did Dorothy
Parker actually say what it means to be a Jew. "For the Gentile," she observed,
"there is always something just a little bit comic about a Jew. That is the
tragedy of Israel."

Her other obsession was the art of Ernest Hemingway. She wrote admir-
ingly of *In Our Time* and *Men Without Women*, she sailed to France to meet him
and write a *New Yorker* profile on him, and she entertained him in Hollywood,
helping to raise funds for his film *The Spanish Earth*. It was his example and
encouragement that persuaded her to risk her life in Spain and his dedication

to art that she most emulated. "A setback with a story or a poem would drive her to the depths of despair," Jane Grant tells us, "and one of her periodic efforts to commit suicide." Although she was prominent in what Morton Cooper calls "a day of giants," her last recorded words, to Beatrice Ames, pursue the relentless worry that her talent did not live up to Hemingway's. "I want you to tell me the truth," she urged. "Did Ernest really like me?"

And the memory from her childhood? She recalled a moment when she was five for *New Masses* when, in 1939, they asked her "What are you doing to combat fascism?" and she replied, "Not enough."

> It was in a brownstone house in New York, and there was a blizzard, and my rich aunt—a horrible woman then and now—had come to visit. I remember going to the window and seeing the street with the men shoveling snow; their hands were purple on their shovels, and their feet were wrapped with burlap. And my aunt, looking over my shoulder, said, "Now isn't it nice there's this blizzard. All those men have work." And I knew then that it was not nice that men could work for their lives only in desperate weather, that there was no work for them when it was fair.

Throughout her life, Dorothy Parker was quick to sympathize with those who suffered or were indentured—those she could pity because of misfortune in politics, money, race, or sex. She admired the servant class and those who, like her "Big Blonde," were defeated by conditions they could not understand or overcome. And she was as quick to attack the causes of their exploitation. From her early poetry of unrequited love to "Clothe the Naked" she attacks pretension and blindness in the middle and upper classes.

But it is equally clear, in studying her work, that she is also attracted to the status and possessions of those who are better off. She sought the stability of Edwin Parker and the Parkers of Hartford. While she understands the awful need to shovel snow to earn keep, such subsistence workers always aspire, as she herself did and partly in awe, to the condition of her aunt. She combines the child's ambition and hope with an adult's sense of outrage and cynicism at shallowness and self-deception, at the uneven and unrequited distribution of favors in this world. She did not always understand that she held mixed loyalties, although they are the foundation for the rueful attitude of much of her early poetry and fiction as well as the disappointment and disgust that characterize her essays and criticism. That memory fixes her for us, as it should, looking out on one activity, looking away from another, yet associated with both, and caught between them.

Her Jewishness gave her the felt roots of her being: a sense of being dispossessed (like the men shoveling snow), a long intellectual heritage personified by her aunt, and the desire for financial success urged by her father. Her means to all their ends were, at her best and most inspired, the means of Hemingway, through total devotion to clean, fine poetry and prose. The consequence would be a corpus of writing which, at its most creative, would be about the world's shovelers of snow designed to be read instructively by persons like her aunt. In that way Dorothy Parker could, finally and forcibly, take part in a dialogue with her aunt and point out the real significance of the blizzard; she could turn it into satire and through that into a kind of mournful, moral fable. Then her Jewishness would be vindicated—and Ernest would like her, too.

—Arthur F. Kinney, "Preface," *Dorothy Parker* (Boston: Twayne Publishers, 1978), iv–vi

George Plimpton

Interviewer ⟨**Marion Capron**⟩: It's a popular supposition that there was much more communication between writers in the twenties. The Round Table discussions in the Algonquin, for example.

Parker: I wasn't there very often—it cost too much. Others went. Kaufman was there. I guess he was sort of funny. Mr. Benchley and Mr. Sherwood went when they had a nickel. Franklin P. Adams, whose column was widely read by people who wanted to write, would sit in occasionally. And Harold Ross, the *New Yorker* editor. He was a professional lunatic, but I don't know if he was a great man. He had a profound ignorance. On one of Mr. Benchley's manuscripts he wrote in the margin opposite "Andromache," "Who he?" Mr. Benchley wrote back, "You keep out of this." The only one with stature who came to the Round Table was Heywood Broun.

Interviewer: What was it about the twenties that inspired people like yourself and Broun?

Parker: Gertrude Stein did us the most harm when she said, "You're all a lost generation." That got around to certain people and we all said, "Whee! We're lost." Perhaps it suddenly brought to us the sense of change. Or irresponsibility. But don't forget that, though the people in the twenties seemed like flops, they weren't. Fitzgerald, the rest of them, reckless as they were, drinkers as they were, they worked damn hard and all the time.

Interviewer: Did the "lost generation" attitude you speak of have a detrimental effect on your own work?

Parker: Silly of me to blame it on dates, but so it happened to be. Dammit, it *was* the twenties and we had to be smarty. I *wanted* to be cute. That's the terrible thing. I should have had more sense.

Interviewer: And during this time you were writing poems?

Parker: My verses. I cannot say poems. Like everybody was then, I was following in the exquisite footsteps of Miss Millay, unhappily in my own horrible sneakers. My verses are no damn good. Let's face it, honey, my verse is terribly dated—as anything once fashionable is dreadful now. I gave it up, knowing it wasn't getting any better, but nobody seemed to notice my magnificent gesture.

Interviewer: Do you think your verse writing has been of any benefit to your prose?

Parker: Franklin P. Adams once gave me a book of French verse forms and told me to copy their design, that by copying them I would get precision in prose. The men you imitate in verse influence your prose, and what I got out of it was precision, all I realize I've ever had in prose writing. ⟨. . .⟩

Interviewer: You have an extensive reputation as a wit. Has this interfered, do you think, with your acceptance as a serious writer?

Parker: I don't want to be classed as a humorist. It makes me feel guilty. I've never read a good tough quotable female humorist, and I never was one myself. I couldn't do it. A "smartcracker" they called me, and that makes me sick and unhappy. There's a hell of a distance between wisecracking and wit. Wit has truth in it; wisecracking is simply calisthenics with words. I didn't mind so much when they were good, but for a long time anything that was called a crack was attributed to me—and then they got the shaggy dogs.

Interviewer: How about satire?

Parker: Ah, satire. That's another matter. They're the big boys. If I'd been called a satirist there'd be no living with me. But by satirist I mean those boys in the other centuries. The people we call satirists now are those who make cracks at topical topics and consider themselves satirists—creatures like George S. Kaufman and such who don't even know what satire is. Lord knows, a writer should show his times, but not show them in wisecracks. Their stuff is not satire; it's as dull as yesterday's newspaper. Successful satire has got to be pretty good the day after tomorrow.

Interviewer: And how about contemporary humorists? Do you feel about them as you do about satirists?

Parker: You get to a certain age and only the tried writers are funny. I read my verses now and I ain't funny. I haven't been funny for twenty years. But anyway there aren't any humorists any more, except for Perelman. There's no need for them. Perelman must be very lonely.

Interviewer: Why is there no need for the humorist?

Parker: It's a question of supply and demand. If we needed them, we'd have them. The new crop of would-be humorists doesn't count. They're like the would-be satirists. They write about topical topics. Not like Thurber and Mr. Benchley. Those two were damn well read and, though I hate the word, they were cultured. What sets them apart is that they both had a point of view to express. That is important to all good writing. It's the difference between Paddy Chayefsky, who just puts down lines, and Clifford Odets, who in his early plays not only sees but has a point of view. The writer must be aware of life around him.

    —George Plimpton, ed., "Dorothy Parker," *Women Writers at Work: The* Paris Review *Interviews*
(New York: Penguin Books, 1989), 112–13, 115–16

EDMUND WILSON

Rereading Dorothy Parker ⟨. . .⟩ has affected me, rather unexpectedly, with an attack of nostalgia. Her poems do seem a little dated. At their best, they are witty light verse, but when they try to be something more serious, they tend to become a kind of dilution of A. E. Housman and Edna Millay. Her prose, however, is still alive. It seems to me as sharp and funny as in the years when it was first coming out. If Ring Lardner outlasts our day, as I do not doubt he will, it is possible that Dorothy Parker will, too.

    But the thing that I have particularly felt is the difference between the general tone, the psychological and literary atmosphere of the period—the twenties and the earlier thirties—when most of these pieces of Mrs. Parker's were written, and the atmosphere of the present time. It was suddenly brought home to me how much freer people were—in their emotion, in their ideas and in expressing themselves. ⟨. . .⟩

It is a relief and a reassurance, in reading her soliloquies and dialogues—her straight short stories, which are sometimes sentimental, do not always wear quite so well—to realize how recklessly clever it used to be possible for people to be, and how personal and how direct. All her books had funereal titles, but the eye was always wide open and the tongue always quick to retort. Even those titles were sardonic exclamations on the part of an individual at the idea of her own demise. The idea of the death of a society had not yet begun working on people to paralyze their response to experience.

⟨. . .⟩ It seems to me, though I shall name no names, that it has been one of the features of this later time that it produces imitation books. There are things of which one cannot really say that they are either good books or bad books; they are really not books at all. When one has bought them, one has only got paper and print. When one has bought Dorothy Parker, however, one has really got a book. She is not Emily Brontë or Jane Austen, but she has been at some pains to write well, and she has put into what she has written a voice, a state of mind, an era, a few moments of human experience that nobody else has conveyed.

—Edmund Wilson, "A Toast and a Tear for Dorothy Parker," (1944), *Classics and Commercials* (1950), in *The Chelsea House Library of Literary Criticism: Twentieth-Century American Literature*, Vol. 5, Harold Bloom, ed. (New York: Chelsea House Publishers, 1987), 3035–36

REGINA BARRECA

Dorothy Parker wrote strong prose for most of her life, and she wrote a lot of it, remaining relentlessly compassionate regarding, and interested in, the sufferings primarily of those who could not extricate themselves from the emotional tortures of unsuccessful personal relationships. Her stories were personal, yes, but also political and have as their shaping principles the larger issues of her day—which remain for the most part the larger issues of our own day (with Prohibition mercifully excepted).

Parker depicted the effects of poverty, economic and spiritual, upon women who remained chronically vulnerable because they received little or no education about the real world—the "real world" being the one outside the fable of love and marriage. But Parker also addressed the ravages of racial discrimination, the effects of war on marriage, the tensions of urban life, and the hollow space between fame and love. Of her domestic portraits one is tempted to say that, for Parker, the words "dysfunctional family" were redundant. She wrote about abortion when you couldn't write the word and wrote about chemical and emotional addiction when the concepts were just a gleam in the analysts' collective eye.

Parker approached these subjects with the courage and intelligence of a woman whose wit refused to permit the absurdities of life to continue along without comment. Irreverent toward anything held sacred—from romance or motherhood to literary teas and ethnic stereotypes—Parker's stories are at once playful, painful, and poignant. Her own characteristic refusal to sit down, shut up, and smile at whoever was footing the bill continues to impress readers who come to her for the first time and delight those who are already familiar with the routine. ⟨. . .⟩

Parker went about the business of writing in a very practical way: she did it and got paid for it. But it seems as if there is a fraternity of disgruntled critics who would like to make her pay for her achievement with her reputation. They speak of her "exile" to Hollywood, where she had the audacity to be successful as a screenwriter and the nerve to be nominated for an Academy Award for writing the cinematic masterpiece *A Star Is Born*. They argue that she "sold out" and "wasted" herself by writing about narrow topics.

Let's clear up this business about narrow topics: Parker concerns herself primarily with the emotional and intellectual landscape of women, the places where a thin overlay of social soil covers the minefields of very personal disaffection, rejection, betrayal, and loss. She manages throughout it all to make her work funny (and that she is funny is one of the most important things about her) while tilling away at this dangerous garden; and for that generations of women and men have thanked her by reading her, memorizing her, making movies about her, performing plays based on her, and writing books analyzing her—but also castigating her most ruthlessly, passing on untruths behind her back and since 1967 speaking most ill of the dead.

Narrow topics? It is true that Parker often viewed her large subjects through small lenses, and that sometimes—sometimes—her fanatic attention to detail can be mistaken for a passion for minutiae instead of a passion for sharply focused observation. But those disparaging Parker's accomplishments usually make only passing (if not parenthetical) reference to the fact that she has remained a popular writer for more than sixty years, a woman who constructed a literary reputation for herself by writing satirical and witty prose and poetry when women were not supposed to have a sense of humor, and writing about the battle between the classes with as much appetite and bite as she brought to the struggle between the sexes.

You might say that Dorothy Parker should be placed at the head of her generation's class, given her ability to willfully and wickedly push, prod, and pinch her readers into thought, emotion, laughter, and the wish to change the world as we've always known it. You might say that she has surely earned recognition by articulating that which is ubiquitous but unspoken, or you might say that she deserves kudos because she managed to say with wit and courage what most of us are too cowardly or silly to admit. Usually when authors manage to do this—write powerfully and passionately about an important and universal topic—they are rewarded.

Not so with Parker. Parker has been slammed for at least thirty years. One recent critic complains that Parker had "no disinterestedness, no imagination," and another bows low to introduce Parker with the gallant phrase "The span of her work is narrow and what it embraces is often slight." It's clear, however, that such critics write not out of their own convictions but out of their own prejudices. How else could they have read Parker with such blinkered vision?

Parker's work is anything—anything—but slight, concerning as it does life, death, marriage, divorce, love, loss, dogs, and whisky. Given the comprehensive nature of her catalog, it is clear that the only important matters untouched by Parker boil down to the impact of microchip technology, sports, and cars. And if you look carefully at her prose, Parker does deal with cars— if only in passing, and only those passing in the fast lane. ⟨. . .⟩

Writing with the full force of true passion—writing the way this character speaks—Parker has indeed been chastised for believing that the literary world was big enough to let her say, in all honesty, whatever she meant. Even as her character misgauges her beloved, so did Parker misgauge a gang of critics who sought to punish her for the authenticity and lack of pretense in her writing. And yet even as her character makes us look at ourselves, and makes us the laugh in the mirror image presented, so does Parker hold a glass up to life, lightly. She wins, finally, because her success affords her the last laugh.

—Regina Barreca, "Introduction," *Dorothy Parker: Complete Stories* (New York: Penguin Books, 1995), vii, ix–x, xix

STUART Y. SILVERSTEIN

In August 1939, Stalin signed the infamous nonaggression pact with Hitler, which caused virtually all of the remaining independent hard left to publicly abandon Stalin. But when the leaders of the Hollywood Anti-Nazi League, including Dorothy, heard of the agreement, they leaped into action—and immediately changed the name of their organization to the Hollywood League for Democratic Action, presumably on orders to avoid offending their new allies. Some of Dorothy's supporters have claimed that she was shocked and appalled by the pact, but there is no contemporaneous evidence to sustain that sublimely convenient assertion. In fact, she doggedly refused to issue any public criticism of it, even though she had been moved to radicalism partly because of the West's lukewarm response to Hitler's Jew-baiting policies.

While it is not certain whether Dorothy formally joined the Communist party, she probably did. She publicly declared herself to be a communist in 1934 (though there was a tinge of adolescent grandiosity to the statement), and she invoked the Fifth Amendment when she was specifically asked twenty years later. But it is clear that despite her emotional sentimentality, her intellectual incoherence, and the utter lack of discipline that characterized, inter alia, her flirtation with the revolutionary struggle, she was by any reasonable definition a Stalinist. Stephen Koch, who has written extensively on the subject, observed that "Parker's union of style and Stalinist attitudes was a natural fit. Through the chic of her hard-left commitments, Parker could both validate her love of glamour, and mask it with an appropriate look of disdain for all the vanities." And according to Bea Stewart, Dorothy "was not a personal friend of the multitudes. She was a very, very *grande dame*, and contrariness was the wellspring of her communism. She was anti. She was anti the Establishment."

If communism helped humanity, then she was, in her own simplistic, romantic way, a communist, and dialectic be damned. Some apologists later excused her actions because she meant well, a useful defense that is routinely employed by erstwhile radicals, but seldom afforded to even the most repentant former reactionaries. But even if Dorothy's intent *was* pure, which is doubtful, she still condoned, and outspokenly supported, and even helped finance the monstrous policies of a hostile and genocidal regime. Determining whether she was a rogue or merely a fool is a melancholy task.

Dorothy's excursion through the hard left cost her many friendships, most notably Robert Benchley's, and her viciously ad hominem intolerance for opposing views caused her to cut loose from most of her remaining longstanding relationships, including those with Bea Stewart and Sara and Gerald Murphy. It ultimately put her name near the top of some of the blacklists that circulated through the industry and effectively destroyed what remained of her screenwriting career, but she never wavered and even attracted a new confidante, with Svengalian overtones, along the way. ⟨. . .⟩

Dorothy told several friends that she was trying to get into the war herself. Perhaps her application to join the Women's Army Corps was denied because of her age, and perhaps she was not allowed a war correspondent's credential because the government would not issue her a passport due to her subversive background, but perhaps not. Meanwhile, her collected fiction was rereleased by Modern Library, and an anthology of her work was selected by Aleck Woollcott as the fourth in a series of volumes intended for soldiers overseas. It was released stateside by Viking in 1944 as *The Portable Dorothy Parker*. Of the original ten volumes in Woollcott's series, only three have continuously remained in print through the interminably evolving tastes of the last half-century: the Bible, the Shakespeare, and the Parker.

But Dorothy wanted to do more. She started giving speeches and raising funds for worthy causes such as war bonds, the USO, and the Emergency Conference to Save the Jews of Europe. At the convention for that last-named group, in July 1943, she passionately appealed for support to assist the removal to Turkey of the four million European Jews she declared were in daily peril of their lives. While the cause was a vital one, and she had even chosen the right side, it emphasized the ambivalence with which she had always regarded her Jewish background. The trauma of her school years had taught her how much of the world regarded Jews. Her usual response had been to obscure her ancestry, which is why some of her acquaintances said that her only happy reminder of her first marriage was the classically Anglo-Saxon surname that allowed her to be "Mrs. Parker." If later in life she would coyly claim that "I was just a little Jewish girl trying to be cute," she could also write a gratuitously anti-Semitic poem, "The Dark Girl's Rhyme," in 1926, when she was making her reputation. In the thirties she had discovered a new god, the deity of radical socialism, which she still served, yet in the midst of a war that nearly destroyed the world's Jewry, she stood up in active support of their survival. Yet in later years, when Jewish survival of another sort was at stake in the State of Israel, she had no interest.

It would be unfair to conclude that her sudden concern for the Jews during the war was insincere, for though Dorothy often engaged in ill-advised conduct, she was seldom disingenuous. However, she soon reverted to more familiar causes, raising funds for children's books as a member of the National Council of American-Soviet Friendship in 1944 and accepting the acting chairmanship of the Spanish Refugee Appeal, another leftist "antifascist" front organization, in 1945. ⟨. . .⟩

Dorothy had lambasted the House Un-American Activities Committee during the late forties and she was often threatened with subpoena, but of more sinister import was the visit from the FBI she received in 1951. They wanted to know about her ties to the Communist party, which she denied had ever existed. In truth, though she still occasionally talked like a radical, her political fires had been largely banked on every issue but civil rights some years earlier. Still, that year HUAC cited her and three hundred other writers, artists, actors, and professors for affiliating with communist front organizations. There were no official punitive repercussions.

Others were not so lucky during the fifteen anxious years that followed the Second World War. Though Dies and Thomas and other self-promoters and zealots perpetrated outrages in pursuit of their "investigations," it is also true that many of their targets were or had been communists. Hellman managed to escape through some clever and seemingly courageous testimony, but Hammett and many others went to prison, and some, like Ella and Donald Ogden Stewart, fled to Britain or other countries. Accusations that Dorothy was either a dangerous communist or merely a subversive dupe effectively

destroyed what was left of her Hollywood career. She was more or less offi-
cially blacklisted through the end of the fifties.

—Stuart Y. Silverstein, "Introduction," *Not Much Fun: The Lost Poems of Dorothy Parker* (New
York: Scribner, 1996), 47–49, 52–53, 55

B I B L I O G R A P H Y

High Society (with George S. Chappell and Frank Crowninshield). 1920.
Men I'm Not Married To. 1922.
Enough Rope. 1926.
Sunset Gun. 1928.
Close Harmony; or, The Lady Next Door (with Elmer Rice). 1929.
Laments for the Living. 1930.
Death and Taxes. 1931.
Collected Poetry. 1931.
After Such Pleasures. 1933.
Collected Poems: Not So Deep as a Well. 1936.
Here Lies: The Collected Stories. 1939.
Collected Stories. 1942.
The Portable Dorothy Parker. 1944.
The Portable F. Scott Fitzgerald (ed.). 1945.
The Ladies of the Corridor (with Arnaud d'Usseau). 1953.
Candide (adaptation; with Lillian Hellman and Richard Wilbur). 1957.
Short Story: A Thematic Anthology (ed., with Frederick B. Shroyer). 1965.
Constant Reader. 1970.
A Month of Saturdays. 1971.
The Collected Dorothy Parker. 1973.

MARGE PIERCY

1936–

MARGE PIERCY was born on March 31, 1936, in Detroit, Michigan, to working-class Jewish parents. The first in her family to attend college, she earned an M.A. from Northwestern University in 1958 and has held various creative writing fellowships at other universities. Between 1958 and 1969 Piercy supported herself with odd jobs while trying to publish her writing. During that time she was active in the civil rights movement and became an organizer for Students for a Democratic Society (SDS).

In 1969 she shifted her political allegiance to the budding women's movement. An openly feminist novelist and poet, Piercy has acknowledged her wish to be "useful" to women. She hoped, she said, "that the poems may give voice to something in the experience of a life. . . . To find ourselves spoken for in art gives dignity to our pain, our anger, our lust, our losses." Though her novels have been criticized as stylistically unsophisticated, the ordinary speech patterns she uses make her poetry both accessible and innovative.

Piercy's first published works were *Breaking Camp* (1968), a volume of poetry, and a novel, *Going Down Fast*, which appeared in 1969. Included among her many volumes of poetry are *Living in the Open* (1976), *The Moon Is Always Female* (1980), and *Stone, Paper, Knife* (1983). She is perhaps better known for her novels, which include *Small Changes* (1973), *Woman on the Edge of Time* (1976), *Vida* (1980), and *Fly Away Home* (1984). She lives in Wellfleet, Massachusetts.

C R I T I C A L E X T R A C T S

RICHARD TODD

The first thing you notice in *Small Changes* ⟨. . .⟩ is the extraordinary confidence that suffuses the prose. It is written with a moralistic insistence that recalls nineteenth-century novels. Beyond questions of individual sensibilities, I'd say there is a cultural explanation for the difference: Marge Piercy is writing about womanhood—about nascent, not waning, attitudes. She writes from an evident feminist perspective, and the book rides a wave of contemporary feeling that seems to free her from self-consciousness. It's a mixed blessing.

Small Changes recounts the tortured young adulthood of two women who come from quite different pasts to Cambridge, where their lives touch. (It's one of the difficulties of the novel that in fact the connection doesn't go very deep. The women serve as symbolic Sisters, demonstrating the essential solidarity of female experience.) Beth: a lower-middle-class Wasp from Syracuse, whom we meet as a timid bride. Denied the college education she wants, she marries her high school sweetheart, who proves to be a lout, and in sudden bold desperation she flees to Boston, where, following an unsatisfying affair, she moves into a woman's commune, and ultimately to lesbianism. Miriam: a Jew from Brooklyn, who spends a long while in the grip of an affair with the man who is her first lover (he had picked her up in the courtyard of the Museum of Modern Art), an affair that ultimately turns into a *ménage à trois*, the third being his best friend. They are louts of a sort, too. A talented and well-educated mathematician, Miriam gets a job with a computer outfit, shakes free of her lovers, and marries her gentle, intellectual boss—only to discover his capacity for loutishness. She ends up where Beth began, institutionalized in marriage.

The vision of marriage in this novel is no cheerier than you'd expect to find by raising the topic in a Los Angeles divorce court. Oppression. Entrapment. Amputated lives. Despair and desperation. That that contract holds some chance of communion is not an allowable idea. Miriam, awash in high hopes, says early in her marriage, "I can enjoy being a woman," explaining that she's learned to like cooking. It is an ironic prelude to the misery ahead. Not that woe is limited to marriage. Wherever they go in this novel's world, women have two roles open to them: they may be prisoners or fugitives.

All the newly classic scenes of womanly suffering that we have read in memoirs of the past half-decade are anthologized here. The anesthetic wedding night. ("They had made love finally, but where was the love they had made?") The wife as unpaid servant. The secretary as sexual object. Dirty socks. Sexist rock lyrics. False moans of sexual pleasure. The discovery by the small-breasted that large breasts are no fun either.

If much of this material is programmatic, though, Marge Piercy's voice has its strengths. What father, for instance, can emerge unshaken from this contemptuous passage: "He was what people called good with his children. He did try hard to teach them things, but he got annoyed if they were not interested. He grew more involved in the course of his exposition than in their reactions. His disappointment was crushing. Ariane was already learning to pretend to understand." There is much else to praise in *Small Changes*. The energy of the book doesn't all go toward polemic; events move along compellingly and the social reportage is acute. Piercy is at ease in the trendy computer company (where the air is full of lingo such as "LISP," "compilers," the "Fall Joint"), as well as in communal apartments. ⟨. . .⟩

⟨. . .⟩ What is absent in this novel is an adequate sense of the oppressor (and his allies), for one thing; and beyond that a recognition that there are limits to a world view that is organized around sexual warfare. It's hard not to think that Piercy feels this, knows that much of the multiplicity and mystery of life is getting squeezed out of her prose, but her polemical urge wins out.

The book ends with the appearance of a new character, to whom Miriam is about to lose her husband. The younger woman, herself divorced, reflects that Miriam hasn't tried hard enough, and she resolves: "Her first marriage had been a disaster, but she thought her second had to be better, with her so willing to work and work at it, unlike some women." How that irony is savored! Marge Piercy gazes down at these hapless characters with the finger-wagging authority of George Eliot. The novel doesn't justify that gusto, though I imagine it's an agreeable feeling.

—Richard Todd, *Atlantic* (September 1973), in *The Chelsea House Library of Literary Criticism: Twentieth-Century American Literature*, Vol. 5, Harold Bloom, ed. (New York: Chelsea House Publishers, 1987), 3089

VICTOR CONTOSKI

Because of Marge Piercy's strong views on social reform, from the very beginning her work has almost automatically divided people into two groups: those opposed to wide-sweeping social reform, and those in favor of it. Nevertheless she finds herself in the rather ambiguous position of being recognized, even embraced, by both the Movement, loosely-bound groups dedicated to radical change in American life, and the Establishment. She writes about radical living styles, communes, war protests, and women's liberation; yet her books are published by such institutions as Pocket Books and Doubleday. The standard technique of propaganda, over-simplification, separates "them" from "us" in her work; yet once this distinction has been made, her best work, while retaining elements of propaganda, notes similarities between the two groups as well as differences. While it focuses on the social problems of America, it focuses also on her own personal problems, so that tension exists not only between "us" and "them" but between "us" and "me."

Not content to wait for happiness and prosperity in some other life, she is driven to find a social and personal happiness on this earth, and the driving force behind her poetry is a stubborn utopian vision. At the same time she remains aware—almost too aware—of the obstacles, social and personal, confronting her. ⟨. . .⟩

Her first book, *Breaking Camp*, presents a rather strange mixture of styles. "Last Scene in the First Act," a clever, ironic meditation on a pair of lovers, shows the slick poetic technique of the academic poets of the 1950's: "Which the lamb and which the tiger / neither knows just yet. / Each lies down in a different bed / to incur a private debt." In "A Cold and Married War" she complains of her lover's indifference: "His cock crowed / I know you not." There is even a sonnet. But in spite of such superficial cleverness, a breathing person moves behind the poetry. We know her life, her concerns.

The first poem in the book, "Visiting a Dead Man on a Summer Day" shows the poet in Graceland cemetery in Chicago where she has gone to visit the tomb of Louis Sullivan. She compares his grave with the Getty tomb and sees the contrast as symbolic of American life.

> All poets are unemployed nowadays.
> My country marches in its sleep.
> The past structures a heavy mausoleum
> hiding its iron frame in masonry.
> Men burn like grass
> while armies grow.
> Thirty years in the vast rumbling gut
> of this society you stormed
> to be used, screamed
> no louder than any other breaking voice.
> The waste of a good man
> bleeds the future that's come
> in Chicago, in flat America,
> where the poor still bleed from the teeth,
> housed in sewers and filing cabinets,
> where prophets may spit into the wind
> till anger sleets their eyes shut,
> where this house that dances the seasons
> and the braid of all living
> and the joy of a man making his new good thing
> is strange, irrelevant as a meteor,
> in Chicago, in flat America
> in this year of our burning.

Such poetry has much in common with propaganda. Its subjects, the country, the past, the poor, are so vast that the poet cannot hope to develop completely her thoughts about them. Instead she relies on a common interpretation of history which she assumes she shares with the reader. The image of the poor housed in sewers and filing cabinets is a startling exaggeration which serves both poetry and propaganda. And the extreme imagery reinforces the basic divisions of the poem. On the one hand we have the heavy, the cold, the mechanical, and the closed-in darkness (mausoleum, iron, sewers, filing cabinets, and Chicago itself); on the other we have the light, the heat, and the organic (men, grass, meteor). Yet much of the impact of the poem comes from imagery that unexpectedly applies to both sides. People burn their body heat naturally, but they are also burned to death by mechanical means in Southeast Asia. And the state, which throughout the poem is associated with the cold and the mechanical, has a "vast rumbling gut" which digests its members—and we are shocked by the natural imagery in its unnatural context.

—Victor Contoski, "Marge Piercy: A Vision of the Peaceable Kingdom," *Modern Poetry Studies* (Winter 1977), in *The Chelsea House Library of Literary Criticism: Twentieth-Century American Literature*, Vol. 5, Harold Bloom, ed. (New York: Chelsea House Publishers, 1987), 3090–91

CELIA BETSKY

Miss Piercy's politics are inseparable from her literary convictions: "The notion that politics have nothing to do with art is a very modern heresy. Alexander Pope wouldn't have known what we were talking about, nor would Catullus. Nor would Homer, for that matter. For most of the world's history, poets have thought of themselves as human beings in a social web, with the same duties in the public sphere as anyone else, with the same set of human interests. My art is political, but no more political than a lot of art not so labeled, which also contains strong notions about what's immoral, moral, what's good and bad, having and getting, who's smart and who's stupid."

In *Vida* Miss Piercy tried "to make real how the war felt to those of us who were living then, how dirty, how compromised—that if you didn't end the war, you didn't deserve to live." For Vida, political responsibility has implications in one's private life. "More things go wrong because of people's inability to deal with each other, with their own feelings about each other or their own reactions, than from any kind of ideological conflict—even though differences may be fought out in the ideological realm."

In the novel, being a fugitive reflects more general conflicts: "The fugitive seemed to be an interesting and rather rich metaphor for an extreme type of woman's experience, but nonetheless one which connected up with all women's experiences. It seems to be one very common dream of women to dream about being hunted, chased, pursued, harried."

Miss Piercy's recent work celebrates the special bond that she feels exists between women. ⟨. . .⟩

Vida is only the most recent in a long line of lesbian or bisexual characters in her work—a reflection of her own involvement with women. "To me it is political for women to be free to choose to have relationships with other women; it's an important option." In *The High Cost of Living* (1978), the novel that preceded *Vida*, she "wanted to write about a lesbian protagonist, and that would just be a given. But the book was much more about class, about how hard it is for working-class kids growing up, kids who could expect to move up in class but find they can't without paying an extravagant price."

Growing up white in a predominantly black community, Miss Piercy thought of herself as "somewhere between black and white." During the 70's, Miss Piercy avoided using minority-group characters in her work. "But I finally decided that I was a writer and that I had to write responsibly, and I couldn't write without writing about racism in the United States. And you can't write about racism if you only write about white people."

Detroit, with its "high energy, good music and its contradictions," was a significant influence on her work. "You see class so clearly there: the indifference of the rich, racism, the strength of different groups, the working-class pitted against itself." Miss Piercy's central characters tend to come from this background, and she ascribes her fascination with "class fate" to her own origins: "My father repaired and installed heavy industrial machinery all over Detroit. My mother was a housewife, she never even finished the 10th grade. My mother made me: she taught me how to look at things, to observe, to notice."

Miss Piercy contends that her mother is a psychic, and she herself is drawn to Tarot cards, the lunar calendar and witchcraft. "I have a strong sense of the power of the nonrational," a sense evident in her poetry: "It is utterance shaped into artifact. It has a healing function. It combines all the different ways of knowing that we have, analytically, synthetically—the sort of gestalt grasping of images. We know through dream images, in many of the same ways that other mammals know, that reptiles know: by senses, sense memory, rhythms. I feel that when I write poems I can speak directly out of my own life, or through masks, when I choose. Other people's lives can speak through me. Art dignifies and validates experience. You can recite poetry to people. A momentary community is created, a ritual."

Poetry can also be the source of what Miss Piercy calls "a new consciousness": "We would be more fully social, more responsible to each other, aware, gentle, open, respectful of our differences. People would be free to concentrate on more creative problems." Best of all, the world would not be run by those who run it now, "nutty and greedy old men."

No matter what the successes and failures of the past few decades, however, there is revolution and revolution. "You know, nothing ever stays the same. The great gift of the 60's was the sense that everybody could change, anything could be done. I still have it, but not with the same euphoria. The other great gift was the sense of community. I learned a lot about other peo-

ple in that time, how they change in struggle, how extraordinarily people
change. The 60's have been caricatured and merchandised. In *Vida*, I wanted
to restore them as they were."

—Celia Betsky, "Talk with Marge Piercy," *New York Times Book Review* (24 February 1980), in
The Chelsea House Library of Literary Criticism: Twentieth-Century American Literature, Vol. 5, Harold
Bloom, ed. (New York: Chelsea House Publishers, 1987), 3094–95

ELINOR LANGER

Almost alone among her American contemporaries, Marge Piercy is radical
and writer simultaneously, her literary identity so indivisible that it is difficult
to say where one leaves off and the other begins. The author of five previous
novels and five books of poetry, ⟨. . .⟩ she has used her prose, particularly, to
chronicle the lives of those society considers marginal—the young, the mad,
the different—or those caught up in the forefront of movements for social
change. Her new novel, *Vida*, which follows the life of a young woman radical from her emergence in the antiwar movement of the 1960's through her life
in the underground network of the 1970's, evokes life in the radical movement
so realistically that it seems at times more literal than imagined. Yet it is also a
fully controlled, tightly structured dramatic narrative of such artful intensity
that it leads the reader on at almost every page. As is often the case with radical fiction, it is the content rather than the formal characteristics that hold the
mind, for it is not "simply" a novel but a political brief. I have my differences
with *Vida*, but I think they are substantive rather than literary. It is an interesting—and challenging—book.

When the novel opens, the time is the present and Vida Asch is returning
East from the West Coast to prepare for a gathering of the underground "network" leaders and to pick up some of the threads of her past. She does not surface—indeed, a large part of the book's action takes place "underground"—but
she does see some of the people she had been close to before, members of that
loose community of former comrades to which even those in the underground
still belong. Her reunions, inevitably, are full of comparisons. Her husband has
a new lover and is becoming less political. Her sister has her family and a full
life in the women's movement. Intelligent, introspective, relatively free of illu-
sions about the role of the underground in the politics of the 1970's, Vida "felt
. . . as if she had outlived her own times, a creature produced by an earlier con-
glomeration of demands, judgments, necessities, passions, crises." But somewhere in her, the old political spirit still burns brightly, and she rarely has
another thought for her future than to continue. ⟨. . .⟩

⟨. . .⟩ Events change, organizations change, beliefs change, relationships
change, all with a microscopic fidelity to actuality that is almost astounding.

How, precisely, was this year different from that year? When, exactly, did one "line" succeed the next? Miss Piercy recalls it all. Demonstrations, political meetings, conversations in movement settings ranging from an apartment in Brooklyn to a hideout in Vermont—these, too, she reproduces with a passion to get it all straight that is the mark of a true calling. With such a mass of characters pulling and hauling in so many directions, it is a wonder that none of them gets away from her, but they do not. Vida, in particular, is completely credible throughout.

Nor does Miss Piercy stop at the past. The present, too, is thoroughly and richly detailed. Life is subtle in the underground, but it is far from over. There are meetings, there are arguments, there are decisions, there are even actions. There are families, there are friends, there are love affairs. 〈. . .〉

Marge Piercy has written about movement people before but never, I think, as lovingly as here. If you are looking to recommend to your students one book that would convey to them how it was in the movement of the 1960's and where it led, you might well want to consider *Vida*.

And yet, in a sense, that is exactly the problem. If a characteristic flaw of the radical literature of the 1930's, taken from the movement that inspired it, was pomposity, a characteristic flaw of the literature stemming from the 1960's may be juvenility. In the "present" sequences the characters are 10 years older than they were, but all their years and experiences have somehow failed to put weight on their bones. Throughout the novel, there is scarcely a significant character who holds views substantially departing from the opinions of the majority—or holds them strongly—and the ones who do are more or less figurine "enemies." In both language and thought, *Vida* is bound by the limitations of its period. The characters are far from stationary—indeed, they remake themselves constantly—but the re-examinations are superficial, taking place only within the framework of the movement. There is no perspective, there are not even any explanations. Why we are against the war, who the enemy is, what measures are justified against the state—all these are simply taken for granted. This hermetic quality is precisely the complaint outsiders had against the movement in life, and now here it is exacerbated in art, for if the movement itself was hermetic, the underground is inevitably more so. To read *Vida* is to be back in the atmosphere of the 1960's movement once again. Suffocating. But righteous.

—Elinor Langer, "After the Movement," *New York Times Book Review* (24 February 1980), in *The Chelsea House Library of Literary Criticism: Twentieth-Century American Literature*, Vol. 5, Harold Bloom, ed. (New York: Chelsea House Publishers, 1987), 3091–92

NATALIE M. ROSINSKY

Marge Piercy's *Woman on the Edge of Time* develops the possibility of coexistence between women and men in a non-sexist future. ⟨. . .⟩ This fictional account of welfare mother Connie Ramos's experiences in twentieth century America and in two disparate, alternative futures ⟨. . .⟩ employs narrative structures that embody its feminist themes and demand active reader involvement to construct textual meaning(s). ⟨. . .⟩

Connie Ramos's social position removes her from the realm of classical heroism. A poor Chicana, she has experienced economic and ethnic discrimination as well as the sexual stereotyping which confronts women of other social backgrounds. Rape, illegal abortion, on-the-job sexual harassment, and confinement for inappropriate or "insane" behavior are all part of this character's gradually revealed past. The novel opens with Connie's latest unjust confinement in a state asylum for "insanely" attacking her niece Dolly's brutal pimp and then alternates between life in this asylum and the future societies to which this character's special telepathic powers give her access. For Connie, like some other women and men whose unconventional perceptions or behavior lead to their forcible confinement, is not the powerless person her society believes; instead, she is a powerful telepathic "catcher" (E, p. 41), capable of receiving the mental impulses of time-travelling Luciente and similarly receptive Gildina. These characters provide the confined woman with access to two possible, conflicting futures: Luciente is from the egalitarian New England community of Mattapoisett in 2137, while Gildina, whom Connie contacts only once, is herself a woman literally as well as figuratively confined. She lives within the purdah-like seclusion and rigid sex roles decreed for women by a second, dystopic future.

Piercy's investiture of power in the conventionally powerless figure of Connie gives fictional life to radical critiques of psychiatric theory and institutions, particularly in relation to women. It also suggests the power the conventionally passive reader may exert in constructing this text's meanings. We may synthesize concepts emerging from the dialectic Piercy establishes through this novel's structural alternation among grim present and disparate, possible futures, or—as Connie has in the past—we may unproductively fragment our perceptions. As Connie tells Luciente,

> in a way I've always had three names inside me. Consuelo, my given name. Consuelo's a Mexican woman, a servant of servants, silent as clay. The woman who suffers. Who bears and endures. Then I'm Connie, who managed to get two years of college—till Consuelo got pregnant. Connie got decent jobs from time to time and fought welfare for a little extra money for Angie [her daughter]. She got me on

a bus when I had to leave Chicago. But it was her who married Eddie, she thought it was smart. Then I'm Conchita, the low-down drunken mean part of me who gets by in jail, in the bug-house, who loves no good men, who hurt my daughter. . . . (E, p. 122)

This character's inability to "claim" under one name the different aspects of her experience reflects the strength of society's wildly conflicting stereotypes for women. The reader may similarly conventionally disown or unconventionally claim the doubled or tripled manifestation of characters in this text. This doubling or tripling does not occur solely within Connie's twentieth century self-fragmentation but in similarities between Connie's contemporary experiences and those of twenty-second century Luciente and Gildina.

These similarities suggest that Connie's visions of Mattapoisett and Gildina's caged existence may just be hallucinations, and that Connie actually *is* mad and merely clothing her hopes and fears in mental fantasy. Regardless of their origins, however, these visions or hallucinations depict society's impact on human potential in ways that make them effective narrative polemic. Thus, an attempt to categorize these chapter-long, futuristic episodes as *either* madness or vision is distortingly irrelevant; these possibilities are complementary rather than mutually exclusive. ⟨. . .⟩

Society's impact on women's appearance and attitude is most dramatically displayed in the character of Gildina. Originally "just a chica" like Connie, her niece Dolly, or Luciente, Gildina has been "cosmetically fixed for sex use" (E, p. 299) until she seems a "cartoon of femininity, with a tiny waist, enormous sharp breasts" and "hips and buttocks . . . oversized and audaciously curved" (E, p. 288). This "gilding" of natural femaleness, reminiscent of Manland's grotesque expectations for womanliness in ⟨Joanna Russ's⟩ *The Female Man*, is but an extension of the cosmetic ordeals that prostitute Dolly inflicts upon herself to achieve a prized "Anglo" look (E, p. 218). Gildina's degraded connection to Luciente is also implicit in the resonance of their names. Conditioned by her dystopic society to live vicariously, attached each day to a "Sense-All" unit for stimulation (E, p. 292) much as twentieth century women (including Connie) depend upon television for entertainment and companionship, Gildina is "gilded" or falsely glittering. Luciente, though, who is active, purposive, and productive, glows with the inner "light" her Spanish name denotes. It does not seem coincidental that Mattapoisett's ritual greeting is a beneficent invocation of "Good light" (E, p. 72). Instead, this greeting is a further link between social norms and individual development. ⟨. . .⟩

Through these and other specific comparisons among the three societies she details, Piercy makes apparent the seeds of both alternative futures within our own time. Indeed, the intrusive corporate control and psychosurgical monitoring of all individuals in Gildina's society are direct outgrowths of the behavior-modifying psychosurgery Connie herself as a mental patient is forced to undergo. As Luciente tells this character, "We are only one possible future. . . . Yours is a crux time. Alternative universes coexist. Probabilities clash and possibilities wink out forever" (E, p. 177). What occurs in Connie's time—our own era—will shape the future.

—Natalie M. Rosinsky, "The Battle of the Sexes: Things to Come," *Feminist Futures: Contemporary Women's Speculative Fiction* (Ann Arbor, MI: UMI Research Press, 1984), 90–93

MARGE PIERCY

There's a general assumption on the part of American critics and academics that anyone who writes fiction or poetry that is politically conscious must be kind of dense—that by its nature the work is cruder than work that simply embodies currently held notions; that, roughly speaking, leftist or feminist work is by definition more naïve, simpler, less profound than right-wing work. What is considered deep is writing that deals with man's fate (always *man's*) in psychospiritual terms, with our heart of darkness, somehow always darker when somebody is thinking that maybe things could be changed a little. Deep work deals with angst-filled alienation (again, always man's, because Mama has a baby and she hasn't got time for the angst). Literature is perceived, as Hans Haacke said about art, "as a mythical entity above mundane interests and ideological conflict." As Haacke also remarked, "In non-dictatorial societies, the induction into and the maintenance of a particular way of thinking and seeing must be performed with subtlety in order to succeed. Staying within the acceptable range of divergent views must be perceived as the natural thing to do." I might add that going beyond that A-to-B circuit must be perceived as unnatural, therefore discordant, strident—inherently less artistic.

As the novelist Joanna Russ has pointed out, "the expectations of the novel have narrowed to the bourgeois novel, with its preoccupation with individual success or failure." She ascribes this to a general Christian bias in favor of individual damnation or salvation, which she opposes to a more collective fiction, more profoundly Jewish, hence communal and socialist and feminist. She has defended my work in these terms, with which I'm comfortable.

I've never been able to understand the assumption that being ignorant of science is good for poets, or that being ignorant of economics and social organization is good for novelists. I've always imagined that the more curious you are about the world around you, the more you'll have to bring to your characters and to the worlds that you spin around them. I've always imagined, too, that one reason many American novelists haven't developed, but, rather, have atrophied, producing their best work out of the concerns of late adolescence and early adulthood, is that since they do not care to grapple with or even to identify the moving forces in their society they can't understand more than a few stories.

Writing that is politically conscious involves freeing the imagination, which is one reason why magic realism has been so energizing to Latin American fiction. If we view the world as static, if we think ahistorically, we lack perspective on the lives we are creating. The more variables we can link and switch in the mind, the greater our potential control over the basic and sometimes unconscious premises of our fiction and our poetry. We must be able to feel ourselves active in time and history. We choose from the infinitely complex past certain stories, certain epochs, certain struggles and battles, certain heroines and heroes that lead to us. We draw strength from them as we create our genealogy, both literarily and personally. Deciding who we are is intimately associated with who we believe our ancestors, our progenitors, our precursors are.

In the arts, particularly, we need our own sense of lineage and our own tradition to work in or to rebel against. Often we must work in a contrapuntal way to a given genre or tradition, taking it apart, slicing it against the grain, making explicit its assumptions. ⟨. . .⟩

A sense of false belonging destroys our ability to think and to feel. A seamless identification with a culture that excludes us as fully human or that impoverishes our options makes us limit our seeing as well as our saying. This is especially true in America, where official history is Disney World. Most of us are the grandchildren of immigrants, with parents who refused to speak whatever language was theirs as a birthright and who considered all the received history and wisdom and stories of their families as so much peasant trash to be dumped and forgotten. Often we have lost not only the names of the villages where our ancestors lived but any knowledge of what they did for a living, what they believed, why they left and came here. We have lost the history of labor and religious struggles they may have bled for. This ignorance makes us shallower than we may want to be. ⟨. . .⟩

Imagination is powerful, whether it's working to make us envision our inner strengths and the vast energy and resources locked into ordinary people and capable of shining out in crisis, capable of breaking out into great good or great evil; or whether imagination is showing us utopias, dystopias or merely societies in which some variable has changed—perhaps a society in which certain women act as incubators for the babies of the upper echelons. When such a society is imagined we can better understand ourselves by seeing what we are not, to better grasp what we are. We can also then understand what we want to move toward and what we want to prevent in the worlds our children must inhabit.

—Marge Piercy, "Active in Time and History," *Paths of Resistance: The Art and Craft of the Political Novel*, William Zinsser, ed. (Boston: Houghton Mifflin Company, 1989), 103–8

ELLEN SERLEN UFFEN

Some of ⟨Piercy's⟩ important works—*Gone to Soldiers* (1987), for one recent example—are set entirely in the past and explore only the period in which the action occurs. As a political feminist, Piercy also views the past as the set of circumstances which was responsible for having formed women—*Small Changes* (1973) is an example here—and for creating the attitudes they use to confront the present. One must attend closely to what was in order to understand and to do battle, if necessary, in the world in which her characters find themselves now.

All of this is evident in *Braided Lives* (1982), which, like Popkin's *Herman Had Two Daughters*, traces the destinies of two women. The "I" narrator here, however, is one of those women and the time span she covers as well as the physical territory, is much more circumscribed than those encompassed by Popkin's panoramic vision. Here, Jill Stuart focuses only on several years during the 1950s, but interrupts her narrative, on occasion, with glimpses into the future, these in the form of italicized passages in which an older Jill speaks and a wiser Jill who has presumably pondered and analyzed the past events she is presenting. But despite these quick views of a time beyond the time covered by the narrative, Jill mainly keeps us in the past. In order to vivify the events and to intensify their immediacy, she relates these occurrences of the past in the present tense. The past, then, comes to us as the present; and what is, in terms of the action, the future, and is related to us as such, is, in fact, Jill Stuart's "real" present.

Each area of time is a different stage on which the events can be viewed and evaluated. The mixture of time schemes functions as a method of analysis in itself, a way for Jill and for us to determine the sense of the past, particularly important in a novel in which past events have formed present feminist political attitudes. That is, the fact of the past occurring in the present tense allows both intimacy and distance. We can believe that Jill is actually living the events, which allows us to respond with appropriate immediacy, and, at the same time, because they exist in the past, we—and Jill—are free to stand back and view the action through a more objective, because temporarily removed, perspective. ⟨. . .⟩

The story Jill goes on to tell us is, most significantly, the story of her relationship with her cousin, Donna Stuart, her father's brother's daughter, who will be her roommate at the University of Michigan. Hers will remain the most important of the lives with which Jill's will become braided. The cousins share the same surname and background and, for awhile, similar fates, similar interests, even a lover. Jill's narrative takes us through their college years, through her own pleasure in the freedom and intellectual openness of university life, the "anxious nonsense" (124) preceding and following her first sexual experience with Mike Loesser and her mother's discovery that she has been sleeping with Mike, through pregnancy and abortion and other lovers and involvements with friends and family and sometimes, less intimately because necessarily viewed from afar, through Donna's experiences and relationships with men. 〈. . .〉

〈. . .〉 The time in which they are living has actively formed them. These were the 1950s in America. There was Korea and McCarthy; there were curfews in university dormitories, but only for the women; there was belief in premarital chastity, yet a girl was expected to have a date every Saturday night; abortion was illegal and birth-control devices were unavailable to unmarried women. Jill and Donna broke the rules, as did many others, and afterwards experienced the guilt of having done what they knew to be right, but were certain was absolutely wrong, nevertheless.

—Ellen Serlen Uffen, "The 1960s to the 80s: Zelda Popkin and Marge Piercy," *Strands of the Cable: The Place of the Past in Jewish American Women's Writing*, Daniel Walden, ed. (New York: Peter Lang Publishing, Inc., 1992), 106–9, 112–14, 118

SHERRY LEE LINKON

In *Gone to Soldiers*, Marge Piercy's multi-perspective novel about World War II, a young French Jew describes her attitude toward her Jewish identity:

> I considered being born in a Jewish family as a contingent peripheral part of my being, not part of my essence, now it defines me. How can I come to master, to own, that definition?
> . . . If I am to be myself, entire, authentic, I must find a way of being Jewish that is mine. I must find an affirmation in this identity. (269)

Her words point to a key theme in contemporary Jewish-American women's writing, the struggle to define a positive Jewish identity near the end of a century of assimilation and after three decades of "second wave" feminism. As Jewish-American women have moved away from traditional Judaism in the twentieth century, they have discovered that they must define for themselves what it means to be a Jewish woman in secular, ethnic terms. And as Adrienne Rich has noted, such a definition does not come easily. The "question of Jewish identity," she notes in a 1982 essay, "float[s] so impalpably, so ungraspably around me, a could I can't quite see the outlines of" (100).

Some Jewish-American women writers have chosen to downplay Jewish identity, giving it only a marginal role in their writing, and most have emphasized issues related to gender and class even when their main characters are Jewish. In most of her work, Piercy has followed this pattern. While she has created many Jewish characters, few of her novels have addressed Jewish identity as a central theme. Yet in three of her later works, Piercy positions Jewish identity at the center of her writing, as a central issue with which her characters struggle. These novels develop variations on Piercy's understanding of Jewish identity, which she explains in a 1984 essay: "A Jew may be anyone the society defines as a Jew and anyone who defines herself as a Jew" (25). This definition sounds simple, but as these novels shows, both external and internal definitions of Jewishness are complex, especially for women.

Piercy's fiction and poetry have received little critical attention, and of that, very few critics have considered her as a Jewish writer or even acknowledged the Jewish content in her work. ⟨. . .⟩

⟨. . .⟩ Only one critic has given serious attention to Piercy within a context of Jewish-American literature. Ellen Serlen Uffen includes Piercy in her book-length study of twentieth-century Jewish American women writers, but even she does not focus on the Jewish content of Piercy's work. Yet Piercy's work offers useful material for developing a more complex understanding of the uses of ethnicity in Jewish-American women's writing.

In several of her early novels, Piercy uses Jewishness as a tool in characterization, a trait that defines some characters as "others" but also explains connections between Jewish characters. These characters do not find much value in their Jewishness, nor does it make any significant difference in their lives. Like Jacqueline in the early part of *Gone to Soldiers*, they see being Jewish as peripheral. In *Gone Down Fast*, Piercy's first published novel (1969), two of the central characters are Jewish. Anna and Leon use a few Yiddish phrases, and Anna's appearance seems intended as "typically Jewish"—dark, curly hair and peasant-like body build. Yet neither character defines his/her identity primarily in terms of being Jewish, and they never experience Judaism in religious terms. ⟨. . .⟩

In three of her later novels, however, Piercy not only draws more fully on Jewish culture in creating characters and plots, she also explores more fully the intersections between Jewish ethnicity, gender, and class. And in her latest work, Jewishness gains a strong, even central position in that triangle. From *Braided Lives* (1982) to *Gone to Soldiers* (1987) to *He, She, and It* (1991), Piercy's Jewish women shift from ambivalence toward their ethnicity to celebration, from seeing Jewishness as just one of several traits that define them as "others" in a mostly Anglo-Christian society to embracing Jewish identity as central, as the defining trait of the "self" against which non-Jews become "others." These novels explore a key problem for Jewish-American women in the late twentieth century. Rather than offering a clear solution, however, Piercy's novels appropriately suggest the complexity of the issue and offer a range of perspectives that illuminate the question of Jewish identity for both Jewish and non-Jewish readers.

As Piercy's definition suggests, Jewish identity can mean almost anything an individual chooses, but it can also come as the result not of self-definition but from others who assign that identity. Indeed, despite the assimilation that has allowed Jews to move into the mainstream of American culture, Jewish identity still includes a basic "otherness," a sense of oneself as separate from the rest of American culture. Twentieth-century American Jews struggle both with a sense of being different from their white, Christian (whether religious or not) neighbors and with a sense of uncertainty about what being Jewish might mean. They are different but not always sure exactly how. ⟨. . .⟩

Gender adds another dimension to this Jewish identity crisis. For Jewish women, especially for Jewish feminists, claiming Jewish identity has often meant identifying with a strongly patriarchal cultural tradition. Adrienne Rich's explanation of her own rejection of Judaism exemplifies the feelings of many Jewish feminists: "I saw Judaism simply as another strand of patriarchy. If asked to choose, I might have said . . . : "I am a woman, not a Jew" (122). If Jews are outsiders in secular culture, Jewish women are outsiders within Jewish culture. They have not traditionally been included in the full practice of religious Judaism, and they have often felt excluded from Jewish cultural life.

This double difference has played an important role in Jewish-American women's writing. Victoria Aarons has argued that the stance of outsider has been common to Jewish-American writing, but that Jewish-American women writers are redefining the relationship between Jewishness and otherness in their work. She sees Jewish-American women writers, such as Hortense Calisher and Grace Paley, creating characters who "find themselves paradoxically alienated from and drawn to a heritage from which they are excluded, and yet in which they play an important function." This paradox leads to "a fragmentation that causes the characters to seek to resolve their ambivalent feelings toward their pasts by trying to recreate them." For the Jewish-American woman, she notes, Jewish identity "remains . . . fraught with ambivalence, with mistrust of one's 'place,' yet with an 'insider's' instinct for continuity and the potential reaffirmation of identity" (393). In her stories of Jill in *Braided Lives*, Jacqueline in *Gone to Soldiers*, and Shira in *He, She, and It*, Piercy traces and finally completes this search for a Jewish identity that might become its own "inside." ⟨. . .⟩

In these three novels, Piercy explores three variations on the internal/external paradigm. While Jill's internal non-definition differs markedly from Jacqueline's mixed experience and the internal/external division of *He, She, and It*, all three highlight issues that are central to contemporary understandings of Jewish identity and its interrelation with gendered identity. Together, they provide a useful map of the meaning of ethnicity for one Jewish-American woman writer and, through Piercy's explorations, of one portion of the Jewish community.

—Sherry Lee Linkon, "'A Way of Being Jewish That Is Mine': Gender and Ethnicity in the Jewish Novels of Marge Piercy," *Studies in American Jewish Literature* 13 (1994): 93–96, 102–3

B I B L I O G R A P H Y

Breaking Camp. 1968.

Hard Loving. 1969.

Going Down Fast. 1969.

Dance the Eagle to Sleep. 1970.

The Grand Coolie Damn. 1970.

A Work of Artifice. 1970.

4-Telling (with others). 1971.

When the Drought Broke. 1971.

To Be of Use. 1973.

Small Changes. 1973.

Living in the Open. 1976.

Woman on the Edge of Time. 1976.

The Twelve-Spoked Wheel Flashing. 1978.

The High Cost of Living. 1978.

The Last White Class: A Play About Neighborhood Terror (with Ira Wood). 1979.

Vida. 1980.

The Moon Is Always Female. 1980.

Braided Lives. 1982.

Parti-Colored Blocks for a Quilt. 1982.

Circles on the Water: Selected Poems. 1982.

Stone, Paper, Knife. 1983.

Fly Away Home. 1984.

My Mother's Body. Ed. Nancy Nicholas. 1985.

Early Ripening: American Women's Poetry Now. 1988.

Gone to Soldiers. 1988.

Available Light. 1988.

Summer People. 1989.

The Earth Shines Secretly: A Book of Days. 1990.

He, She, and It. 1991.
Mars and Her Children. 1992.
Longings of Women. 1994.
City of Darkness, City of Light. 1996.

GERTRUDE STEIN

1874–1946

GERTRUDE STEIN was born on February 3, 1874, in Allegheny, Pennsylvania, the youngest of five surviving children of Daniel and Amelia Stein. She spent her childhood in Vienna, Paris, and Oakland, California, and later attended Radcliffe College, where she studied under philosopher and psychologist William James.

Stein was especially interested in psychology, and her first published work, "Normal Motor Automatism," written with Leon Solomons, was published in the *Psychological Review* in 1896. She studied medicine at Johns Hopkins University from 1897 to 1901 but left without receiving a degree. In 1903 she moved to Paris with her brother Leo and lived there for the rest of her life. She returned to the United States only once.

In 1904, Stein and her brother began collecting paintings, including early works of Cézanne, Matisse, Picasso, and Braque, and started what became their famous Saturday evening gatherings frequented by members of the expatriate and French avant-garde. In 1907 Stein met Alice B. Toklas, who became her lifelong lover and assistant; they lived together until Stein's death.

Inspired by the aesthetic philosophies and styles of the artists she collected and by Flaubert's *Trois contes*, Stein wrote *Three Lives* (1909). Likewise, the cubism of Picasso—for whom Stein sat for a portrait—influenced her astonishing prose-poem, *Tender Buttons* (1914). Over the next 40 years she wrote almost constantly, producing nearly 500 works, including portraits, plays, poems, and scores of books, only a few of which were published in her lifetime. While some critics hailed her stream-of-consciousness technique as liberating and illuminating, others thought her work self-indulgent, deliberately obscure, and intellectually dishonest.

Among her best-known works are *Tender Buttons, The Making of Americans* (1925), and the popular *The Autobiography of Alice B. Toklas* (1933). The opera *Four Saints in Three Acts* (written with composer Virgil Thomson) premiered in the United States in 1934. That year she also embarked on a highly successful lecture tour in the United States, and in 1935 her essay collection *Lectures in America* appeared, followed by *Narration*.

During World War II, Stein and Toklas lived in the countryside in Nazi-occupied France under the protection of villagers and a friend with government connections. By the time Stein recorded her experiences in France during the war in *Wars I Have Seen* (1945), her reputation in America was firmly established. She died on July 27, 1946.

Stein was undoubtedly one of the most influential writers of her time and was central to a significant segment of the European artistic community; Sherwood Anderson and Ernest Hemingway are among those most directly in her debt.

CRITICAL EXTRACTS

SHERWOOD ANDERSON

Since Miss Stein's work was first brought to my attention I have been thinking of it as the most important pioneer work done in the field of letters in my time. The loud guffaws of the general that must inevitably follow the bringing forward of more of her work do not irritate me but I would like it if writers, and particularly young writers, would come to understand a little what she is trying to do and what she is in my opinion doing.

My thought in the matter is something like this—that every artist working with words as his medium, must at times be profoundly irritated by what seems the limitations of his medium. What things does he not wish to create with words! There is the mind of the reader before him and he would like to create in that reader's mind a whole new world of sensations, or rather one might better say he would like to call back into life all of the dead and sleeping senses.

There is a thing one might call "the extension of the province of his art" one wants to achieve. One works with words and one would like words that have a taste on the lips, that have a perfume to the nostrils, rattling words one can throw into a box and shake, making a sharp, jingling sound, words that, when seen on the printed page, have a distinct arresting effect upon the eye, words that when they jump out from under the pen one may feel with the fingers as one might caress the cheeks of his beloved.

And what I think is that these books of Gertrude Stein's do in a very real sense recreate life in words. ⟨. . .⟩

For me the work of Gertrude Stein consists in a rebuilding, an entire new recasting of life, in the city of words. Here is one artist who has been able to accept ridicule, who has even foregone the privilege of writing the great American novel, uplifting our English speaking stage, and wearing the bays of the great poets, to go live among the little housekeeping words, the swaggering bullying street-corner words, the honest working, money saving words, and all the other forgotten and neglected citizens of the sacred and half forgotten city.

Would it not be a lovely and charmingly ironic gesture of the gods if, in the end, the work of this artist were to prove the most lasting and important of all the word slingers of our generation!

—Sherwood Anderson, "The Work of Gertrude Stein," *Geography and Plays* (1922), in *The Chelsea House Library of Literary Criticism: Twentieth-Century American Literature*, Vol. 6, Harold Bloom, ed. (New York: Chelsea House Publishers, 1987), 3766

THORNTON WILDER

Miss Gertrude Stein, answering a question about her line

A rose is a rose is a rose is a rose,

once said with characteristic vehemence:

"Now listen! I'm no fool. I know that in daily life we don't say 'is a . . . is a . . . is a . . .'"

She knew that she was a difficult and an idiosyncratic author. She pursued her aims, however, with such conviction and intensity that occasionally she forgot that the results could be difficult to others. At such times the achievements she had made in writing, in "telling what she knew" (her most frequent formulization of the aim of writing) had to her the character of self-evident beauty and clarity. A friend, to whom she showed recently completed examples of her poetry, was frequently driven to reply sadly: "But you forget that I don't understand examples of your extremer styles." To this she would reply with a mixture of bewilderment, distress, and exasperation:

"But what's the difficulty? Just read the words on the paper. They're in English. Just read them. Be simple and you'll understand these things."

Now let me quote the whole speech from which the opening remark in this introduction has been extracted. A student in her seminar at the University of Chicago had asked her for an "explanation" of the famous line. She leaned forward giving all of herself to the questioner in that unforgettable way which has endeared her to hundreds of students and to hundreds of soldiers in two wars, trenchant, humorous, but above all urgently concerned over the enlightenment of even the most obtuse questioner:

Now listen! Can't you see that when the language was new—as it was with Chaucer and Homer—the poet could use the name of a thing and the thing was really there? He could say "O moon," "O sea," "O love" and the moon and the sea and love were really there. And can't you see that after hundreds of years had gone by and thousands of poems had been written, he could call on those words and find that they were just wornout literary words? The excitingness of pure being had withdrawn from them; they were just rather stale literary words. Now the poet has to work in the excitingness of pure being; he has to get back that intensity into the language. We all know that it's hard to write poetry in a late age; and we know that you have to put some strangeness, something unexpected, into the structure of the sentence in order to bring back vitality to the noun. Now it's not enough to be bizarre; the strangeness in the sentence structure has to come from the poetic gift, too. That's why it's doubly hard to be a poet in a late age. Now you all have seen hundreds of poems about roses and you know in your bones that the rose is not there. All those songs that sopranos sing as encores about "I have a garden; oh, what a garden!" Now I don't want to put too much emphasis on that line, because it's just one line in a longer poem. But I notice that you all know it; you make fun of it, but you know it. Now listen! I'm no fool. I know that in daily life we don't go around saying "is a . . . is a . . . is a . . ." Yes, I'm no fool; but I think that in that line the rose is red for the first time in English poetry for a hundred years.

This book is full of that "strangeness which must come from the poetic gift" in order to restore intensity to images dusted over with accustomedness and routine. It is not required in poetry alone; for Miss Stein all intellectual activities—philosophical speculation, literary criticism, narration—had to be refreshed at the source.

There are certain of her idiosyncrasies which by this time should not require discussion—for example, her punctuation and her recourse to repetition. Readers who still baulk at these should not attempt to read this volume, for it contains idiosyncrasies far more taxing to conventional taste. The majority of readers ask of literature the kind of pleasure they have always received; they want "more of the same"; they accept idiosyncrasy in author and period only when it has been consecrated by a long-accumulated prestige, as in the cases of the earliest and the latest of Shakespeare's styles, and in the poetry of Donne, Gerard Manley Hopkins, or Emily Dickinson. They arrogate to themselves a superiority in condemning the novels of Kafka or of the later Joyce or the later Henry James, forgetting that they allow a no less astonishing individuality to Laurence Sterne and to Rabelais.

This work is for those who not only largely accord to others "another's way," but who rejoice in the diversity of minds and the tension of difference. Miss Stein once said:

Every masterpiece came into the world with a measure of ugliness in it. That ugliness is the sign of the creator's struggle to say a new thing in a new way, for an artist can never repeat yesterday's success. And after every great creator there follows a second man who shows how it can be done easily. Picasso struggled and made his new thing and then Braque came along and showed how it could be done without pain. The Sistine Madonna of Raphael is all over the world, on grocers' calendars and on Christmas cards; everybody thinks it's an easy picture. It's our business as critics to stand in front of it and recover its ugliness.

This book is full of that kind of ugliness. It is perhaps not enough to say: "Be simple and you will understand these things"; but it is necessary to say: "Relax your predilection for the accustomed, the received, and be ready to accept an extreme example of idiosyncratic writing."

—Thornton Wilder, "Introduction," *Four in America* (1947), in *The Chelsea House Library of Literary Criticism: Twentieth-Century American Literature*, Vol. 6, Harold Bloom, ed. (New York: Chelsea House Publishers, 1987), 3768–69

ALLEGRA STEWART

Whitehead once remarked that "it requires an unusual mind to undertake the analysis of the obvious. Familiar things happen, and mankind does not bother about them." Gertrude Stein's analysis of the obvious, however, confronts the given in ordinary human experience with full awareness of its mystery. She raises questions as to the nature of perception, the meaning of being, the boundlessness of space and the roundness of the world, the passage of time and the nature of personality and identity, and the activities of genius. To contemplate the obvious is to confront the polarities in the universe and the contradictions in man. It is to become aware of the dualism which runs through all things. ⟨. . .⟩

The meditative element became dominant in the writings of Gertrude Stein when she began to write portraits—in other words, at the time when she ceased to worry about communication and emphasized communion. During the writing of *The Geographical History of America*, she was concerned primarily with being, not with time and change. From *Tender Buttons* on, however, all her work is a kind of communion. She detached herself from "mechanical civilizations and the world being round," convinced that the dialectical process in time leads only from one pole to another—from communism to individualism and back again in a never-ending cycle, in which the individual is always lost in the collective or the solipsistic. The union of opposites is a creative act, but that action itself can never become the object of knowledge. To perform the act is to assert man's freedom from every necessity except that of existence itself. ⟨. . .⟩

For Gertrude Stein, meditation is more than reflection: it is communion, participation—an act of presence. Direct, immediate—it is the only way to master the contradictions and oppositions of discursive thinking and experience and to give a content to the "now." Only through participation will the word have life, and only through the written word can life be immortalized. The written word is the one medium in which all mediation disappears. Words on the written page bear no resemblance to the things they signify, and they are therefore entirely closed to sense perception and open immediately to the inward eye. Through written words one can commune in silence across space and time by signs which in themselves need make no appeal to the senses.

—Allegra Stewart, "The Quality of Gertrude Stein's Creativity," *American Literature*, Vol. 28 (January 1957), in *Gertrude Stein*, Harold Bloom, ed. (New York: Chelsea House Publishers, 1986), 69–71, 74–75

VIRGIL THOMSON

Just as Gertrude kept up friendships among the amazons, though she did not share their lives, she held certain Jews in attachment for their family-like warmth, though she felt no solidarity with Jewry. Tristan Tzara—French-language poet from Romania, Dada pioneer, early surrealist, and battler for the Communist party—she said was "like a cousin." Miss Etta and Dr. Claribel Cone, picture buyers and friends from Baltimore days, she handled almost as if they were her sisters. The sculptors Jo Davidson and Jacques Lipschitz, the painter Man Ray she accepted as though they had a second cousin's right to be part of her life. About men or goyim, even about her oldest man friend, Picasso, she could feel unsure; but a woman or a Jew she could size up quickly. She accepted without cavil, indeed, all the conditionings of her Jewish background. And if, as she would boast, she was "a bad Jew," she at least did not think of herself as Christian. Of heaven and salvation and all that she would say, "When a Jew dies he's dead." We used to talk a great deal, in fact, about our very different religious conditionings, the subject having come up through my remarking the frequency with which my Jewish friends would break with certain of theirs and then never make up. Gertrude's life had contained many people that she still spoke of (Mabel Dodge, for instance) but from whom she refused all communication. The Stettheimers' conversation was also full of references to people they had known well but did not wish to know any more. And I began to imagine this definitiveness about separations as possibly a Jewish trait. I was especially struck by Gertrude's rupture with her brother Leo, with whom she had lived for many years in intellectual and no doubt affectionate communion, but to whom she never spoke again after they had divided their pictures and furniture, taken up separate domiciles.

The explanation I offered for such independent behavior was that the Jewish religion, though it sets aside a day for private Atonement, offers no mechanics for forgiveness save for offenses against one's own patriarch, and even he is not obliged to pardon. When a Christian, on the other hand, knows he has done wrong to anyone, he is obliged in all honesty to attempt restitution; and the person he has wronged must thereupon forgive. So that if Jews seem readier to quarrel than to make up, that fact seems possibly to be the result of their having no confession-and-forgiveness formula, whereas Christians, who experience none of the embarrassment that Jews find in admitting misdeeds, arrange their lives, in consequence, with greater flexibility, though possibly, to a non-Christian view, with less dignity.

Gertrude liked this explanation, and for nearly twenty years it remained our convention. It was not till after her death that Alice said one day,

> You and Gertrude had it settled between you as to why Jews don't make up their quarrels, and I went along with you. But now I've found a better reason for it. Gertrude was right, of course, to believe that "when a Jew dies he's dead." And that's exactly why Jews don't need to make up. When we've had enough of someone we can get rid of him. You Christians can't, because you've got to spend eternity together.

—Virgil Thomson, "A Portrait of Gertrude Stein," *Virgil Thomson* (1966), in *The Chelsea House Library of Literary Criticism: Twentieth-Century American Literature*, Vol. 6, Harold Bloom, ed. (New York: Chelsea House Publishers, 1987), 3767

NORMAN WEINSTEIN

Surely one of the pleasures of reading Proust's *Remembrance of Things Past* in its entirety is the sense of final cohesion that brings together the enormous weight of detail with which Proust so liberally decorates his narrative.

By contrast, one of the severe difficulties of even reading *The Making of Americans* in its entirety is the narrative discontinuities in a book that purports to be a "family history." For example the book opens with Gertrude Stein's reworking of a quote from Aristotle's ethics:

> Once an angry man dragged his father along the ground through his own orchard. "Stop!" cried the groaning old man at last, "Stop! I did not drag my father beyond this tree."
> It is hard living down the tempers we are born with. We all begin well, for in our youth there is nothing we are more intolerant of than our own sins writ large in others and we fight them fiercely in ourselves; but we grow old and we see that these sins our sins are of all sins the really harmless ones to own, nay that they give charm to any character. . . .

This is Gertrude Stein speaking. And it is Gertrude Stein's omnipresent voice as narrator that resounds through the half million words of narrative. From the very start there is no ambiguity as to the nature of the narrator. She is perfectly in control of the thematic flow at all times. She is repetitious, for our particular storyteller is also a theorizing psychologist who believes the essence of the human personality is revealed in repetition.

> Repeating then is in every one, in every one their being and
> their feeling and their way of realizing everything and every one of
> them comes out in repeating. More and more then every one comes
> to be clear to some one.

But the most striking characteristic of our narrator is her astonishing verbosity. Nearly a thousand pages of closely packed prose and a half million words are employed to depict the progress of the Dehning and Hersland families. Why this prolixity? Is the verbosity an outgrowth of the author's attempt to write the complete family chronicle of these families with every detail clear and intact? ⟨. . .⟩

Gertrude Stein gives the raison d'être for such a technique in the lecture "Composition as Explanation."

> There is singularly nothing that makes a difference a difference
> in beginning and in the middle and in ending except that each
> generation has something different at which they are all looking. . . .
> There was [in making] a groping for using everything and there was a
> groping for a continuous present and there was an evitable beginning
> of beginning again and again.

All of these ideas become translated into the following paragraph in *The Making of Americans*:

> Sometime there is a history of each one, of every one who ever
> has living in them and repeating in them and has their being coming
> out from them in their repeating that is always in all being. Sometime
> there is a history of everyone.

The Making of Americans can be considered a "history of everyone who ever lived, is living and will live" because for Gertrude Stein all persons can be fitted into her characterology. The roots for her characterology are found in *Three Lives*. Melanctha Herbert and Doctor Campbell were unable to love because of an essential discrepancy in the rhythm, the speed of their personalities. The same is true of Julia and Alfred, but in *The Making of Americans* the attempt is made to trace the roots of their discord all the way back—three generations back to European soil. The title "making of Americans" is meant to be taken literally. From the immigration of grandparents to the youngest American in the book, David Hersland, Jr., the aim is to show how the *American* consciousness is forged through the passage of generations. ⟨. . .⟩

So what changes from generation to generation is not the type of psychological phenomenon but the distribution. What changes is not the fact that men perceive reality but what they choose to single out in their perception of reality. So we are dealing with a highly peculiar variety of family history in *The Making of Americans*. We are concerned with the gradualness of a change in viewing the objects of consciousness through a family's history.

—Norman Weinstein, "*The Making of Americans*: The Narrative Redefined," *Gertrude Stein and the Literature of the Modern Consciousness* (1970), in *The Chelsea House Library of Literary Criticism: Twentieth-Century American Literature*, Vol. 6, Harold Bloom, ed. (New York: Chelsea House Publishers, 1987), 3771–72

Frederick J. Hoffman

Miss Stein was above all convinced that the twentieth century was interested, as she put it in *Lectures in America*, in *feeling a thing existing*: "we that is any human being living has inevitably to feel the thing anything being existing, but the name of that thing of that anything is no longer anything to thrill any one but children." And this leads us, finally, to her genuine value as a critic of modern literature: she is above all the most important sponsor of what we have called "presentational immediacy," of the integrity and the uniqueness of the "thing seen at the moment it is seen." Though she read widely and even exhaustively in the classics, they had no meaning for her except as they pointed to parallels with the present. Most importantly, it was the *visual* sense that intrigued her, the shape, color, depth, dimension, and texture of the thing seen. In the grain of that texture lie the differences from one generation to another. Her sense of time was limited to two things: the alterations (subtle as they may be) in the way of seeing things; the effect of force on surfaces. Of war she said that it speeds up change, that it makes spectacular differences not only in the arrangements of objects in space but also in the ways in which one "feels existence." In the case of World War II, which she described in *Wars I Have Seen* as an unheroic war, when the "nice heroic deeds" were no longer possible, it made a radical difference. In any case, the twentieth century was remarkably different from the nineteenth, and the difference simply emphasized the need for a radical change in sensibilities, so that it could be honestly and faithfully recorded.

The essential difference was fragmentation, or the separation of objects and persons from each other so that they could no longer feel securely dependent upon one another. This change the Americans understood far more clearly than the Europeans; Miss Stein was convinced that the twentieth cen-

GERTRUDE STEIN

tury was American and that Europe was able only after World War II to break
from the nineteenth. Partly this was because the American space enabled
Americans to see things in a "cubist way," and their speed of movement above
or along the landscape made them see reality as a disembodied, geometrical
series of forms. But it was mostly because of that remarkable convergence of
self-consciousness and science, which nourished each other, the one forcing
analysis, the other reducing it to a study of pure and impersonal forms.
  —Frederick J. Hoffman, "Gertrude Stein," *Seven American Stylists from Poe to Mailer: An
  Introduction* (Minneapolis, MN: University of Minnesota Press, 1973), 143–44

JANE RULE

Like Radclyffe Hall, but not so extreme in her pose, Gertrude Stein could not
identify herself as a woman. Adele says in *Q.E.D.*, after witnessing a complex
scene between Mabel and Helen, "I always did thank God I wasn't born a
woman." Gertrude Stein could not align herself with the cause of women,
either when she was chided by her friend Marion Walker about the slur
against women it would be if she dropped out of medical school or years later
when Marion again asked her to support the women's movement. "Not that
she at all minds the cause of women or any other cause but it does not happen
to be her business." It was obviously a defensive stance, as was her attitude
toward psychology. "You don't know how little I like pathological psychology,
and how all medicine bores me." And she reports of herself through Alice,
"She always says she dislikes the abnormal, it is so obvious. She says the normal is so much more simply complicated and interesting." Though she cut her
hair off and assumed the social role of husband, providing money and learning to drive a car (very badly), "whenever there was a soldier or a chauffeur or
any kind of man anywhere, she never did anything for herself, neither changing a tyre, cranking the car or repairing it." Having been raised by a tyrannical father and having fought bitterly with a beloved brother for the right to
her own identity, she did not easily identify with men either. She explained
the help she got from men along the road in these terms: "The important
thing, she insists, is that you must have deep down as the deepest thing in you
a sense of equality. Then anybody will do anything for you." It's a fine Steinian
contradiction on the surface of it, but like so many of her paradoxes, it also
contains deep, good sense. As early as in *Q.E.D.* she was expressing her perceptive theories about the nature of power in a relationship. Of Mabel's
attempt to manipulate, she explains, "The subtlety and impersonality of her
atmosphere which in a position of recognized power would have compelling
attraction, here in a community of equals . . . lacked the vital force necessary
to win." With whatever arrogance she asserted her own genius, with whatever
egotism she controlled a room with a monologue, she had a deep understand-

ing and real suspicion of the use of power. "Father Mussolini and father Hitler and father Roosevelt, and father Stalin and father Lewis and father Blum and father Franco . . . There is too much fathering going on just now and there is no doubt about it fathers are depressing." In *Brewsie and Willie* she went so far as to explore the need for revolution to destroy industrialism in America. Though she never became a supporter of the women's movement, she wrote a play about Susan B. Anthony called *The Mother of Us All* in which men are seen as poor things, pitiful, blustering, fearful, but with the essential power to get what they want. Still, Gertrude Stein was afraid that women in the struggle for the vote would become more like men, for whom she obviously had very little general respect, though she probably numbered more men than women among her numerous friends.

Gertrude Stein wanted to be a middle-class, ordinary, honest genius, and at her very best she probably was, teaching, through her own extremes, generations of writers after her what the limits of language are. Whether her whole body of work would have been greater or less interesting if she had lived either in a climate of more acceptance or in a personal style more continuously open is impossible to say. Not even at her most obscure did she ever give up the temptation to be "selfishly honest," nor did she at the height of her popular fame. Twice in the third lecture in *Narration*, about journalism, one of the last of her lecture series in America, the exposition is interrupted with the non sequitur, "I love my love with a b because she is peculiar." But her audience had to wait until long after her death to understand the power of that need, not in her greatest work but in a book important for those who would follow. "As Pablo once remarked, when you make a thing, it is so complicated making it that it is bound to be ugly, but those that do it after you they don't have to worry about making it and they can make it pretty, and so everyone can like it when the others make it." No one will ever write a "pretty" *Q.E.D.*, but the courage to write with such selfish honesty comes from a woman who did not want to be a hero but could not finally accept cowardice either.

—Jane Rule, "Gertrude Stein 1874–1946," *Lesbian Images* (Garden City, New York: Doubleday & Company, Inc., 1975), 71–73

LYNN Z. BLOOM

Narration of one's own autobiography through the persona of the individual about whom the biography was supposedly written is, to the best of my knowledge of autobiographies in English, completely innovative and utterly unique. By the very nature of its form, autobiography-by-*Doppelgänger* veritably precludes repetition or imitation. The wit intrinsic in the initial endeavor becomes a joke progressively more stale with each repetition, guaranteed to annoy the readers of successive works, even though they are in the joke because they are cozily in league with the author, who has made the *real* subject of the autobiography unmistakable from the third page on. Imagine the third volume of Stein's autobiography, *Wars I Have Seen*, rewritten as *Wars Alice B. Toklas Has Seen!* Once is genius; twice is gimmickry; thrice is boredom. The form itself is almost self-destructing.

Let us see why this is so, for the form has a number of advantages both literary and autobiographical which should surely have tempted imitators if the imitations were feasible.

In conventional autobiographies the form is usually quite commonplace—either a chronological or a topical presentation of its author's life. In these numerous instances, the reader's familiarity with the form breeds indifference or oblivion to it. As a result, he is much more likely to concentrate on the content and perhaps on the style.

Such cannot be the case when the form is so compellingly unique. It obliges attention, which is to Stein's advantage, for her skill and innovative craftsmanship warrant notice. The reader wonders what Gertrude will have Alice will have Gertrude say or do next; what Alice will reply; how Gertrude will react in this dialogue spoken by a monologist. ⟨. . .⟩

This ventriloquistic persona performs a number of functions which may be grouped into three major categories with several subtle variations on each: the egotistical, the interpretive, and the objective. These overlap and blend to produce a work far more interesting than one without such variety would be. One of the most important aspects of the *egotistical function* is to *disarm* or *distract* the reader from the egotism inherent in conventional autobiography. By consistently employing "Gertrude Stein" or "Miss Stein" when referring to the *Autobiography's* real subject, and by using third-person pronouns less often than expected, *The Autobiography of Alice B. Toklas* escapes the egotism of the consistent first-person usage that is otherwise inevitable in conventional autobiography. This is an extraordinarily clever way to eliminate a plethora of I's; "I" here refers to Alice B. Toklas and her persona uses it sparingly. ⟨. . .⟩

The innovative device of a ventriloquizing persona of Alice B. Toklas in the *Autobiography* also performs a number of functions related to *interpreting* Gertrude Stein. A common aspect of this function is that of *reporter*. The persona of Alice can quote Gertrude Stein secondhand or refer (and defer) to Stein's opinions. This allows Stein-as-autobiographer much greater freedom and latitude of expression, with greater literary tact than she might have had if she had been speaking in the first person. For instance, Alice-as-reporter observes, "The young often when they have learnt all they can learn accuse her [Gertrude Stein] of an inordinate pride" (p. 94), and then quotes Stein indirectly:

> She says yes of course. She realizes that in english literature in
> her time she is the only one. She has always known it and now she
> says it.
>   She understands very well the basis of creation and therefore her
> advice and criticism is invaluable to all her friends. (p. 94)

This sort of self-congratulation, even if true, would appear insufferably egotistical if spoken directly by a first-person autobiographer, and as such would be likely to antagonize most readers, if it would not alienate them completely. So Stein's strategy is sound. *Alice-as-intermediary* softens the direct thrust, blunts the egotism, evades the hubris, and communicates her own appreciation of the rightness of Stein's opinion of herself. ⟨. . .⟩

In imposing such control, Stein also imposes *objectivity*, the third major function of her autobiographical point of view. Gertrude Stein as autobiographer, of course, has absolute control not only over the literary image and personality of Alice B. Toklas but over the persona and personality of herself that she chooses to present to the readers. This in itself, being germane to autobiography as a genre, is not particularly innovative, but Stein's apparent objectivity in that presentation is highly unusual and innovative in autobiography.

It is hard for the autobiographer to be objective in conventional autobiography, when the self is talking directly about the self. But Stein-the-writer has created both the ventriloquist, Alice Toklas, and Stein-the-puppet, who actually though subtly controls the ventriloquist. The continuous presence of two personages in action and interaction enables Stein to *appear* to present Gertrude Stein from the *outside*, rather than from the autobiographer's almost inevitable *inside*, perspective, for the reader sees her as she is allegedly seen by Toklas. "Sentences not only words but sentences and always sentences have been Gertrude Stein's life long passion" (p. 50) is much more external, impersonal than the conventional alternative, "I have always loved long sentences passionately." Likewise, secondhand fury is somewhat milder than firsthand wrath in such observations as: "Gertrude Stein used to get furious when the english all talked about german organisation. She used to insist that the germans had no organisation, they had method but no organisation" (pp. 187–88). As a result, Stein appears as solid and as foursquare as Jo Davidson's seated, washerwomanlike sculpture of her, and, like the sculpture, a human entity visible essentially from the outside.

—Lynn Z. Bloom, "Gertrude Is Alice Is Everybody: Innovation and Point of View in Gertrude Stein's Autobiographies," *Twentieth Century Literature* (Spring 1978), in *The Chelsea House Library of Literary Criticism: Twentieth-Century American Literature*, Vol. 6, Harold Bloom, ed. (New York: Chelsea House Publishers, 1987), 3775–77

JAMES E. BRESLIN

When she was asked to write her autobiography, Stein replied, "Not possibly," and it is easier to imagine her writing an essay called "What Are Autobiographies and Why Are None of Them Masterpieces" than it is to imagine her writing her own autobiography. Of course, she did not write her own autobiography; she wrote *The Autobiography of Alice B. Toklas*. Or did she? Some writers have speculated that Alice B. Toklas wrote her own autobiography or at least substantial parts of it. But perhaps the most important point about this debate is that it seems to have been generated not just by an extraliterary curiosity about the book's composition, but by an actual literary effect the book has on its readers—namely, the effect of raising questions about just whose book it is.

I will return to this issue; for the moment, assuming (as I have been) Stein to be the book's author, I want to suggest how she took up the formal challenge of autobiography by recalling a young man named Andrew Green, who appears briefly in the third chapter of *The Autobiography*. Andrew Green "hated everything modern." Once while staying at 27 rue de Fleurus for a month he covered "all the pictures with cashmere shawls"; he "could not bear" to look at the strange, frightening paintings. Significantly, "he had a prodigious *memory* and could recite all of Milton's *Paradise Lost* by heart" (my emphasis). "He adored as he said a simple centre and a continuous design." Green *has* an identity, so much so that his character can be fixed in a single, brief paragraph. Gertrude Stein does not have an identity; in attempting to represent her "self" she created in *The Autobiography of Alice B. Toklas* a book with an elusive center and a discontinuous design. ⟨. . .⟩

But most readers are more like Andrew Green than Gertrude Stein; they don't like to dwell in uncertainties, and so most discussions of *The Autobiography* begin by assuming the character of Stein to be its easily identifiable center, and they proceed to discuss this character as if it were not mediated for the reader by a perspective that is to *some* degree external to it. Yet, even if we proceed along these lines, the character of Stein turns out to be an elusive and enigmatic "center." Stein, Toklas tells us, sought in her writing to give "the inside as seen from the outside" (p. 156); that is one reason she creates herself through the external perspective of Toklas. What she mans by "the inside" can be clarified through *The Autobiography*'s account of Picasso's famous portrait of Stein; it was with this painting, we are told, that Picasso "passed from the Harlequin, the *charming* early italian period to the *intensive struggle* which was to end in cubism" (p. 54; my emphasis). Stein emphasizes the "intensive struggle" that went into the painting of the portrait itself. During the winter of 1907 Stein patiently posed for Picasso some eighty or ninety times, but then he abruptly "painted out the whole head." "I can't see you any longer when I look, he said irritably" (p. 53). At this point both Stein and Picasso left Paris for the summer, but the day he returned "Picasso sat down and out of his head painted the head in without having seen Gertrude Stein again." In the enigmatic sentence, "I can't see you any longer when I look," what is the referent of "you"? On the one hand, it is not the external, literal Stein, recognizable to her little dog or a realistic novelist. That is why, when Stein later cuts her hair short, Picasso, at first disturbed, can conclude that "all the same it is all there." He was not striving for a realistic mimesis, as Stein stresses in her account of Picasso's difficulties with what turned out to be the least realistic feature of the portrait, the face. On the other hand, Picasso was not trying to evoke the inner, subconscious depths of Stein, of the sort that might fascinate a psychological novelist; in fact, Toklas later claims that Stein had no subconscious (p. 79). ⟨. . .⟩

⟨. . .⟩ Anyone who reads *The Autobiography* looking for a "key" to Stein's fictional works—and many do, as Stein knew they would—will be just as frustrated as the one who reads it looking for the "key" to Stein's private psychology. "Observation and construction make imagination," Stein says (p. 76), as if she were demystifying the imagination, making it a matter of perception and craft, but Stein, of course, *goes on*: "Observation and construction make imagination, that is granting the possession of imagination," and imagination and Stein herself remain playfully mystified. Oracular and witty, Stein is a sibylline presence, no village or even a Parisian explainer.

—James E. Breslin, "Gertrude Stein and the Problems of Autobiography," *Georgia Review* (Winter 1979), in *The Chelsea House Library of Literary Criticism: Twentieth-Century American Literature*, Vol. 6, Harold Bloom, ed. (New York: Chelsea House Publishers, 1987), 3779–81

MARIANNE DeKOVEN

Like a good deal of early modern fiction, *Three Lives* employs the device of obtuse or unrealiable narration. Generally, obtuse narration is a function of subjectivity: the narrator's psychology and involvement in the story determine her or his version of it. By allowing for this subjective structuring, we are able simultaneously to chart the limits of the narrator's perception and to see beyond them (this process is often facilitated by multiple narration, as in Conrad's *Nostromo*, Woolf's *To the Lighthouse*, etc.). In *Three Lives*, the narration is "omniscient third," yet nonetheless obtuse: there is a discrepancy, sometimes to the point of contradiction, between the tone of the narrative voice and the content of the narrative. Some such discrepancy is, as we know, characteristic of fiction, where irony, understatement, or a conflict of conscious and unconscious creation so often generates a complex vision. But in *Three Lives*, the discrepancy is so extreme that the narrator seems at times entirely blind to the import of what she narrates.

While the narrative voice of *Three Lives* is consistently innocent, straightforward, mildly jolly, and approving, the content is often grotesque, sinister, ridiculous. The gulf between what the narrator tells us and what we see is most vivid in some of the brilliant brief portraits, such as this one of Mrs. Haydon, Lena's aunt:

> This aunt, who had brought Lena, four years before, to Bridgepoint, was a hard, ambitious, well meaning, german woman. . . . Mrs. Haydon was a short, stout, hard built, german woman. She always hit the ground very firmly and compactly as she walked. Mrs. Haydon was all a compact and well hardened mass, even to her face, reddish and darkened from its early blonde, with its hearty, shiny cheeks, and doubled chin well covered over with the uproll from her short, square neck.

The avuncular simplicity, the cheerful straightforwardness of the narrator's tone, the words "well meaning" and "hearty," muffle the frightening, repulsive discord of the "hardened mass" and the "doubled chin well covered over with the uproll from her short, square neck." If we visualize Mrs. Haydon from this description, we see a monster, which is precisely what she becomes in the course of the story. ⟨. . .⟩

The narrative voice in *Three Lives* is not only straightforward, factual, reassuring; it is also childish, whimsical, consciously naive: the baker is "a queer kind of a man," "all puffed out all over," who "sits and puffs" in the kitchens of his customers. The diction and tone could be those of a children's story. This childish language heightens the discrepancy between narrative voice and content, here and elsewhere by means of its implied innocence concerning what seems a sexually charged disgust, and more generally in the novellas by masking the sophisticated complexity and somber implications of Stein's "imagined reality."

The three women's lives of the title all end in defeated, lonely death, a fact one would never surmise from the narrative tone. Anna, a generous, hardworking, stubborn, managing German immigrant (based on one of Stein's Baltimore servants), works herself to death for a series of selfish employers and friends who take all she offers, allow her to run their lives (the only repayment she exacts), then desert her when she has outlived her usefulness or when they are tired of her rigid control. She dies poor, of an unnamed disease, alone except for the one friend (Mrs. Drehten, the long-suffering, passive victim of poverty and a tyrannical husband) whose society represents no hope whatever of improving Anna's lot. ⟨. . .⟩

These plot summaries are accurate and yet misleading. The bitter implications, the powerful feminist morals of these stories (the "good" woman who dies of service to others, the "gentle" woman who dies in unwanted childbirth, the "complex, desiring" woman who dies of self-defeating complexity and unsatisfied desire) are concealed or overruled not only by the narrator's tone and diction but also by narrative emphasis and temporal structure. While Stein's uses of obtuse narration to distance language ironically from content and to avoid forcing on the reader any judgment of the story seem intentional (she was translating Flaubert's *Un Coeur simple* when she began *Three Lives*), her use of narrative tone and temporal structure as a defense against her own anger and despair appears unconscious. Throughout the novellas, Stein seems primarily interested in the comic manifestations of her heroines' psychologies, or in the inverse relation, among friends and lovers, between power and need, or in clashes resulting from the attraction of opposite temperaments. One has no sense that Stein recognizes what is clear in each plot: the defeat of a woman by dominant personality traits which are culturally defined as female. The three deaths of this trilogy are achieved in quick closing sections, almost appended as afterthought or postscript (only *The Good Anna* is divided into parts; "Part III, The Death of the Good Anna" takes up six of the story's seventy-one pages; Melanctha dies in half a page, Lena in half a paragraph).

—Marianne DeKoven, "*Three Lives*," *A Different Language: Gertrude Stein's Experimental Writing* (1983), in *The Chelsea House Library of Literary Criticism: Twentieth-Century American Literature*, Vol. 6, Harold Bloom, ed. (New York: Chelsea House Publishers, 1987), 3788–89

RANDA K. DUBNICK

The key stylistic interest in *The Making of Americans*, and in other works of Stein's participial style, is syntax. Grammatically correct but eccentric sentences spin themselves out and grow, clause linked to clause, until they are of paragraph length. She asserts that nothing "has ever been more exciting than diagramming sentences. . . . I like the feeling the everlasting feeling of sentences as they diagram themselves." Her long, repetitive sentences convey the feeling of process and duration, and of the time it gradually takes to get to know a person or to come to grips with an idea. She felt that sentences were not emotional (i.e., the syntax or "internal balance" of the sentence is a given) but that paragraphs were. She illustrates this principle by reference to her dog's drinking water from a dish. The paragraph is emotional in that it prolongs the duration of the idea or perception until the writer feels satisfied. This feeling of satisfaction is subjective and not arrived at by following rules of grammar. By extending the sentence to the length approximately of a short paragraph, Stein was trying to achieve an emotional sentence. Many of the stylistic idiosyncracies of her "participial" style function to extend the length of the sentence. What follows is a passage located near the end of *The Making of Americans*:

> Certainly he was one being living when he was being a being young one, he was often then quite certainly one being almost completely interested in being one being living, he was then quite often wanting to be one being completely interested in being one being living. He certainly then went on being living, he did this thing certainly all of his being living in being young living. He certainly when he was a young one was needing then sometimes to be sure that he was one being living, this is certainly what some being living are needing when they are ones being young ones in being living. David Hersland certainly was one almost completely one being one being living when he was being a young one. Some he was knowing then were certainly being completely living then and being then being young ones in being living then, some were quite a good deal not being one being completely living then when they were being young ones in being living. David Hersland did a good deal of living in being living then when he was a young one. He was knowing very many men and very many knew him then. He remembered some of them in his later living and he did not remember some of them. He certainly was one almost completely then interested in being one being living then. ⟨. . .⟩

In *The Making of Americans*, Stein stretches syntax almost to the breaking point and simultaneously limits her vocabulary. She moves farther and farther away from the concrete noun-centered vocabulary of the realistic novel. In part, the movement is due to her subject matter. *The Making of Americans* is a monumental attempt to create a chronicle of one family which could serve as an eternally valid history of all people, past, present, and future. Herein, she presents people as generalized types, and uses the characters in the novel to represent all human possibilities. This method led her from the essentially conventional narrative which dominates the beginning of the book to the generalized and theoretical kind of digression dispersed throughout the novel, but especially prominent towards the end of the book.

—Randa K. Dubnick, "Two Types of Obscurity in the Writings of Gertrude Stein," *Emporia State Research Studies* 24, No. 3 (Winter 1976), in *American Women Poets*, Harold Bloom, ed. (New York: Chelsea House Publishers, 1986), 80–82

MARY ALLEN

As children perceive objects by quaint analogy, so Stein freshens monotonous vision. A James study shows how a child mistakes an egg for a potato because he is used to seeing the potato without the peel. In *Tender Buttons* Stein writes, "A shawl is a hat," as indeed it is to the child who sees a shawl used to cover the head. To allow one thing the function of another is to open the world not only to a poetic interpretation but to a fascinating realistic one, as the ingenious Don Quixote demonstrates when he turns a shaving basin over and creates a helmet. As a child does not limit the description of an object to the single conventional function assigned to it by the adult world, he may not separate the object from the emotions it evokes. Thus, buttons put into buttonholes by tender fingers are, then, tender buttons.

The marvelously playful *Tender Buttons* is a logic-defying work that has received a due amount of ridicule. But where it refuses analysis, it does not refuse pleasure, yielding the fun a child gets from poking at a world he would not expect to understand. A curious enjoyment can be derived from not "understanding" *Tender Buttons*, with its conscious attempt to dislodge logic. Critics continue, however, in their efforts to establish connections in this book of non sequiturs. In *Gertrude Stein in Pieces*, Richard Bridgman observes that objects share common qualities: a tiger skin and a coin are the same color. But when a common characteristic is located, with the suggestion of a true association, the essential differentness and impossibility of connection become even more noticeable. A coin and a tiger skin are so very *unlike*. *Tender Buttons* makes sly fun of the predilection of the highly trained, logical mind in its attempt to create meaningful wholes. The fresher child's approach is to accept the individual object and to probe it for new significance. He plays with it. The art of play is the method of *Tender Buttons*, although the book is touched by a maternal tenderness for the strangely arranged "Objects," "Food," and "Rooms." Nothing in this small world, however, is grown up or dead. Things smash, but they are not destroyed. In fact, Stein had a particular weakness for breakable objects.

Gertrude loved to eat and was delighted by the French cuisine, with its adherence to every particular, as the familiar was made marvelous. As Bridgman notes, for Stein the "culinary mystery" is the "aesthetic one: . . . the whole can be sectioned and prepared, but never lost . . . obtaining, cooking, serving, slicing, eating, and digesting the outside world," even with images of ingestion and absorption as the food is transformed, cannot cause it to lose its integrity. Vegetables are chopped into marvelously small particles; celery is cut into extravagant curls. But all flavors and propensities remain. Even fluids, as Stein sees them, begin with tiny units that contain the essence: "a piece of coffee."

As each entity has its own essence, it also contains its own energy. The work of art itself is imbued with the potential to leap its boundaries—a picture to spring out of its frame. But as Stein attributes motion to matter, she produces this paradox: if wholeness is to be found only in the smallest unit, but that unit is endowed with the capacity for movement, the resultant motion appears to be a drive toward a greater wholeness. And yet, as the flow continues, without a limit, no sense of a greater wholeness can be achieved. With no frame for a picture and no end to the way an object may appear, there is no finality and not unity. The total effect in many of Stein's works, then, is that of a mass in movement going nowhere, in which the particle within it remains the most interesting aspect.

—Mary Allen, "Gertrude Stein's Sense of Oneness," *Southwest Review* (Winter 1981), in *The Chelsea House Library of Literary Criticism: Twentieth-Century American Literature*, Vol. 6, Harold Bloom, ed. (New York: Chelsea House Publishers, 1987), 3782

B I B L I O G R A P H Y

Three Lives. 1909.
Portrait of Mabel Dodge at the Villa Curonia. 1912.
Tender Buttons. 1914.
Have They Attacked Mary. He Giggled. 1917.
Geography and Plays. 1922.
The Making of Americans. 1925.
Descriptions of Literature. 1926.
Composition as Explanation. 1926.
A Book Concluding with As a Wife Has a Cow: A Love Story. 1926.
An Elucidation. 1927.
A Village. 1928.
Useful Knowledge. 1928.
An Acquaintance with Description. 1929.
Lucy Church Amiably. 1930.
Dix Portraits (with English translation by G. Huguet and V. Thomson). 1930.
Before the Flowers of Friendship Faded Friendship Faded. 1931.
How to Write. 1931.
A Long Gay Book. 1932.
Operas and Plays. 1932.
The Autobiography of Alice B. Toklas. 1933.
Four Saints in Three Acts. 1934.
Portaits and Prayers. 1934.
Chicago Inscriptions. 1934.

Lectures in America. 1935.
Narration: Four Lectures. 1935.
The Geographical History of America. 1936.
Is Dead. 1937.
Everybody's Autobiography. 1937.
A Wedding Banquet. 1938.
Picasso. 1938.
The World Is Round. 1939.
Prothalamium. 1939.
Paris France. 1940.
What Are Masterpieces. 1940.
Ida. 1941.
Wars I Have Seen. 1945.
Brewsie and Willie. 1946.
Selected Writings (Carl Van Vechten, ed.). 1946.
The First Reader and Three Plays. 1946.
In Savoy. 1946.
Four in America. 1947.
Kisses Can. 1947.
The Mother of Us All (with Virgil Thomson). 1947.
Literally True. 1947.
Two (Hitherto Unpublished) Poems. 1948.
Blood on the Dining-Room Floor. 1948.
Last Operas and Plays (Carl Van Vechten, ed.). 1949.
Things as They Are. 1950.
Unpublished Work (Yale ed., 8 vols.). 1951–58.
In a Garden. 1951.
Absolutely Bob Brown, or Bobbed Brown. 1955.
On Our Way (with Alice B. Toklas). 1959.
Yes Is For a Very Young Man. 1964.
Writings and Lectures 1911–1945 (Patricia Meyerowitz, ed.). 1967.
Lines. 1967.
Lucretia Borgia. 1968.
Motor Automation. 1969.
A Christmas Greeting. 1969.
Selected Operas and Plays (John Malcolm Brinnin, ed.). 1970.
Gertrude Stein on Picasso (Edward Burns, ed.). 1970.
I Am Rose. 1971.
Fernhurst, Q.E.D., and Other Early Writings. 1971.

Sherwood Anderson/Gertrude Stein: Correspondence and Personal Essays (Ray Lewis White, ed.). 1972.

Why Are There Whites to Console. 1973.

Reflection on the Atomic Bomb (Robert Bartlett Haas, ed.). 1973.

Money. 1973.

How Writing Is Written (Robert Bartlett Haas, ed.). 1974.

Last Will and Testament. 1974.

Dear Sammy: Letters from Gertrude Stein and Alice B. Toklas (Samuel M. Steward, ed.). 1977.

ANZIA YEZIERSKA

1885–1970

ANZIA YEZIERSKA was born in a mud hut in Plinsk on the Russian-Polish border in 1885, the daughter of Pearl and Baruch Yezierska. Some time between 1890 and 1895, her parents emigrated to the United States with their nine children. She later worked in a sweat-shop while attending night school to learn English. Columbia University admitted her to its Teacher's College in 1900. While attending school she struggled to find her own personality. Her orthodox family offered little solace and her marriages, to attorney Jacob Gordon in 1910 and to teacher Arnold Levitas in 1911, were short-lived.

Yezierska's first published story, "The Free Vacation House," appeared in *Forum* magazine in 1915. She won the O'Brien Award for "The Fat of the Land" in 1919, and in 1920 she was paid $10,000 by Samuel Goldwyn for rights to her first novel, *Hungry Hearts*, an accomplishment that attracted the attention of others in Hollywood. Her works include *Salome of the Tenements* (1922), *Arrogant Beggar* (1927), *Children of Loneliness* (1923), and *Bread Givers* (1925), an autobiographical novel reflecting her struggles with her father.

Yezierska's works chronicle the lives of Jewish immigrants in America, in particular the struggles of Jewish women to escape drudgery and realize their dreams. She was critical of the patriarchal religious culture of Orthodox Judaism that transported old-world oppression to America. Her semifictional autobiography, *Red Ribbon on a White Horse*, was published in 1950.

CRITICAL EXTRACTS

ALLEN GUTTMAN

Anzia Yezierska was a more fluent but less profound writer than Abraham Cahan. Like him, she wrote essentially of the first generation. Her collection of stories, *Hungry Hearts*, came out in 1920. The first, allegorical story sets the pattern for the entire book. Shenah Pessah, a twenty-two-year-old dowryless girl, works as a janitor, lives in an almost sunless basement apartment, and bewails her outcast fate: "My heart chokes in me like a prison!" (p. 1) Into her life, like the prince of the fairy tales, steps the handsome stranger, an instructor in sociology busy with field work on "Educational Problems of the Russian Jews." He rents an apartment in Shenah's building and is soon charmed by her innocence and by her untutored desire for an education. (Of a book, she says, "It lifts me on wings with high thoughts." [p. 7]) He seems to Shenah to be, quite literally, a God-sent alternative to the wife-seeking Motkeh, an illiterate fish peddler. The sociologist takes her to the Boston Public Library, where Mary Antin found what *she* hungered for, and begins to fall in love with her. But America is no fairyland. He moves from the apartment and leaves Cinderella (Shenah) to console herself with the possibility of escape through education. Sociological princes know that love seldom survives the movement across class and religious lines.

Shenah appears in the second story, "Hunger," to tell sympathetic Sam Arkin of her love for the village she left to come to loveless America: "I love the houses and the straw roofs, the mud streets, the cows, the chickens and the goats. My heart always hurts me for what is no more." (p. 56) But when Sam Arkin proposes marriage, Shenah reveals that she still loves her lost sociology instructor and the wider world that he symbolizes: "This fire in me, it's not just the hunger of a woman for a man—it's the hunger of all my people back of me, from all ages, for light for the life higher!" (p. 63)

The reader never learns whether or not Shenah's hungry heart is to be satisfied, but the characters of other stories suggest that she had better settle for minimal satisfactions. In one story, the narrator feels that a single act of kindness is compensation for years of disappointed struggle. In another, the effort to create "beautifulness" in the form of a newly painted kitchen is thwarted by the greed of the landlord (also a Jew), who raises the rent beyond his desperate tenant's ability to pay. Still another story ends with the night-school teacher's declaration of love for his hungry-hearted student, but this story is appropriately entitled "The Miracle."

The best story moves beyond the first generation and anticipates the novels of generational conflict that appeared in the 1930s and 1940s. The irony of "The Fat of the Land" is that fulfillment is also disappointment. Hannah Breineh is introduced in her crowded tenement, where she knocks across an air shaft to borrow a wash boiler from kindly Mrs. Pelz. While she gossips, her youngest child topples over with the chair he had been strapped into. "For what did I need yet the sixth one?" (p. 185) The children fight over their food, except for Benny, who is delivered by the police who picked him up for truancy. From this squalor, the scene shifts to the opulence into which Mrs. Breineh's grown-up children have placed her. The trouble is, of course, that the "successful" children are ashamed of their mother and want to Americanize her. She finds her plight unbearable, flings groceries all over her Persian rug, and rushes off to live with Mrs. Pelz. But she is too old and pampered to live in poverty and must return to the hateful elegance of Riverside Drive. What does it profit a woman to have her wishes granted when they were not what she wanted after all?

—Allen Guttman, "The Promised Land," *The Jewish Writer in America: Assimilation and the Crisis of Identity* (New York: Oxford University Press, 1971), 33–35

ELLEN GOLUB

Yezierska wrote more in her long life: a few novels, some stories, an autobiography. And truthfully, their quality does not often match that of other Jewish writers of her generation for subtlety or art. Yet her fiction compels our attention for its boldness, its vitality, and its insatiability. In writing of the America she found and the way of life she left behind, Yezierska unfolds the central metaphor of her generation: hunger. For the promise of America, its language, its natives, and her rapidly Americanizing Lower East Side of New York, she has but one metaphor. For beauty, language, love, achievement—for all the desires she confronts in the immigrants' name, issues of the mouth color and define her prose.

In Yezierska's world, food is animate and it animates people who have "cheeks like red apples" and shapes "like a squashed barrel of yeast." One character finds a hat "with cherries so red, so luscious, that they cried out to her, 'Bite me!'"; another defines social equality as people who come together and "eat by the same table," tasting "the bread and wine of equality"; yet another finds the attention of men as "melting looks . . . something to eat and something to drink." Whole menus are cast in Yezierska's fiction, lists of bread, chicken, strudel, nuts, raisins, almonds, gefülte fish, onions, herring. And so many stories take place in cafeterias and kitchens; even her own writing she defines as "a feast of language." People bend "ravenously" over stolen meals, their "starved nerves" tantalized by the savor of butter and eggs. They daydream meals of the past and, "savagely hungry," they torture each other with fantasies of dinners unattainable. ⟨. . .⟩

Aside from its obvious value in a world of famine, food is as well a destructive force, as in "Children of Loneliness," where a woman leaves home because she cannot tolerate her immigrant parents' table manners. Her father tirades, "The old Jewish eating is poison to her; she must have *trefa* ham—only forbidden food." Satisfaction, not ham, is the true forbidden here. In another story, secret eating brings tragedy to a starving woman on relief; a daydreaming laundress loses her job for mooning over memories of her mother's home-made gefülte fish. Dissatisfaction is as much a way of life as hunger. Indeed, they are one, the same. ⟨. . .⟩

The Russian Jew, symbolized by Yezierska's downtrodden women, uses hunger to articulate her peculiar discontent. Picture, for example, Hanneh Breineh, the ambivalent mother of six hungry children whose interminable complaint is their vigorous appetites. "Eating is dearer than diamonds," she moans. Yet when her children grow up and become wealthy, and she lives on "the fat of the land" (the story's title), she is equally, perhaps more, distressed. She has not adjusted to either America or wealth. ⟨. . .⟩

The restlessness of Hanneh Breineh is like the exasperation of Rachel in "Children of Loneliness." "It drives me wild to hear you crunching bones like savages," she screams at her parents. Yet the distant cool of the more polite Frank *Baker* (my emphasis) is equally repellent to her. So Rachel abandons all of them to seek out a "fruit" from loneliness, asking, "But am I really alone in my seeking? I'm one of the millions of immigrant children, children of loneliness, wandering between worlds that are at once too old and too new to live in."

Rachel seeks company for her solitude as a child seeks family in the new world. For her and for Hanneh Breineh, "the fat of the land" which they have received in America is ironic. For now, with bellies full, they hunger even more intensely. Still wailing their desires in the language of the mouth, they betray their longings to be more psychological than physiological. Yezierska gives us the key to this mystery when she presents Shenah Pessah (a woman described as "Her mother's milk still fresh on her lips"). In telling of her love for an American professor, Shenah Pessah connects her own personal desire with the needs and history of the Jewish people:

> the hunger in me for the life that ain't just eating and sleeping and slaving for bread. . . . This fire in me, it's not just the hunger of a woman for a man—it's the hunger of all my people back of me, from all ages, for light, for the life higher!

Shenah Pessah has penetrated the most meaningful and oft-employed of her author's symbols. ⟨. . .⟩

David Levinsky emigrates only after his mother dies and, arriving on these shores, claims to be reborn "like a new babe" in America. Yezierska, disappointed by the obstacles of the United States to the immigrant, claims that her generation are among the "orphans" and "stepchildren" of America—not her natural born heirs. Perhaps this is why Yezierska's heroines seem untrusting and unhappy, unable to sustain satisfying relationships in their new haven. They feel that they do not belong. Thus Yezierska's metaphor is of chronic oral dissatisfaction which derives from the locus of mother-child interaction, the getting and giving of food. Orality means mother, her loss, and the insatiable longing for her. For a hunger which is not hunger; for food which is not food. The novelist has located in these themes a libidinal language which speaks for her generation's great angst. "America was in everyone's mouth," wrote her contemporary Mary Antin, in *The Promised Land*. This gusto and subsequent disgust with that morsel became Yezierska's most telling explanation of that remarkable cultural transition.

> —Ellen Golub, "Eat Your Heart Out: The Fiction of Anzia Yezierska," *Studies in American Jewish Literature* 3 (Albany: State University of New York Press, 1983), 51–56, 59–60

ROSE KAMEL

It is easy to see why *Hungry Hearts* was made into a film. Loosely episodic, sentimental, at times melodramatic, it follows the predictable format of the silent movies Yezierska must have watched, though she does not mention them. Stock characters: heartless factory foremen, landlords, "charity ladies," aspiring poets with eyes burning like flames, vamps, suffering Jewish mothers and sternly orthodox fathers have the traits personified by actors in a Griffith or an Eisenstein film. Moreover, her fiction has essentially the same plot. A would-be writer, almost always a poor young immigrant woman, tries to find love and self-fulfillment in a strange land. The narrator-personae may have different names—Shenah Pessah and Sophie Sapinsky in *Hungry Hearts*, Fania Ivanowa in *All I Could Never Be*, Sarah Smolinsky in *Bread Givers*, but they speak in the voice of the pariah determined to flower in the promised land:

> When I only begin to read, I forget I'm in this world. It lifts me on wings with higher thoughts.
>
> I, soaking in the foul vapors of the streaming laundry, I with my dirty, tired hands, I am ironing the clean, immaculate shirtwaists of . . . society. I, the unclean one, am actually fashioning the pedestal of their cleanliness, from which they reach down, hoping to lift me to the height I have created for them.
>
> Once I had been elated at the thought that a man had wanted me. How much more thrilling to feel that I had made my work wanted.
>
> Trying to recapture the vanished dream that had for a moment brought them together, forced her to write. Through her writing, she still hoped to reach him who had gone beyond reach.

The power of Yezierska's prose lies in her strong sense of contrasts—parvenu and pariah, Jewish women avid for learning confronting patronizing

middle-class WASPS—and in her ambivalent need for self-scrutiny while seeking the communality of other women:

> "Ach. If I could only write like Hanneh Breineh talks!" thought
> Sophie. "Her words dance with a thousand colors. Like a rainbow it
> flows from her lips." Sentences from her own essays marched before
> her stiff and wooden. How clumsy, how unreal were most labored
> phrases compared to Hanneh Breineh's spontaneity.
>
> Suddenly Sophie's resentment for her lost morning was forgotten.
> The crying waste of Hanneh Breineh's life lay open before her like
> pictures in a book. She saw her own life in Hanneh Breineh's life.
> Her efforts to write were like Hanneh Breineh's efforts to feed her
> children (*HH*, pp. 235–236). ⟨. . .⟩

In her creation of Hanneh Breineh whose speech comes replete with lita-
nies of curses reminiscent of Sholem Aleichem's characters, Yezierska moves
from self-consciousness to otherness, providing the reader with a refreshing
narrative distance from her characters. Hanneh is palpably comic—an amal-
gam of old word stamina and Hester Street aggressiveness. ⟨. . .⟩

In *Children of Loneliness* Hanneh Breineh participates vociferously in the rising and falling fortunes of her lodgers. She cooks their suppers and offers them
unsolicited advice. When they cannot pay their rent she is compassionate;
when they make good in America she is delighted, but will not allow them to
forget their origins and denigrate her. ⟨. . .⟩

Hanneh Breineh's diatribes have their dark side, however, not only in their
depiction of the hand-to-mouth existence of the ghetto, but in evoking the
Jewish woman's wasted potential. An elegiac quality underscores the prolifer-
ation of household images—samovars and sabbath candles, feather beds and
pillows, hand-made quilts and hand-embroidered sheets, Yezierska's mother's
exquisite shawl—reminders of how easily the hope of immigrant women was
eroded by brutish labor in factories and in the dingy tenements of New York.
"The hand," a noun resonating throughout the writer's prose signifies manual
drudgery at the expense of the spirit. Unceasing hand labor has turned her
mother's "cheeks like red apples" gray and wan so that she resembles "a
squashed barrel of yeast" with only a vague memory that once in the old country she danced like a Cossack (*BG*, p. 303).

Nor can the parvenu escape spiritual starvation. In "Fat of the Land,"
Hanneh Breineh's children, grown-up and well-to-do, have installed her in an
apartment on Riverside Drive which boasts of a doorman in the lobby.
Estranged from her teeming ghetto, she is miserable:

"My heart is dying in me like in a prison," . . .

"I am starved out for a piece of real eating. In that swell restaurant is nothing but napkins and forks and lettuce leaves. There are a dozen plates to every bite of food. And it looks so fancy on the plate but it's nothing but straw in the mouth" (*HH*, p. 218) ⟨. . .⟩

The would-be writer discovers that she must avoid the limitations inherent in her mother's life. Exacerbated by the treatment her father metes out to the women in his family, Sarah Smolinsky moves away, finds a dank room, and begins training as a schoolteacher. Lonely, she warms to her mother's first visit, especially since the latter has come with filling food and a feather bed. However, when Mrs. Smolinsky pleads with her to return the visit, Sarah responds impatiently that there will be time enough for that and her studies must come first. Shortly afterward, Mrs. Smolinsky falls ill and dies. Sarah is overcome with guilt: "All became dark. Blackness drowned me." "I had failed to give mother the understanding of her deeper self during her lifetime" (*BG*, pp. 251–252, 257). ⟨. . .⟩

Had Yezierska not been so undermined by her father's obstinate refusal to recognize the validity of her talent—"a woman alone, not a wife and not a mother has no *existence* [italics, mine] no joy in earth, no hope of heaven"—she might have convinced herself that her response to him, "My children were the people I wrote about," sufficed. She might have acquired the aggressiveness of male immigrant writers of her generation developing their craft in patriarchal America. But her remarkable emergence as a writer using, as did Joseph Conrad, an adopted language was heart-breakingly short-lived. Unable to affect the distance that could have perfected her craft, she proved unable to convince herself that in recreating both Sophie Sapinsky and Hanneh Breineh she had also brought forth life.

—Rose Kamel, "'Anzia Yezierska, Get Out of Your Own Way': Selfhood and Otherness in the Autobiographical Fiction of Anzia Yezierska," *Studies in American Jewish Literature* 3 (Albany: State University of New York Press, 1983), 42–43, 45–50

EVELYN AVERY

More than seventy years ago, an ambitious, bright, young Jewish immigrant observed the unsettling effects America had on newcomers. While the "land of opportunity" offered freedom and prosperity, it often exacted a steep price—first, the transformation of family structure, then, the dissolution of family bonds. In *The Promised Land* (1912), a tribute to her adopted country, Mary Antin conceded that such painful sacrifices were necessary for survival in America. "The older generation," she noted, "must step down from their throne of parental authority, and take the law from their [more Americanized]

children . . . the result," Antin acknowledged, "was an inversion of normal rela-
tions, which sometimes [disrupted] families that were formerly united and
happy."

For Mary Antin and another immigrant Jewish author, Anzia Yezierska,
the sacrifices were costly but appeared warranted, the passports to professional success and American identities. Part of a generation bridging Yiddish
culture and Yankee experience, Antin and Yezierska passionately described the
struggles and changes within the immigrant Jewish family. More than half a
century ago, the autobiographical *Promised Land* and the novel, *Bread Givers*,
anticipated the concerns of such later authors as Tillie Olsen, Grace Paley,
Cynthia Ozick, Norma Rosen and Joanne Greenberg. ⟨. . .⟩

Antin's self-centeredness, her religious skepticism, and her enthusiasm for
America resemble Sara Smolinsky's characteristics in Anzia Yezierska's novel
Bread Givers. Published thirteen years apart, the two works share other elements. Though *Bread Givers* is set primarily on New York's Lower East Side,
"shtetl" values dominate as they had in Antin's Polotzk. Moisheh Smolinsky,
like Pinchus Antin, is an old-fashioned patriarch, convinced of his wisdom and
authority. In contrast to Mr. Antin's secularism, however, Reb Smolinsky justifies his actions according to Orthodox Judaism. Thus, his four daughters and
wife exist to serve him, to enable him to study Torah. Their salvation is rooted
in his proximity to God. So persuaded is Smolinsky of this heavenly scheme
that he arranges his daughter's marriages for his own profit. Predictably, his ill-
conceived plans fail: the marriages are disastrous and his one business venture
ruins him. Even his devoted wife Shenah warns him against investing their
meager funds, but he arrogantly ignores her and the money is lost.

In many ways, Shenah, almost a stereotype of the "shtetl" woman is
changed in America. Early in the novel she worships her pious husband, for-
giving his egotism and ineptitude. With the rent unpaid and the table bare,
Shenah defends Moisheh, captivated by his holy manner.

> Mother's face lost all earthly worries. Forgotten were beds, mattresses,
> boarders and doweries. Father's holiness filled her eyes with light.

Moved by their father's religious spirit, the daughters are also spellbound,
"straining not to miss a word" (11), temporarily forgetting their earthly woes.
But the mood cannot last in America which values pragmatism, independence,
and above all, success. More importantly, from Yezierska's viewpoint, Reb
Smolinsky's piety is shallow, a cloak for his selfishness, and a justification for
his tyranny. Though the three older daughters agree to his matchmaking, they
never forgive him for their bitter lives. Eventually Shenah's patience is also
exhausted; her earlier, more muted criticism grows louder, climaxing in an ugly
scene in New Jersey where he had just purchased a worthless store. "Why do

you never trust your own wife?" She cries. "Why do you only trust strange people? To whom can I go with my bitter heart?" (126). Despite the outburst, however, she remains "bargaining with the wholesalers . . . pleading to be trusted and getting the goods on time" (128). While insisting that Sara respect her father "even if he was a drunkard and a card-player" (130), she also slips her daughter the rent money so she can escape. Paradoxically, it is Shenah's dying wish, "be good to father" (245), which draws Sara back to the Lower East Side, where she is melodramatically reunited with her father.

Stubborn and strong willed, sensitive and generous, Sara has inherited personality traits which vie for her allegiance. As an immigrant child, Yezierska, like Antin, applauded American opportunity but also longed for the Yiddish community's warmth and vitality. Where *The Promised Land* celebrates Americanization, *Bread Givers* concludes ambiguously, with Sara's misgivings about living with her father. Such cultural and generational conflicts, Yezierska suggests, can only be resolved through the younger generation's willingness to compromise that honor their heritage, while they pursue the new. Despite her good fortune, Sara realizes that she could not "escape by running away . . . that the shadow of the burden was always following her" (295).

—Evelyn Avery, "Oh My 'Mishpocha'! Some Jewish Women Writers from Antin to Kaplan View the Family," *Studies in American Jewish Literature* 5 (Albany: State University of New York Press, 1986), 44–48

SHELLY REGENBAUM

Asher and Anzia, the outcast artists, create their art under the heavy burden of guilt. Asher is haunted in his dreams by the "dark-bearded and dark-visaged" (300) ancestor who threatens to destroy him and his art. Anzia for many years struggles with the feeling that her creative urge is "murderous" and likens herself to the biblical Cain, "'forever bound to the brother he slew with hate'" (73). Through their sense of loss and guilt, both Asher and Anzia come to regard art as a power that can destroy and create, bring pleasure and pain—a power both demonic and divine.

Although burdened by guilt, the two artists do not reject the Jewish tradition. Instead, they remain loyal to Jewish values and attempt to integrate them with the Western tradition they admire. Their initial artistic efforts in the American world are successful. Asher has one-man exhibitions and his paintings are bought by museums; Anzia's book *Hungry Hearts* is made into a movie, and she is transported overnight from the Lower East Side to Hollywood, from rags to riches. However, it is in the way success affects them and their struggle to fuse the two traditions that the differences between them begin to show. Asher's art deepens and develops through progressively complex forms and themes. Anzia's art becomes uncertain and progresses only by fits and starts. Asher's exhibitions dovetail each other; Anzia's writing comes to a standstill. Success invigorates Asher and, although it signals the pain of separation from his parents, gives him courage. Success terrifies Anzia and stills her strong voice. In his controversial and powerful painting, the *Brooklyn Crucifixion*, Asher integrates the Jewish and the artistic aspects of his being and thus becomes a strong and free man. Anzia's fame brings about such confusion, doubts, and misgivings that she feels "lost in chaos, wandering between worlds" (73). Her reconciliation with the Jewish tradition is finally effected only through the sacrifice of her art.

In wrestling with the dictates of the Jewish religion, the artists share a similar predicament. However, Anzia must also cope with added burdens from which Asher is free: she is poor; she is an immigrant and thus twice removed from the American culture she admires; and, most importantly, she is a woman. Her female identity is responsible for many of her anxieties, self-doubts, and bitter expressions of self-hatred throughout the novel. As a woman, she is expected to become a wife and a mother, not a writer. In choosing to write, Anzia not only defies the moral tenets of the Jewish tradition, a defiance which she shares with Asher Lev, but she also defies the sex role assigned to her by that tradition. Thus, her burden of guilt is heavier than his and less manageable, and she fails where he succeeds.

In the society of orthodox Judaism, everywhere and at all times, as Cynthia Ozick points out, "communal responsibility is left exclusively to males" (125). The woman's position in the community is above all biological and is defined by "a dependent and subordinate connection" (125). Women are exempted (really excluded) from important prayers and rituals, and, when they do pray in the synagogue, they are hidden behind a wall. Furthermore, for thousands of years, women have been barred from study and intellectual endeavors. Thus, Jewish history, as Cynthia Ozick describes it, "has excised an army of poets, thinkers, juridical figures; it has cut them off and erased them" (137) ⟨. . .⟩

Although in her life Yezierska was more successful than her heroine in the novel (who can only in part be identified with her), she sought to emphasize her turmoils in the patriarchal world. In the novel, she makes no mention of her two brief marriages and her daughter. By omitting the relationships which mellowed her loneliness (a husband and a daughter), Yezierska brings into sharp relief the isolation of the Jewish woman artist and dramatizes her bitter bewilderment over her role in life. ⟨. . .⟩

—Shelly Regenbaum, "Art, Gender, and the Jewish Tradition in Yezierska's *Red Ribbon on a White Horse* and Potok's *My Name Is Asher Lev*," *Studies in American Jewish Literature* 7 (Kent, Ohio: Kent State University Press, 1988), 56–60, 64–65

SUSAN HERSH SACHS

Johanna Kaplan, in a *New York Times* book review (February 24, 1980), of *The Open Cage* edited by Alice Kessler-Harris, wrote of the bitterness of the familial relationships in Yezierska's works. "Anzia Yezierska saw that there could be in parental love a terrible, haunting descent from envy to malediction." Yet, when giving a reading of her stories to a group of Senior Adults, primarily women, at the local Jewish Community Center, this writer was confused by the response of the listeners to material that one might have thought incredibly bitter. These elderly women, most of them immigrants themselves, personally familiar with Yezierska's territory, exploded into laughter—exhuberant laughter.

To be sure, the Yiddish language accounts for such a paradox, a *finster gelichter*—bitter humor. When Hanneh Breineh rages at her starving children, modern sensibilities perceive malediction, but the women closest to Yezierska's background respond to the *gelichter* aspect of Hanneh Breineh's words. "'Gluttons—wolves—thieves!' Hanneh Breineh shrieked. 'I should only live to bury you all in one day!'" But just before she had said, "How it chokes me the tears every morning when I got to wake her [her 13 year old daughter] and push her out to the shop. . ."

The "haunting descent" of Hanneh Breineh's visions are not universal to parental ties; they are universal to parental ties in situations of dire stress. The women at today's J.C.C.'s are safely long removed from those dire straits: They are even well past the pains of becoming nouveau middle-class. Now, far from being an embarrassment to their children, these women enjoy their grandchildren's pride in that ethnicity which they represent. Now they can laugh.

Their laughter, though, isn't aroused only from the *finster gelichter* nor just from distance between themselves and Hanneh Breineh or their own pasts. The laughter also comes from the very character of the fiery Hanneh Breineh. By herself she is theater: bigger than life, overstating everything, throwing herself from the extreme end of one stage of life to the opposite side. She leaps from the vale of lamentation to a high on grape juice, "thrilled into ecstasy with each lingering drop, 'How it laughs yet in me, the life, the minute I turn my head from my worries!'" she enthralls. Fine points, proportion, nuance— these are not her style, nor are they the style of other Yezierska protagonists. The laughing women at a Senior Citizens luncheon may have clearer insight into the author's intentions than the rest of us, whose vision might be dimmed by over-education. Sophie, the young author-tenant, saw in Hanneh Breineh's burning words a rainbow of colors that she emulated in her own writing. "If I could only write like Hanneh Breineh talks! Her words dance with a thousand colors."

In the pied-beauty of her writing, Yezierska drew well the polarities of life. Despite the paradoxes in her shifting points of view, she sketched the counter forces clearly: youth—age, poor—rich, modern—traditional, native—foreign, assimilated—Orthodox, accepted—rejected, isolated—part of community, and, certainly, love—hate. All of these tensions, delineated so starkly in her works of the 1920s in particular (which have often been called her best) undoubtedly had their echoes in her real life. Because the tensions in her experiences were never as completely resolved as she would have liked, they continued to spark her creativity. Her creative writing, dramatic that it is, in turn sheds light on the vivacity of many immigrant women of her generation who sought a place for themselves in America.

She illuminated some basic truths, if not all of the facts of her time.

—Susan Hersh Sachs, "Anzia Yezierska: 'Her Words Dance with a Thousand Colors,'" *Studies in American Jewish Literature* 3 (Albany: State University of New York Press, 1983), 65–66

MARK SHECHNER

From Mendele Mocher Sforim's *The Travels of Benjamin III*, in which Benjamin deserts his wife to go off in search of the Ten Tribes, to the novels of Saul Bellow and Philip Roth, where the family is already a museum piece and the Jewish man is usually found casting off his first (or second or third) *shikse* amid much wailing and gnashing of teeth, the decline of the Jewish family under the impact of modern conditions seems to be the most hackneyed of Jewish themes.

⟨. . .⟩ Indeed some of the bitterest portrayals of it are to be found in the domestic storm and stress literature of the 1920s and 1930s: in the explosive battles of father and daughter in Anzia Yezierska's *Bread Givers*; in the blows visited by father upon son in Henry Roth's *Call It Sleep*; in the omnibus bickerings and betrayals that mark Clifford Odets' *Awake and Sing*. In such company, ⟨Isaac Rosenfeld's⟩ *Passage from Home* seems to be a routine dramatization of Jewish civilization and its discontents, the son longing to take flight from the father, the father distant and inscrutable, given to sudden rages and bursts of rejection. But in *Passage from Home*, a book published twenty-one years, and thus a generation, after Yezierska's account of a young woman's bid for liberation from the family, the father's world is already a threadbare remnant of the Jewish tradition. In *Bread Givers*, at least, the father is a student of Torah, his iron dominion over his daughters sanctioned by his role as the keeper of law and preserver of memory. It is not an appealing picture of the Jewish tradition, since the father's immersion in study appears to be a mask for self-interest, but it is one in which the traditional elements of the family are initially in place, even if they must be shattered for the next generation to breathe freely. ⟨. . .⟩

Where Yezierska's father sat wrapped in phylacteries, Rosenfeld's sits wrapped only in sadness, and the son's revolt is infused with pity for the father and a nostalgia for a past with which he has no contact except through the grandfather.

—Mark Shechner, *The Conversion of the Jews and Other Essays* (New York: St. Martin's Press, 1990), 21–22

ELLEN SERLEN UFFEN

The fiction of Anzia Yezierska is obviously presented to us as fiction, although it is constructed of variations on the "real" themes evident in Antin and Stern. In Yezierska's stories and novels there are young women who desire better, who long to leave the ghetto; there are non-Jewish lovers; there are tyrant fathers ruled here, too, and ruling by their religious orthodoxy. Most notably there is the father in *Bread Givers* (1925), who is unlike Leah Morton's father, however, in that in Yezierska's version, he is relentless in his selfishness and blindness to his family's needs. His portrait is unrelieved by kindness or humor. There is frequently in Yezierska's writing, a concern with the troubled relationships of parents and children as they confront America.

But the tone of Yezierska, the flavor of her fiction, differs radically from that of either of her contemporaries. Her stories have the intensity of silent films—perhaps because the reality upon which they are based was so intense. She presents emotional extremes: depths of poverty and despair, flights of lyrical longing. Her women mostly are not thinkers and intellectuals whose language is the refined English of educated America, but are rather natural poets and dreamers who speak the woman's language of the ghetto, the Yiddish-English dialect which Yezierska knew how to use better than anyone, says Sally Ann Drucker: "Only Yezierska used it to show that her characters come from the culture of the ghetto, but without that culture denigrating or debasing them" (99). Yezierska's work was written in English, but it sings with the wonderfully rich and dramatic and comic cadences of her characters' Yiddish.

There are two grand themes in her writing, and perhaps in the writing of Antin and Stern as well, which, when understood in all their implications, subsume every other concern: hunger and flying. The novels, really only types of the stories writ large, clearly are based on these concerns, but they are best seen, variously, in Yezierska's early collection of stories, *Hungry Hearts*, from 1920, and republished only recently with the addition of several stories written later, one when she was in her eighties.

Hunger is, of course, a literal fact in Yezierska's work, as it was in the Jewish ghetto of New York's Lower East Side, where the stories take place. That people do not have enough to eat and that a great part of one's waking hours is spent finding ways to provide food for oneself and one's family must affect, in significant ways, relationships, beliefs, behavior. It also prevents entry into mainstream America and makes of the ghetto a prison. Hunger as metaphor suggests desire to escape the ghetto, desire for love, for life, success, happiness, for the orderly and clean and accentless America outside those prison walls.

To attain the desire, or to sate the hunger, is to fly: to be creative, to be in love, to feel passion, to embrace reality completely and unselfconsciously and with absolute freedom and transcendant abandon, like the fiddlers and lovers of the canvases of Marc Chagall, or later, but now with innocence complicated by narrative ambiguity, like all those levitators in the work of Cynthia Ozick. In Yezierska the innocence is still mostly intact. To her young women, to attain the ability to fly is to take the first step into America. But Yezierska, if not her dreamers, knows that America, often masquerading as a WASP lover, while it longs for the dreamers, and longs itself to dream, is terrified of those who can.

—Ellen Serlen Uffen, "The Beginnings: Mary Antin, Elizabeth Gertrude Levin Stern, Anzia Yezierska," *Strands of the Cable: The Place of the Past in Jewish American Women's Writing*, Daniel Walden, ed. (New York: Peter Lang Publishing, Inc., 1992), 17–19, 33–36

MELANIE LEVINSON

The experiences of the African-American and Jewish-American communities have varied widely, but as perpetual outsiders in a land which professes equality for all, their traditions logically, at certain points, intersect. The notion of passing, though informed by an experience which differs from the African-American—that of a female Old World immigrant—frequently appears in Anzia Yezierska's fiction. Her heroines keenly feel their "difference" and while each longs "to become an American: to look and dress with the assurance of the native born," they equate achieving that status with breaking into the white, middle- to upper-middle class Christian sphere—the same class, generally, used to define "American" in African-American passing narratives.

The psychological questions passing raises for any participant are disconcerting—should those who are able to pass for "white" (and I use this term as one having little to do with color) do so? The authors of these narratives explored many questions: Is it ethical to abandon one's birth culture if to do so offers you other opportunities, or is an individual's primary responsibility to him or herself? Is it psychologically possible to "pass" and still retain a sense of personal integrity? Frances E. W. Harper unequivocally answered no to these questions—when Iola, her heroine, discovers that her mother was and is a slave, she refuses to return to her white friends and her white life after the

Civil War. Most characters who pass cannot come to terms with their liminality so easily, and, like Rena "Warwick" are rarely at home in either their birth
or chosen community.

Anzia Yezierska's heroines seem to struggle with this dilemma—she terms
it not as "passing" but rather as the hunger to be a person. ⟨. . .⟩

To "pass," however, as we see with Charles Chesnutt's Rena and John
Warwick in *The House Behind the Cedars*, means more than merely improving your
social graces—it requires severing one's past life completely, and Yezierska's
fictions repeatedly pose this question: If shedding the past requires relin-
quishing everything you hold dear (even your mother's bridal shawl) but offers
new opportunities for an economically better life, is it right or ethical to
do so?

> How often when I had sought work in Christian offices had I been
> tempted to hide my Jewishness—for a job! It was like cutting off a
> part of myself. That was why there was no wholeness, no honesty, in
> anything I did.

Although Yezierska grapples with this issue to some extent in a number of her
short stories and novels, there is never a sense of final reconciliation between
the Old World and the New.

In the title story of Yezierska's "Children of Loneliness," Rachel Ravinsky,
just returned from Cornell University to her parent's home in a New York
ghetto, bemoans her dilemma: "Ah, I don't want to abandon them!" she
thought; "I only want to get to the place where I belong." It is this sense of
liminality: "I can't live with the old world, and I'm yet too green for the
new" which informs Yezierska's depiction and investigation of each heroine's
life. ⟨. . .⟩

Bread Givers, probably Yezierska's best-known work, is divided into three
sections: "Hester Street," "Between Two Worlds," and "The New World."
Despite Yezierska's titles, Sara never reaches the New World entirely. While
she believes that her degree from college and her new-found financial freedom
have miraculously changed her "into a person!" her return to Hester Street
reveals that her status as a Jewish woman has changed very little. Sara tries, as
does Chesnutt's Rena, to balance her love for her family and her desire to be
a member of a privileged class, but discovers that she no longer belongs to or
is unquestioningly accepted by her birth culture. The disparity between Sara's
self-image and the position which she is required to fulfill as a daughter and a
woman in the Jewish community on Hester Street are irreconcilable. When
she refuses, upon her mother's death, to rend her suit as religious tradition
demands, stating: "I don't believe in this. It's my only suit, and I need it for
work. Tearing it wouldn't bring Mother back to life again" she is scorned by

her former neighbors: "A hundred eyes burned on me their condemnation. 'Look at her, the Americanerin':! Sara has become an American, at least to the Jewish people of Hester Street, but has not achieved the fulfillment she thought it must bring: "The goal was here. Why was I so silent, so empty" [269]?

Sara is empty because it is psychologically necessary for her to function in both the modern American world and her birth culture—the Old World Jewish community of Hester Street. She finds that neither community is willing to allow this sort of dual citizenship, that she has become "a stranger among her own people." After six years, Sara has received enough training to finally "pass" as "a person". Instead of maintaining the silence between herself and her family, however, she returns to share her accomplishments with them. By returning, and by resuming her obligations as a daughter in the Old World sense, she is forfeiting her chance to "be a person" or, perhaps more accurately, to "pass" for an American.

—Melanie Levinson, "'To Make Myself for a Person': 'Passing' Narratives and the Divided Self in the Work of Anzia Yezierska," *Studies in American Jewish Literature* 13 (University Park, PA: Pennsylvania State University, 1994), 5–7

EDITH C. WEINTHAL

Bread Givers addresses itself to the problem of the traditional, Jewish cultural norm of valuing women in the domestic sphere alone. Shtetl women, whose very selves were defined by the men of the family, lived in constant subordination within a male-dominated society. Led to believe that their very existence was to procreate and to serve those who dominated them, these women rarely felt that they could have an impact upon any aspect of public society. Even when economic reality demanded that these women become "bread givers," this role was one which was devalued and considered insignificant. The emphasis on woman's maternal roles, strongly reaffirmed in the traditional Jewish household, confines a woman to gaining prestige and value solely within the domestic sphere. Men, on the other hand, can achieve authority, prestige, and cultural value by playing out more public roles. Nowhere are these divergent roles more evident than in a city setting.

Sara Smolinsky's world on Hester Street depicts the crowded, noisy, ghetto-like existence of many first-generation Jewish American immigrants. As the novel opens, one of the initial violent images is of life on the streets. Fania tells of combing the streets for work, competing with hundreds for a single position, literally fighting through a crowd and "tearing the clothes from our bodies and scratching out each other's eyes in the mad pushing to get in first" (2). Two armed policemen are called to maintain the order in the street. The pushcarts and marketplace become a daily ordeal for the Smolinsky

women who must plead, bargain, promise, and humiliate themselves to sustain
the family. On the other hand, Reb Smolinsky, the father, utilizes his religion
to remove himself from any negative interaction with the city. He prays in his
neighborhood shul, he studies in his own room in the tiny, overcrowded apartment, while allowing the women to attend to his worldly comforts.
Surrounded by his books, he is undisturbed by city life. For Smolinsky, his life
is ". . . like living in a beautiful garden" (294). And it is Reb Smolinsky who is
elevated to a special position in the society. He says of himself, "The whole
world would be in thick darkness if not for men like me who give their lives
to spread the light of the Holy Torah" (24).

In contrast, Mrs. Smolinsky, sacrificing daily, starving, overworked, end-
lessly fighting the grime, the crowds, and the ordeals of life in the ghetto, is
only considered "a servant of a man who studies the Torah" (9). It is a she who
must face the bleak, sterile, often hostile world of a city which has imposed
total anonymity upon her.

Life in an apartment house is a world away from the home which the
Smolinskys left in Poland-Russia. Because it belongs to the domestic realm, the
women attempt to make their own small space into a "safe" haven in the midst
of the chaos and dangers which the city outside imposes upon them. It
becomes impossible, however, for they can never find a place to be alone; can
never find a way to become isolated so that nothing can penetrate their
fortress. Rev Smolinsky rules this domain, the land. Lady enters to collect her
overdue rent, and would-be suitors intrude to take the Smolinsky females into
situations which would parallel that of the life of the mother.

The dream in America becomes, for Mrs. Smolinsky, one of having "the
money for our own bought house, with steam heat and hot running water and
a white marble sink" (116). It represents an escape from the city and all it
implies. When Rev Smolinsky is swindled into buying a failing grocery store
in Elizabeth, New Jersey, Mrs. Smolinsky finds some relief from her sorrow
because, according to Sara, she is "drunk with the green grass and the blue sky"
(130). "It's the first time since we came to America that we have a little light
and air," says Mrs. Smolinsky. "When I look out of the window, it's not into a
black airshaft. I see a tree, the sky, green grass" (130). ⟨. . .⟩

The city as portrayed in Yezierska's *Bread Givers* supposes the superiority of
culture over nature, and does not nurture either a sense of sharing or a sense
of community. Furthermore, domestic life, usually associated with females, is
considered of little or no worth when compared to an urban system which is
dictated by males in public roles. Sara, as rebel, can find no validation for her
life within the traditional Jewish cultural model nor within an urban model
which has long devalued the place and voice of women. Not unlike Anzia

Yezierska herself, Sara Smolinsky's dilemma is unresolved at the end of the novel. She remains suspended between maternal and paternal cultural perceptions, forever attempting to forge a new identity. The city, for Yezierska, becomes the arena for the confrontation between these widely diverse images.

—Edith C. Weinthal, "The Image of the City in Yezierska's *Bread Givers*," *Studies in American Jewish Literature* 13 (University Park, PA: Pennsylvania State University, 1994), 11–13

B I B L I O G R A P H Y

Hungry Hearts. 1920.
Salome of the Tenements. 1922.
Children of Loneliness. 1923.
Bread Givers. 1925.
Arrogant Beggar. 1927.
All I Could Never Be. 1932.
Red Ribbon on a White Horse. 1950.
The Open Cage (including previously unpublished work). 1979.